Managing the
Customer
Experience

Turning customers into advocates

FORUM®

where learning means business

PEARSON

Custom
Publishing

FT Prentice Hall

FINANCIAL TIMES

PEARSON CUSTOM PUBLISHING
75 Arlington Street, Suite 300, Boston, MA 02116
A Pearson Education Company

Advance praise

"Refreshing and practical. *Managing the Customer Experience* shows companies how to build the power of their brand. The Forum Corporation inspires your organization to deliver a different and more valuable offering to your targeted customers."

Bradley T. Gale, author of *Managing Customer Value*, and President, Customer Value, Inc.

"Delivering customers a consistently superior set of benefits is probably the most important driver of value creation. This book provides a number of practical insights which will guide the reader on the difficult but fascinating path leading to great customer value delivery."

Jean-Claude Larréché, The Alfred H. Heineken Professor of Marketing, INSEAD

"A fascinating and insightful book which is equally relevant for the leaders of professional services firms looking to build 'trusted advisor' relationships with their key clients."

Michael Bray, Chief Executive, Clifford Chance

"*Managing the Customer Experience* is an incredibly practical guide for building customer loyalty in the new century."

Marshall Goldsmith, Founding Director of the Financial Times Knowledge Dialogue and the Alliance for Strategic Leadership.

"The Forum Corporation shows us what the 21st Century Company has to look like if it is to be successful. They show that great brands are not primarily built through advertising but by the experience and value they offer customers."

Professor Peter Doyle, Warwick Business School, University of Warwick

"This book shows how to unlock the full value potential of the customer experience, supported by a wealth of examples from world leaders such as Tesco and Harley-Davidson. The connection made between the Marketing, Human Resources and Customer Service functions is very powerful. This, combined with the emphasis on the role of leadership, makes *Managing the Customer Experience* required reading for CEO's, Marketing, Human Resource, and Operations Directors, and their teams."

William Gordon, Strategy Partner, Accenture and co-author of
Brand Manners

"In their book, *Managing the Customer Experience*, the authors bring forward the concept of loyalty and advocacy in customer experience in a very targeted way...unearthing one of the most essential branding rules, which is to make your preferred customers your best ambassadors."

Marc Gobé, President and Executive Creative Director,
Desgrippes Gobé Group, author of *Emotional Branding: the New*
Paradigm for Connecting Brands to People

"If you are interested in increasing customer loyalty, *Managing the Customer Experience* is the book for you. Most books on the subject focus on your company's image and tell you why it's important. This book makes the business case for branding but then shows you how to do it. Full of practical 'how to' advice, illustrative anecdotes, and application exercises, it is not only a good read, but a significant investment in your future success."

Richard Whiteley, author of *The Customer Driven Company*

"Great brands stand for great things ... great products, great services, and more importantly – great experiences. Forum are experts on branded customer experiences and this book details their research, experiences, challenges and successes. It's required reading for our entire organization."

Mark Snyder, Senior Vice President,
Holiday Inn Brand, InterContinental Hotels Group

Contents

████████████████████

Foreword

"The customer experience is bigger than customer service in that it is the full, end-to-end experience. It starts when you first hear about Amazon from a friend, and ends when you get the package in the mail and open it. We want to raise the worldwide bar for customer experience," declares Jeff Bezos of internet giant Amazon.com.

In that one comment, Jeff captures the power and promise of Managing the Customer Experience. This is not a book that espouses someone's theory about how to improve customer loyalty, but rather is the result of ground-breaking research into the best practices of companies that are creating an unbeatable competitive advantage by focusing on the customer experience and are enjoying substantial business success as a result.

Managing the customer experience was written by a team of Forum experts to fully explore successful strategies of many of the world's leading brands and to share with you the "secret sauce" that makes them the names that everyone recognizes. This book will take you on an exploration of how a handful of leading companies have achieved almost unbeatable competitive advantage, by focusing on the experience they create for their customers. These organizations are absolutely passionate about this idea — that the experiences that their customers have with their people, products and services redefine the concept of customer loyalty. "We want to be the world's most loved brand," announces Jack McAleer, executive vice-president of the fast growing doughnut chain, Krispy Kreme.

In an era where companies have reduced costs as a matter of survival, and markets have become even more competitive, we see over and over again that the true differentiator of successful brands is the link forged between a brand's promise and how customers experience the brand. It's not about who has the biggest advertising budget or who is achieving top scores in customer satisfaction ratings. Rather, it is about the experiences your people and products deliver to your customers at every touchpoint, direct and indirect, that makes the difference. In the end, nothing else matters as much…your experience is your brand.

Our goal in writing this book is to provide you with a practical guide and inspiration to begin the journey towards lasting customer loyalty. But what consultant wouldn't think that their approach is the best path forward? That's why this book is different. Don't take it from us but rather from the world-class companies that have informed our approach and continue to validate the Branded Customer Experience® as a business strategy for today and for the days to come.

So don't let me hold you up any longer. Go to chapter one and get started on your customer experience journey.

Tom Knighton
Executive Vice President
The Forum Corporation

Acknowledgments

*The brands that will be big in the future will be
those that tap into the social changes that are
taking place*

Sir Michael Perry chairman, Centrica plc

Our thanks to the many people who made this book possible,
in particular:

Ed Boswell	Ronan Knox	Tracey Richardson
Ken Brown	Anne Lockhart	Jonathan Rosin
David Carder	Carmelita Lubos	David Simmons
Jackie Draper	Wayne Marks	Shaun Smith
Bill Fonvielle	Sarah McIntosh	Diann Strausberg
Bill Ghormley	Jane Palmer	Jane Weinstein
Stacy Hatcher	Laura Perryman	Joe Wheeler
Diane Hessan	Peter Pickus	Jennifer Wolf
Galina Jeffrey	Jan Porell	Diane Woodworth-Jordan
Tom Knighton	Alison Rawlinson	Bill Woolfolk

And our partners at:

Interbrand
Experience Engineering
Heath Wallace
Satmetrix
Accenture

And our many clients throughout the world who constantly challenge
our thinking.

The Forum Corporation

Introduction

■■■■■■■■■■■■■■■■■■■

I believe there is almost no limit to what a brand can do, but only if used properly

Richard Branson founder of the Virgin empire

Are you a loyal customer? Can you think of companies you buy from which have earned your repeat business? Which companies go out of their way to make you feel special? Probably not many. If you are lucky, perhaps you can think of one or two – a book store, a pizza parlor, or clothing store that provides a level of product and service quality that you feel has earned some measure of loyalty.

Think again. Can you name a company that you buy from that you would *proactively* recommend to others, defend from criticism, perhaps even have their logo tattooed on your arm? Is there a company you would advocate for? Being an advocate is not a half-hearted commitment. As an advocate you will drive past dozens of competitors to experience a company's product or be prepared to fly with them on a route with more frequent stops than their closest competitor.

We wouldn't be surprised if you can't think of a single company.

Some readers may already be shaking their heads. However, if you own a Harley-Davidson motorcycle, are a lifetime patron of Krispy Kreme Donuts, or are a frequent flyer member of Virgin Atlantic, you know what we are talking about. Customers of these companies are much more than loyal customers, they are advocates – customers who identify with not only the brand promise associated with these firms, but with the customer experience that these companies have created.

So, how can you raise the bar for customer experience? It isn't easy. For a start, you must re-think who your customers are; what they deeply value; and how your organization can deliver a customer experience that is consistent, intentional, differentiated, and valuable.

Understanding how you can make this step-change happen for your organization is what this book is all about. First, we review why the customer experience has evolved from an interesting concept to a proven business model. We explore how industry innovators are aggressively pursuing customer experience as the route to long-term competitive advantage and consistent profitability. We examine customer advocacy. How far does it go beyond customer satisfaction? Why is advocacy the only true form of loyalty?

Then we will show you how it is done. In Chapter 3, Loyalty by design, we will take you through the steps that world-class companies go through to re-think their business from the customer's point of view. We look at how they design and deliver a customer experience that drives loyalty and profitability. The remainder of the book highlights the results of our research into what distinguishes organizations delivering superior customer experiences. This includes new, innovative approaches to leadership, performance management, and the importance of what we call "triad power." Throughout we will draw heavily on the research and interviews we conducted with executives from leading brands for our recent book *Uncommon Practice: People who deliver great brand experience*.[1] Whereas that book focussed on the *who* and *what*, this one will focus on the *why* and *how*.

Why and how means learning about new approaches to selling that increase revenue without driving product quotas; successful approaches to product management that have little to do with the actual product itself. Finally, we look at what it takes to keep the edge and retain market leadership in a world of diminishing customer loyalty. We review some extraordinary examples of companies that are demonstrating unrivaled determination and leadership in making their brand promise icons in the markets they are choosing to serve.

Throughout the book you will find contributions from companies that we partner with, or whose perspective we value. We believe we can best serve our clients by partnering with the very best in the field, when required, rather than trying to be expert in every facet of the customer experience. We thank them for their collaboration.

The Appendix is rich in resources and tools for charting your own course in pursuing a Branded Customer Experience.® We hope you find these tools and approaches useful and insightful. They will only be so if they are able to help you and your organization win in the tough times as well as the good ones.

As a good starting point, Steve Anderson, director of customer experience at Krispy Kreme, describes perfectly the required approach: "I have found the most important thing to do is to decide what you're about, decide who you are, what you hold as important, and what you value. Make sure that whatever you're doing is about becoming more of what you really are and not about plans and strategies that have financial gain as the starting point. That doesn't mean you can't have aggressive goals. It does mean that you're in for the long run and when times get difficult you have a place to come back to and reaffirm who you are, what you're about; it gives you comfort and confidence in the tough times."

The approach, stories, and practices shared in this book, in relation to Managing the Customer Experience will enable you to lay a foundation for enduring success in the future.

The Forum Corporation

Note   1   Unless otherwise stated, quotes from executives are drawn from the interviews for *Uncommon Practice: People who deliver a great brand experience*, FT/Prentice Hall, 2002, ISBN 0 273 65936 7.

1

■■■■■■■■■■■■■■■■■■■

The age of experience

*The customer experience is the next
competitive battleground*

Jerry Gregoire CIO, Dell Computers

Experience is everything. And never have so many experiences been available.

Do you have the urge to fly a MIG 21 at twice the speed of sound? No problem, pick up a voucher at your local retailer. How about undertaking a James Bond mission and, in the process, getting the weapons training and gadgets? Just drop into the UK retail chain WH Smith and buy a gift certificate. Perhaps you would like to share a kitchen with a celebrity chef? That too is just a phone call away.

These adventures and many more are now available to consumers. But this is not just a retailing phenomenon. The same thing is happening in every sector of the economy. Consumers are looking for experiences that enable them to realize their dreams and achieve their desired lifestyle. Climbing Everest or flying into space are just a credit card transaction away.

This trend is crossing over to the service sector. From hotels to restaurants to airlines, consumers are looking for suppliers who go beyond the basics to meet their unique needs. They are looking for what we at Forum call a Branded Customer Experience®, a service experience that is intentional, consistent, differentiated, and valuable.

Author and consultant Patricia Seybold agrees: "To win in the customer economy you need to build and sustain an exquisite branded experience and to measure and monitor what matters to customers. That's new." She goes on to recommend that companies appoint a high-level executive responsible for the total customer experience across product lines and distribution channels.[1]

Companies are listening. Hewlett-Packard, for example, now has two large customer enterprises – one for consumers and one for business customers. Each one has a president, and reporting directly to that president is a vice-president responsible for the total customer experience. Scott Livengood, CEO of Krispy Kreme, says: "Instead of a customer service department – words are important and what things are called is very important – we developed and implemented a customer experience group."

Experience is about more than semantics. Creating a customer experience that becomes synonymous with your brand is increasingly recognized as a vital driver of corporate performance. Disney started the trend. Southwest Airlines adapted it to the airline sector. In the UK, First Direct started a new concept in banking using it. Howard Schultz of Starbucks applied it to selling coffee. Ian Schrager is perfecting it in the hotel sector and Amazon.com is applying it in the online environment. All of these companies are creating loyal customers by delivering Branded Customer Experiences that create value for customers beyond the products or services the companies happen to sell. Why this, why now?

> **Creating a customer experience that becomes synonymous with your brand is increasingly recognized as a vital driver of corporate performance.**

Psychologist Abraham Maslow conceived his theory of motivation more than 50 years ago. Maslow believed that humans evolve through five stages of motivation: first, the physical need for food and shelter; second, the need for longer-term security and protection; then, the social need for a mate, friends, and family. Only as we answer these needs do our ego needs for achievement and recognition become dominant. At the highest level of motivation, realizing our dreams becomes the driving force.

For many people of Maslow's generation, moving up this hierarchy of needs was a lifelong struggle. They lived in the dark shadows of need, the bitter experiences of the depressions of the 1920s and 1930s, and two world wars.

Today, most young people take meeting the physical needs for granted, and their social and ego needs become their starting point.

Wearing a pair of Timberland boots is as much about making a statement as it is about keeping the feet dry. The need fulfilled by the boots is much more than a humble physical one. The boots are a means of expression, of belonging to a "tribe." This phenomenon has been colorfully described by the British economist John Kay: "I am irresistible, I say, as I put on my designer fragrance. I am a merchant banker, I say, as I climb out of my BMW. I am a juvenile lout, I say, as I down a glass of extra strong lager. I am handsome, I say, as I don my Levi's jeans."[2] The brand is a means of self-expression.

For increasing numbers of consumers, Maslow's higher order needs have become the drivers. Maslow called it "self-actualization," the desire to fulfill one's potential. For many people in developed societies, income levels are such that people have the freedom and choice to pursue their desired lifestyle. Self-actualization is their most deeply felt need. Witness the profusion of books on self-development, on nurturing our souls, reaching individual enlightenment. No one thinks of nurturing their inner self when putting food on the table is an issue.

Allied to the drive to achieve one's full potential is the need for the time to do it. Convenience has become increasingly valuable. We want to be at one with our souls, but would rather it was a speedy experience. We are impatient. We want it all and we want it now.

Think back to how things have changed and by how much. In their book *The Experience Economy*, Joseph Pine and James Gilmore relate this shift in service to the birthday party.[3] When our parents were young, their parents would visit the local store to purchase the ingredients to bake a birthday cake. When we were small, our parents would buy ready-made cakes with all the trimmings from the supermarket. Our birthday celebration involved our friends and our parents making amateur efforts to provide the entertainment. Now, our children are taken to McDonald's with a few friends for their birthday treats. Increasingly, parents will pay to delegate the entire birthday experience, complete with decorations and entertainment, to a T.G.I. Friday's, Chuck E. Cheese's, or Rainforest Café.

Each generation of consumers has enhanced the buying experience. Consumers are willing to pay an increasingly large premium for the extra value represented by each succeeding one. Evolution rules.

Evolving brands

So how does the development of this experience-rich world relate to brands?

If we go back to the beginning of the twentieth century, brands were simply a means of identifying goods. Our need for safety and security created brands that, over time, became proxies for quality and dependability. Apply Maslow's hierarchy to brands and we were at the basic level of seeking security.

Brands reassured. They were warm, domestic, comforters. Kellogg's became synonymous with healthy breakfasts, Gillette with safety razors, and so on. Then, as consumers became more affluent and motivated by ego needs, brands became more aspirational and visible signs of success. We wore them like badges.

And the power of the badges has steadily increased. Karl-Heinz Kalbfell, BMW's global head of marketing, now talks about "wearing a lifestyle." For many consumers in the 1990s, driving a BMW was as much about making a statement about who they were as was wearing a pair of Armani jeans or Nike cross-trainers.

At one level this could be dismissed as incredibly superficial. But people have always sought to express themselves through their clothes and possessions. People like being badged, the feeling of belonging, the sense of identity with a group – however distant this may be from their reality.

This use of brands as a means of expression has grown over recent years. In today's economy, brands say something about what is important to us, about our values and our lifestyle. They are much more than superficial statements of taste. What they express is much more important, more personal. The Body Shop, First Direct, Four Seasons Hotels, Virgin, Saturn, Amazon.com, Quicksilver, Linda McCartney meals, and Home Depot are all brands that have intentionally created products and services aimed at particular consumers and their lifestyles.

Brands have moved from being names of products to badges of success to a means of enjoying the kind of life we wish for ourselves.

Think of Starbucks. The now ubiquitous coffee shop chain started life in 1971 when Gerald Baldwin, Gordon Bowker, and Zev Siegl opened a gourmet coffee store in Seattle's Pike Place Market. To launch the business they raised $10,000. The trio called their enterprise Starbucks.

Starbucks really took off after Howard Schultz joined in 1982 to help with its marketing. Schultz had grown up in Brooklyn and went to college on a football scholarship at North Michigan University. He later became a Xerox salesman. In 1987 Schultz bought out the Starbucks management team for $4 million and set about broadening the company's horizons. He opened a store in Chicago. It took off. More followed. And then more. Today, the company has over 2,000 stores worldwide. The approach was a branding classic. "The goal was to add value to a commodity typically purchased on supermarket aisles," said Schultz. "At our stores our baristas [bartenders] introduce customers to the fine coffees of the world the way wine stewards bring forward the world's fine wines."[4]

Starbucks offered excellent service combined with a rejuvenated product. "Starbucks is not a trend. We're a lifestyle," proclaimed Schultz. The Starbucks training manual explains: "As Americans, we have grown up thinking of coffee primarily as a hot, tan liquid dispensed from fairly automatic appliances, then 'doctored' as needed to make it drinkable... The opposite of this approach is to treat coffee making as a brand of cooking. You start with the best beans you can buy, making sure they are fresh. You use your favorite recipe. You grind the beans to the right consistency and add delicious, fresh-tasting water."

Starbucks did little advertising to build its brand strength. "We concentrated on creating value and customer service," says Schultz. "Our success proves you can build a national brand without 30-second sound bites."[5] Between 1987 and 1998 Starbucks spent less than $10 million on advertising. It recognized that great experiences are worth much more than Super Bowl ad slots.

"What we've done is we've said the most important component in our brand is the employee," says Schultz. "The people have created the magic. The people have created the experience." His autobiography is suitably entitled *Pour Your Heart Into It*.

Howard Schultz believes that the advantage Starbucks has over other brands is that "our customers see themselves inside our company, inside our brand – because they're part of the Starbucks experience." Brands are us.

Consumers are looking for service experiences that complement their lifestyle, and brands that say something about their aspirations. Put these two things together and you have the Branded Customer

Consumers are looking for service experiences that complement their lifestyle, and brands that say something about their aspirations.

Experience®. This is not simply a neat phrase. Commercially it is irresistible – or should be. The potential benefits of a Branded Customer Experience® to the organization are enhanced loyalty, higher margins, and an increased share of spend.

The cost of the coffee in your $2.25 cappuccino may only be 18 cents. You are paying for the experience (see Fig. 1.1). Little wonder that competition to create such experiences is hotting up faster than milk in a Gaggia coffee machine. According to one report, the number of "branded" chain outlets in the UK, such as Starbucks and Pret A Manger, will grow from 1,300 today to more than 2,400 by 2003.[6]

Figure 1.1   *Welcome to the experience economy*

Commodities	Goods	Services	Experiences
Coffee	Nescafé	McDonald's	Starbucks

18¢ ————————————————————▶ $2.25

Based on The Experience Economy.

Creating and managing brands

Technically speaking a brand is a trademark which differentiates the goods and services of one supplier from that of another. This trademark might be a name, a logo, a color, a shape, even a smell or a sound (anything in fact that is capable of being written down – yes, the particular description of the smell of a tire is a trademark, as Sumitomo's lawyers will tell you!).

But of course, we know that brands are so much more than that. A brand represents a pact between supplier and customer. The brand owner promises to deliver a particular experience and the purchaser promises his business in return. Like all pacts its strength depends on the brand owner's ability to deliver and to ensure constantly that the promise and the delivery are kept relevant. And, like all pacts, the more consistently it is delivered over time, the deeper and more secure the relationship that is built between the two parties. From an economic point of view it is the security of this brand relationship that provides a reliable guarantee of future earnings for businesses – and that is why brands become valuable.

However, to understand the true value of brands and the loyalty they engender among customers, one has to understand what comprises a brand.

"Products are built in factories, brands are built in the mind" has become a cliché but, like all clichés, retains a strong element of truth. People buy brands for three main reasons:

- At a basic level they provide a functional need which customers consider necessary, e.g. clothing, sustenance, taste, communications, financial security, or traveling from A to B. Meeting this need is the traditional role of the product and the focus of much product marketing.

- The possession of a brand makes a social statement about the desired self-image of the customer (to be seen as fashionable, traditional, smart, reliable, whatever). Meeting this need is primarily the role of promotions and packaging, and particularly of advertising.

- At a more profound level, the buyer identifies with and philosophically or emotionally connects with the attitude or the ethos that the brand represents (be it innovation, trust, hope, environmental concern, radicalism, conservatism, safety, etc.). This requires a business-wide belief system that delivers the promise to customers.

The brands that create the strongest relationships and therefore the greatest economic value are the ones that provide great products, distinctively promoted but above all delivered with an almost philosophical commitment. Coca-Cola, BMW, Sony, Virgin, Disney, IBM, and Nike are examples of such brands.

So what should we look for in a great brand? There are six broad processes that brand management needs to focus on if it is to create sustainable brand value:

1 **Developing and maintaining a differentiated point of view that is credible and relevant to customers:** great brands have a different way of looking at the world from their competitors. This differentiation is the key to their appeal to customers. Harley-Davidson has a different belief about the role of the motorbike than Suzuki, Apple has a different point of view about computers than IBM, and so on. Understanding the mindset of your customers and how to appeal to them begins with an understanding of what makes you different.

2 **Creating a differentiated visual identity consistently applied across every aspect of the brand:** great brands do not just think differently, they look different. They own, legally or by popular perception, an icon, color, style, imagery that makes any communication instantly recognizable. BMW dealerships would be instantly recognizable even if you took the BMW logo off them, so consistently applied and differentiated is their design. Nike advertisements ooze "Nikeness" to the point that they only have to put the swoosh symbols at the end and we all know who it is from. Too many brands copy their visual cues from market norms (white colors for detergents, footballs for sports brands, etc.). This makes them inherently unrecognizable. And if they are easily confused with another brand why should anyone bother to buy them?

3 **Communicating powerfully, consistently, and empathetically with all external stakeholders:** great brands develop communication strategies that are not only creative in their choice of style and content (Budweiser's reptile ads, for example) but also in their choice of media (the legendary Apple ad at the Super Bowl, a gigantic Swatch dressing a building, etc.). Their choice of communication is always relevant to the audience that they are trying to reach. Moreover, the great brands realize that it is often as important to communicate with the influencers in a marketplace (be it government, charities, or even parents).

No matter to whom they talk, it is always with the same voice – but with different accents.

4 **Communicating powerfully, consistently, and empathetically with all internal stakeholders:** it is becoming understood that brands that earn their customers' loyalty are characterized by employees who understand and identify with the brand. Leading-edge communications that target and inspire employees, combined with a form of one-to-one relationship marketing by managers with their staff (understanding their needs, explaining their objectives, helping them attain their goals), is critical to the development of a positive brand-centric culture.

5 **Aligning processes, systems and training, development, and management structures and style with the brand promise:** this is where the difference between great authentic brands and the great creative advertiser is seen. Organizations that put their promise to the customer at the heart of their operations ensure that:

- people are recruited who have an attitude consistent with the brand;
- human resources, operations (R&D, customer service, requisition), and marketing work together and share best practice;
- management style reflects the behaviors that would be expected of staff dealing with customers.

Nowhere is the gap between perceived brand promise and actual brand delivery more frequently apparent than in service industries. Too often, the internal imperative in businesses like airlines, financial services, and restaurant chains has been about protecting the cost base while the external promise has been about growing the customer franchise.

6 **Measuring what contributes to brand value, not what creates short-term sales:** there is not necessarily a conflict between short-term sales and brand building but too much of the sales growth companies encourage is often at the expense of long-term brand value. Businesses that care

> about their brand will take into account a wide range of
> factors, both those which can best be described as "lag"
> indicators, i.e. those which indicate historic performance –
> such as market share, sales turnover, and profits – and as
> importantly, those "lead" indicators which predict market
> behavior – such as customer satisfaction, brand equity, and
> brand value.
>
> **Andy Milligan, director, Interbrand**

The future of the developed world's economies will be about creating for customers a perceived "value for experience." The future of brands will lie with those who ensure that those experiences are delivered internally and externally. If one takes this view on the value, appeal, and management of brands, then the importance of culture, leadership, and an organizational focus on the delivery of an outstanding customer experience is critical to the creation and maintenance of brand value. That is what this book is about.

Experiencing the brand

There are two routes to creating a Branded Customer Experience®. The first is *experiencing the brand*; the second is *branding the experience*. They are similar – but differ in their starting point. For organizations that are established brands in mature markets, experiencing the brand is the way to go. In other words, what does the organization need to do to bring the brand to life and deliver on its advertising promises?

Sometimes brands can become a liability because of their historical associations in the minds of consumers. In this case there is a need to create a totally new experience and brand. This is when branding the experience is the route to take, as in the case of First Direct in the UK and Saturn in the US. This route also works for new organizations seeking to differentiate themselves. Look at the UK airline easyJet. Stelios Haji-Ioannou, the company's chairman says: "I did not start a brand. I started an airline which became a brand." Haji-Ioannou started with a market opportunity, conceived a customer proposition, created a customer experience, developed the route to market, and then, finally, designed the brand to communicate it.

First, let's look at the experiencing the brand route. Experiencing the brand is basically the customer realization of the Branded Customer Experience®. Organizations start with the brand and what it represents and then intentionally create an experience that delivers it to customers.

One organization that successfully embarked on a process to completely rethink how it wished to deliver its brand was the UK supermarket Tesco. Ten years ago the brand was lagging behind in the grocery market and was known for its "pile it high – sell it cheap" mentality. Today it is the UK's most successful retailer and the largest online grocer in the world, and Sir Terry Leahy, the CEO of Tesco, was recently voted one of the UK's most admired leaders.[7] Tesco's mission is to "create value for customers, to earn their lifetime loyalty." Over recent years, Tesco has embarked on a complete change program to focus on the customer and deliver against its "Every little helps" promise. This has led the retailer to pioneer the Tesco Clubcard to better understand the buying patterns and needs of its most loyal customers; the introduction of new format stores ranging from Metro stores in city centers to destination hyperstores; and home shopping for those who would prefer not to shop in stores at all. At the heart of this change has been the Tesco brand and what it represents to customers. Terry Leahy makes this point very clearly: "Our business strategy and our brand strategy are almost inseparable because one so closely defines the other."

> **Delivering on promises is rarer than you might imagine.**

Experiencing the brand begins with the brand and its desired values, turns these into a promise for target customers, and delivers the promise in a way which brings the brand alive (see Fig. 1.2). "A brand is a promise, and in the end, you have to keep your promises. A product is the artefact of the truth of a promise. Coke promises refreshment… There is no difference between what you sell and what you believe," observes the futurist, Watts Wacker.[8]

Delivering on promises is rarer than you might imagine. Next time you are watching television, take note of the promises the advertisements make. How many of those promises are actually delivered? Not many. Yet broken promises are a huge cause of customer dissatisfaction and turnover.

Fulfilling the promise requires engaging and aligning every employee, every department, and every process with the values of a brand. It entails significant investment in education and training, effective teamwork, performance management, communication, and systems that provide the skills and information everyone needs to succeed.

This holistic view of the brand and the organization creates an opportunity to define what the organization is and why it should matter. "Companies must be able to describe themselves – both internally and externally – because they are no longer adequately defined by the products they make. Customers buy the company and everything it stands for. So the company must be able to define itself in a connected and coherent way," says Jesper Kunde, author of *Corporate Religion*.[9]

One of the executives we interviewed for *Uncommon Practice* was John Whitaker of the charity Oxfam. "The brand and our beliefs influence and affect the way we work," he told us. "While our brand is a vehicle to achieve our beliefs, it's also all about our people. It's the people that we're working with – whether they're employees or volunteers or partners."

Figure 1.2   *Experiencing the brand*

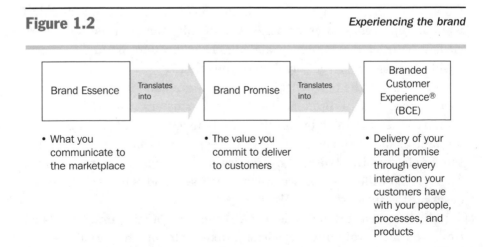

Brand Essence	Translates into	Brand Promise	Translates into	Branded Customer Experience® (BCE)
• What you communicate to the marketplace		• The value you commit to deliver to customers		• Delivery of your brand promise through every interaction your customers have with your people, processes, and products

It seems that values are increasingly becoming the cornerstones of brands. In 1998, Forte, the hotel group, went through a systematic process of articulating values for each of the four brands in its portfolio (Le Meridien, Post House, Heritage, and Signature). This process was based on extensive customer research. The company then invested $15million over a three-year period, cascading the values and be-haviors to 47,000 employees in a program called "Commitment to Excellence." Forte's efforts and substantial investment sought to ensure that it would move beyond promising to begin delivering the brand values for its customers.

All too often, organizations stop at high-level brand values – such as responsiveness, trustworthiness, and friendliness – without ever articulating how those values will be brought to life for customers in a way that differentiates the organization from competitors and without ever articulating how employees will need to behave to deliver on the promise. But all the values in the world are meaningless corporate decoration unless they're translated into consistent action. The customer experience is where the corporate rubber makes contact with the market highway.

Branding the experience

It has always seemed to me that your brand is formed primarily, not by what your company says about itself, but what the company does.

Jeff Bezos CEO, Amazon.com

Brands are powerful because of what they say about an organization. Sometimes this can be a limitation because of the associations consumers hold about the brand and the experience it represents. For example, some years ago, the UK's Midland Bank identified that there was a profitable and growing segment of the population that values time and convenience above all else. People in this segment lead busy lives and want to bank with an organization that is always available and easy to access, and one that provides quality service. Midland recognized that it could not credibly meet this segment's need with its own brand and its legacy of traditional offices.

The result was the creation of First Direct, a new brand and a new concept. First Direct customers can access their accounts any time of the day or night on the telephone. Staff are responsive and friendly. One of the key recruitment criteria for frontline staff is communication skills rather than previous bank employment! Midland first created the experience and then created the brand to market it. Today, First Direct has the highest satisfaction levels in the market, gains one-third of all of its new business through referrals, and is recommended by its customers every four seconds.

Branding the experience involves organizations setting out to create a new experience for target customers and then branding it accordingly. The starting point is the customer and what he or she values. This may not be the same as what the customer wants, however. Sometimes customers don't know what they don't know simply because they have never considered it possible. So bank customers would have experienced difficulty in suggesting the First Direct telephone banking model before it was offered but they certainly knew that they wanted more convenience and better service.

In the US automotive industry, General Motors created a new brand and branded experience with Saturn. GM knew that to successfully compete against the Japanese imports it needed to totally rethink how cars are sold. Its slogan – "A different kind of car; a different kind of company" – summed up the need to create distance from the GM brand and the traditional associations car buyers held of the experience. GM's complete engineering of the customer experience and the brand was neatly summarized by Stuart Lasser, a Saturn dealer: "We knew from the beginning that, if Saturn was to succeed, we'd have to do more than just sell a good car. We'd also have to change the way the cars are sold, the way the people who sell are perceived, and the way the customers feel about the experience of shopping for a car." Within five years of its launch, Saturn was the #2 car in US retail sales in the market and enjoyed the highest customer retention rate (61 percent) in the market.[10]

The other main use of this second route takes place during start-ups where the market opportunity and customer need can be used to create the brand. You start with the customer experience and then develop the brand to reflect it (see Fig. 1.3). As easyJet's Stelios Haji-Ioannou recalls: "If I am honest with myself I have to admit that I did not start a brand. I started an airline which became a brand."

Figure 1.3 *Branding the experience*

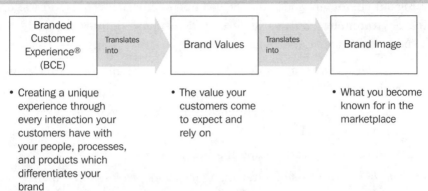

An extreme form of branding the experience occurs when the experience is so unique that it requires no obvious visual identity at all. A case in point is a collection of hotels in the US and UK developed by Ian Schrager. Schrager has been so successful in branding the experience with his St Martin's Lane hotel in London that, unless you know it is there, you will not find it. It does not have a sign, nor does it look like a hotel. You cannot even see into the lobby through the frosted glass of the main doors. Yet, the hotel and its three restaurants are always fully booked. St Martin's is a unique hotel experience. So much so, that satisfied customers promote the brand through word of mouth and obviate the need for billboards or advertising. Ian Schrager has successfully branded the experience. The question is will he be able to sustain the quality of that experience so that it continues to thrive on word of mouth alone?

The Branded Customer Experience®

Common to both routes we have described is the notion of the Branded Customer Experience®. This is a powerful driver of customer loyalty. In a survey forum conducted with the UK retail research consultancy, Verdict (described in more detail in the next chapter), we found that the supermarket chain William Morrison has the most loyal customers of all UK food retailers. We subsequently had a chance to ask Michael Bates,

William Morrison's marketing director, what the company's secret was. "I really don't know," he said. "We are just passionate about consistently giving our customers good quality food at a keen price in a friendly shopping environment." Bates's understated response defines precisely the Branded Customer Experience® in that it is:

- *Consistent* – in terms of delivering that experience over time and location.
- *Intentional* – in terms of delivering a customer experience to support the brand.
- *Differentiated* – from competing brands.
- *Valuable* – in terms of offering a customer proposition which meets target customer needs.

Passion sums up the approach taken by one of London's rising branding stars, Pret A Manger, the fast-growing coffee and sandwich chain. Pret's slogan is "Passionate About Food." It sets out to offer fresh food served quickly by friendly employees. Large posters on the walls in Pret stores spell out what "Passionate About Food" means in terms of the ingredients the company buys, the way its coffee is grown, selected, and so on.

Wanting a coffee, we called into a local Pret A Manger during a busy lunchtime. As usual, the place was packed and the staff very busy. Nevertheless, the service was prompt and friendly. When we came to pay, the young lady said: "The coffees are on the house." When we asked her why, she said we had waited longer than we should have. Her action in itself created a Branded Customer Experience®; it reinforced our already positive impression of this exceptional company. Do you think that Pret will cover the cost of those free coffees in our future purchases? Of course. We have been converted from consumers into "brand advocates."®

Though Michael Bates of Morrison's summed up the essence of his organization's Branded Customer Experience® with admirable simplicity, we cannot pretend that creating such an experience is easy. If it was straightforward companies would all be offering truly memorable experiences. They do not. In a world of complexity, simplicity is as rare and elusive as the Siberian Tiger.

For many companies, branding itself was the source of the problem. For years, branding was the domain of marketers and creative people from the advertising industry. Only consumer product companies scrupulously examined their brand identity and distilled what it is that makes their company special. Creating a Branded Customer Experience® requires a new and enhanced understanding of the notion of what a brand is, what a brand involves, and what a brand does.

Norman Blackwell, former director of group development at the bank NatWest, has observed: "Brands are not something created by advertising, they are created primarily by what we do." Brands are not empty statements or meaningless stamps, but actions. What companies *do* – as opposed to the material goods or specific services they provide – is the means by which customers experience a brand.

The best way to examine the Branded Customer Experience® is to set it at the opposite end of the spectrum from random experience (see Fig. 1.4). Most mass market shoe stores offer a random service experience. It varies from store to store, day to day, and sales assistant to sales assistant. There is little intentionality evident in the service the customer receives. As such there is little loyalty to any particular store, and most consumers simply window-shop whenever they need shoes.

Few large brands leave customer service entirely to chance; they invest in service training, standards, and processes to intentionally shape the customer experience to make it more predictable and consistent with

---

Figure 1.4   *Branded Customer Experience® drives customer loyalty and profits*

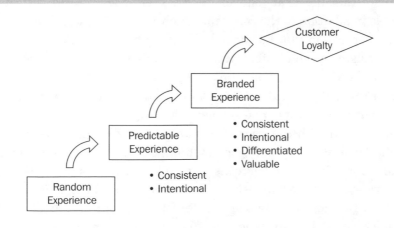

their brand. Their doing so is certainly important; we know that one of the biggest causes of dissatisfaction is unpredictability – not knowing if the product will be in stock, if the plane will leave on time, if the table reservation will be made – but it is not enough. Take McDonald's for example. This brand became famous by introducing predictability into the fast food industry. Customers were attracted by consistent standards, predictable service, and reassuringly identical food wherever the restaurant happened to be. However, this soon became the price of entry for any large fast food chain and now customers take consistency for granted. They are increasingly favoring outlets that provide this and more.

ATMs (cash dispensers) are another example. Banks were certainly "intentional" when adding this element to the customer's experience, and they succeeded in making that experience highly consistent. However, what bank has significantly differentiated the ATM experience? A large section of the market – typically older, wealthier, and potentially valuable customers – simply do not value the convenience offered by ATMs. First Direct, on the other hand, has taken a conscious decision to use technology in general and telecommunications in particular to provide a "high-touch" service that provides convenience *and* builds lasting customer relationships because it provides enhanced value. (It has also done this with its website, as described in Chapter 8.)

Branded Customer Experiences are created rather than conjured up from the marketer's box of branding tricks. They are intentionally and carefully designed to meet target customer needs, are consistent in meeting these needs, and are differentiated from competing offers. The difference that the Branded Customer Experience® creates is in itself valuable in addition to the core product or service that is offered.

An organization that has done well on the three counts of intentionality, consistency, and differentiation, but has yet to fully address the final hurdle of creating a *valuable difference,* is the Rainforest Café, a chain of restaurants which sets out to create a "jungle experience" for diners. The restaurants are festooned with tropical plants and creepers, the air is filled with the cries of monkeys and exotic birds. Is it intentional? Certainly. The management has gone to enormous trouble to create the jungle effects. Is it consistent? Certainly. It is the same experience whatever store you visit and whenever you visit it. Is it differentiated? Very. There is only one Rainforest Café. But is that difference valuable? The answer depends on if you are a target customer or not.

If you are, then the themed approach may be enough to keep you coming back. If you are not, the experience may be satisfying once or twice but the novelty can wear off unless it has intrinsic value and satisfies your needs in a way that no one else can.

The failure of the Fashion Café – the international restaurant chain supported by various supermodels – can be attributed to the fact that the theme of the chain did not create lasting value for its customers over time. Compare T.G.I. Friday's, which serves a similar market. The organization provides a customer experience which is intentional, consistent, and different from that of other fast food restaurants – and one which provides value. T.G.I. Friday's friendly staff and its fun atmosphere, interesting food, and reasonable prices create an experience which is so unique to T.G.I. Friday's that it is branded. The secret ingredient is the staff. They have taken the brand and made it their own with their zany hats and badges and very individual style of service to customers. Clever themes are not enough to sustain a leading position. They can be copied and become commonplace. It is only when the experience is so embedded in the culture of the organization that every single employee delivers the promise again and again that the organization thrives.

> **Brand themes and gimmicks don't last. They are the branding equivalent of one-night stands.**

Woody Allen noted that "Sex without love is an empty experience but, as empty experiences go, it is one of the best." Brand themes and gimmicks don't last. They are the branding equivalent of one-night stands. Creating a Branded Customer Experience® – one that really drives customer loyalty – requires thought, effort, and resources. It requires careful design, it requires new forms of collaboration between marketing, HR and operations, and it requires the means to harness the power of your people to turn them into brand ambassadors. It also requires the seamless integration of high-tech and high-touch, the powerful combination of processes, products, and people. But most of all it requires managers to understand what it means to lead the brand.

Experiencing the brand and branding the experience take different routes but have the same concept at their heart – the Branded Customer Experience®. The model that we use for depicting the BCE is shown in Fig. 1.5.

Figure 1.5 *The Branded Customer Experience® management model*

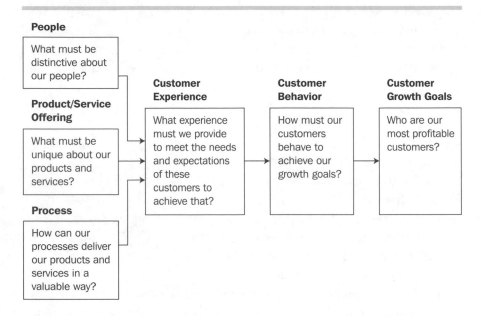

In the next chapter we will describe our approach to creating these experiences. The results are worth the journey. A study by Accenture and Montgomery in 2000 found that if a $1 billion enterprise increased its investment in customer interactions from average to high, it could anticipate a $42 million return on investment. They concluded that "superior relationship management is worth half your bottom line." The payoff is in the experience.

Starting points

Consider your own brand and ask yourself:

1 What are our key growth goals?
2 How do our customers need to behave to achieve them?
   - try
   - buy
   - buy more

- buy more often
- buy exclusively from us
- pay more
- refer others

3 What experience do we create for our customers?

4 Is it sufficiently valuable and differentiated to cause our customers to behave as we wish?

5 What promise does our brand make?

6 Do our customers believe that we deliver on the promise?

7 How must our people, processes, or products perform differently to deliver on the promise?

These questions are simple. Their answers are complex. Nonetheless, they can be – and *need* to be – addressed, as rapidly growing companies in every industry are proving. Innovative companies are beginning to equate their brand with everything that shapes the customer experience – so that their brand embodies such superior and distinct value that customers can neither overlook nor forget it. The goal is an emotional and practical barrier to switching which is so high that competitors have to work near miracles to lure customers away (as opposed to so-called loyalty programs many of which simply lock in customers with incentives until the loyalty points are spent or a competitor comes up with a more attractive scheme).

The C-O-O-L customer experience in lodging

The Hudson in Manhattan was voted the world's coolest hotel closely followed by W in New York's Union Square. While wealthy American tourists still flock to the Dorchester, the Ritz, or the George V in Paris, the people "in the know" can be seen parking their Ferraris outside the Sanderson and the Colonnade in London or the Montalembert in Paris.

The coolest hotels are those that deliver a Branded Customer Experience®. The once sedate world of exclusive hotels has been reinvented. What is going on?

The answer is that pampering is passé. Sophisticated travelers now expect an experience. In the words of Ian Schrager, who developed the concept of London's St Martin's Lane, the hotel "represents the first hotel of the next wave – a hotel for modern people that crave something original, different, and magical."

So why the shift toward boutique and designer hotels? First some history. Hotels started out as lodges, accommodation for travelers on the road. They provided a bed and board, albeit in a range of different grades from the simple inn to the sublime Raffles Hotel in Singapore. With the advent of business travel, guests wanted a "home away from home." In-room televisions, mini-bars, and beverage-makers became the norm. Holiday Inn created a worldwide design which promised uniformity wherever you stayed and became a virtual home for many frequent travelers.

With the growth in leisure travel, hotels became destinations, resorts in their own right offering spas, activities, and entertainment. Fairmont Hotels and Resorts create guest experiences that make the most of the locations in which they are situated. The Banff Springs Hotel is a perfect place to ski and stay, for example. If romance is more your thing, the Banyan Tree chain offers "Intimate Moments Packages," romance neatly packaged as a hotel experience. While you are at dinner the hotel will decorate your pavilion room with 50 candles, run the water for your outdoor bath, lay out a tray of aromatic oils for your massage, and be on hand to provide the massage, teach your partner to give it, or just leave you alone.

People want to experience their desired lifestyles. Why have a Philippe Starck designed bathroom in your new loft apartment and then be forced to use some mock marble monstrosity straight out of the 1980s when you stay in your very expensive city center hotel?

Skeptics may suggest that boutique hotels are triumphs of form over function. Not so. There is more to them than minimalist foyers and eclectic restaurants. They provide a customer experience and a style of service which is technically excellent but also informal and a long way removed from that of the condescending maîtres d'hôtel who continue to inhabit some grand dining rooms.

Do not think that Branded Customer Experiences are reserved for the very rich or those in search of decadence and luxury. This trend is not restricted to upmarket brands alone. Malmaison Hotels, voted UK hotel group of the year in 1999, offers in-room artwork, entertainment centers and "cool" CDs at a very reasonable rack rate. Its brand promises "Hotels that dare to be different," its website features a virtual room tour, and its people have acquired a reputation for being friendly.

This shift is being fuelled by the continued growth in tourism and business travel as well as the increasing trend toward eating out and weekend breaks for affluent young professionals. In the UK, for example, the hospitality market is forecast to grow by 50 percent to reach $21.9 billion by 2004, according to Euromonitor.[11]

Even the large chains are bringing designer brands to market. Starwood, owner of the Sheraton and Westin Hotels, launched its W brand in New York and since then has opened a further 12 properties. Like the Ian Schrager properties, the W brand offers few clues to its ownership. The designer hotels set out to intentionally create a customer experience that is different and valuable. "We find a Sheraton customer goes to a Sheraton and a W customer to a W. Our W guests are some of the most loyal we have," says Barry Sternlicht, Starwood's chairman and CEO.[12] As a result, margins are often far higher than for most traditional hotels.

So is the day of the grand old hotel over? No there will always be a market for hotels like the Ritz-Carlton, the Dorchester, Raffles, and Savoy for example, because their attention to detail, opulence, and outstanding service are timeless. They have long realized that the experience is the thing. The difference is that the experience they offer appeals to a different audience than to the Ferrari set. Perhaps that is why you are more likely to see a Rolls Royce parked outside.

Put all this together and the conclusion is that hotels are finally waking up to the fact that they will be more successful if they are more intentional in targeting customers, understanding what these customers value, and then designing an experience which delivers that. If they get it right, business trips may well become fun again.

Notes

1 Dearlove, Des, "When the Customer Clicks, Jump," *The Times,* June 30 2001.

2 Crainer, Stuart and Dearlove, Des, *The Ultimate Book of Business Brands*, Capstone, 1988.

3 B Joseph Pine II and James Gilmore, *The Experience Economy – Work is Theatre and Every Business is a Stage!* Harvard Business Press.

4 Ioannon, Lori, "Making Customers Come Back for More," *Fortune,* March 16, 1998.

5 Ioannon, Lori, "Making Customers Come Back for More," *Fortune,* March 16, 1998.

6 *Evening Standard*, January 16, 2001.

7 *Management Today*, December 2001.

8 Crainer, Stuart and Dearlove, Des, *The Ultimate Book of Business Brands*, Capstone, 1988.

9 Kunde, Jesper, *Corporate Religion*, FT/Prentice Hall, 1999.

10 Whiteley, Richard and Hessan, Diane, *Customer-Centered Growth,* Addison Wesley, 1996.

11 "Hotels in the UK," Euromonitor, September 2000.

12 www.brandchannel.com

2

■■■■■■■■■■■■■■■■■■

Beyond satisfaction

Brand loyalty is very much like an onion.
It has layers and a core. The core is the user
who will stick with you until the very end

Edward Artzt former CEO, Procter & Gamble

In 1979 when Terry Leahy joined the UK retail chain Tesco as commercial director for fresh foods, Tesco was, as Leahy puts it, 'a struggling organization with a poor self-image." Things didn't change overnight. Even as recently as the early nineties, many customers were saying that Tesco was in it more for the profit than for them.

When he became marketing director in 1992, Leahy knew what he was up against: "Essentially what happened was that we were so busy benchmarking another company that we'd lost focus on our own customers, and they had been hard hit by the recession. They needed Tesco to give them better value and we weren't doing that. Paraphrasing reams and reams of research, what they were saying was 'You have been too busy following that other company and haven't been following us.' And so from that day on we really changed the philosophy and direction of the business, and we determined to follow our own customers, rather than follow everybody else."

By 1995, Tesco was breaking new ground in food retailing by introducing the first customer loyalty card as a way of offering benefits to shoppers while also helping the company to discover more about its customers' needs. In the same year Tesco overtook its main rival to become the largest food retailer in the UK. It is still leading the pack with Leahy now at the helm as CEO.

How did Tesco manage its impressive turnaround? Initially, it was the strategic decision to follow the customer rather than competitors. Immediately after that, a whole recovery strategy was laid out based on listening very carefully to customers and changing the organization in order to earn their loyalty. What the customers consistently said was that they came into Tesco because of the staff. "It's not about customers being loyal to you. It's about you being loyal to your customers. You earn loyalty by giving it," says Clive Humby of Dunhumby Associates, which helped develop the Tesco Clubcard.

Loyalty, as managers increasingly realize, has a lucrative effect on bottom-line performance – loyalty helped Tesco rise to become the UK's leading supermarket retailer. Companies with satisfied, loyal customers enjoy higher margins, greater profits – and consequently, higher stock-price earnings (P/E) multiples – than businesses that fail to retain and satisfy their customers.

In his book *The Loyalty Effect,* Frederick Reichheld of Bain & Co. identifies that loyal customers are more profitable, because the costs of sales are amortized over a longer period, they increase their purchases and percentage of spend with you, cost less to administer, refer others, and are willing to pay a premium.

The economics of customer loyalty equally apply to e-commerce. Bain has undertaken two years of research into e-loyalty. Bain's Reichheld and Phil Schefter simply conclude: "Price does not rule the web; trust does. Without the glue of loyalty, even the best-designed e-business model will collapse."[1] This explains why CEOs at the cutting edge of e-commerce – from Michael Dell, to eBay's Meg Whitman – care deeply about customer retention. Loyalty, say Reichheld and Schefter, is an economic necessity: "Acquiring customers on the internet is enormously expensive, and unless those customers stick around and make lots of repeat purchases over the years, then profits will remain elusive."

In the fall of 2001, researchers at Satmetrix Systems conducted a study to empirically determine if there were any links between improved customer satisfaction and higher price-to-earnings ratios. What they discovered proved more startling than anticipated. The research revealed that the P/E ratios of companies with above average customer loyalty index scores were more than double those of their competitors. That spread translated into a $1 billion market valuation for even the smallest Fortune 1000 firm.

The Satmetrix study showed that as customer satisfaction increases, so do retention and referral rates, proving in resounding terms that satisfied and loyal customers are the principal drivers of profits. Not only do they continue to purchase products and services, the value of satisfied and loyal customers exponentially increases as they refer new business, acting (as they do) as the most ardent evangelists, spreading good news across markets. Equally important, there is a direct correlation between customer satisfaction and that of employees – companies with loyal customers typically enjoy loyalty in the workplace as well.

> **"It's not about customers being loyal to you. It's about you being loyal to your customers. You earn loyalty by giving it."**

These findings empirically demonstrate what has always been intuitively understood in the business world – that to create happier shareholders, organizations must create experiences that make happier customers.

The Satmetrix research echoes other research findings of recent years. According to a Conference Board study, customer loyalty is the number one issue on the minds of CEOs.[9] The role of loyalty as a powerful profit generator is increasingly being recognized. In the Conference Board research, a total of 37 percent of CEOs, from North America, Europe, and Asia, identified customer retention and loyalty as the greatest management challenge facing their companies. An increase in the importance of retention was particularly evident in Europe. Much hyped issues, such as increasing flexibility and speed, competing for talent, and reducing costs, trailed behind.

Of course, growing senior management enthusiasm for customer loyalty does not mean that companies have suddenly become adept at retaining customers or that their investment priorities have dramatically shifted.

The fact remains that most companies invest more in acquiring new customers than they do in keeping the customers they have. On the surface this does not seem a particularly startling fact. The need to attract a continuing stream of new customers is conventional commercial wisdom. Much of the initial frenzy surrounding the new economy concerned large sums of money being directed at acquiring customers, with little thought to sustaining the relationship over time.

In this instance, conventional wisdom is fatally flawed. The economics are simple. It costs six times more to acquire a new customer than it does to keep an existing customer. At the same time, a 5 percent increase in customer loyalty increases the lifetime profits of a customer by as much as 95 percent. Investing in building loyal customers is an investment in profitable growth.

Knowing the economic facts – and these are facts – does not make retaining customers any easier. Capturing this largely untapped source of profit potential is demanding. To do so, a company has to go beyond customer satisfaction and create an indelible impression that results in customers becoming true advocates for the company and its products and services. The best companies do not leave loyalty to chance – they design it in so that it is part of their raison d'être, integral to their culture, performance, outlook, and brand. Creating and nurturing loyalty is the driving force behind the way the company is organized and structured, as well as the way it behaves.

Gimmicks don't buy loyalty

The first important realization for companies coming to terms with the nature and meaning of loyalty must be that loyalty is not the same as satisfaction. Our research shows that many customers who switch suppliers are satisfied with their previous supplier. Neither is loyalty the same thing as repeat purchases.

Indeed, for a number of industries, what are perceived as loyal customers are actually lazy customers or, in some cases, customers who have few alternatives and are, therefore, locked in. Until First Direct came along and made it attractive and easy to switch banks, few customers would entertain the inconvenience of closing their account and applying for one elsewhere, yet the retail financial segment has generally low levels of satisfaction among consumers. What kept customers coming back was not loyalty, but the hassle factor and the fact that most banks offered equally poor service. Not any longer. First Direct tells its prospective customers: "We can now transfer your standing orders and direct debits for you – so transferring bank accounts has never been easier." Locked in customers, resigned to poor service, have been galvanized. First Direct has raised expectations and reaped the benefits.

Loyalty is more than an initiative or a program. This has not prevented thousands of loyalty programs being launched. Research by the consulting firm McKinsey and Company found that about half of the ten largest US retailers in each of seven sectors have launched loyalty programs, which give consumers rewards for repeat purchases from particular merchants. In the US, 53 percent of grocery customers are enrolled in them.[3]

While many loyalty programs are successful, they also struggle with three stubborn facts: they are expensive (16 major European retailers had a total of some $1.2 billion tied up in annual discounts to customers); they are easy to start but hard to finish; they often fail to increase customers' loyalty (70 percent of grocery customers say they are always seeking alternatives to their current retailers).

According to McKinsey, ineffective programs often fall into one or more of four traps:

- They attract free riders (as many as half of all members of loyalty programs enjoy benefits without spending more).

- There are slim margins versus attractive rewards (a retailer's two percent rebate on $500 worth of annual household sales translates into a rebate check of $10 a year – not much in absolute terms and trivial compared with the 25 to 40 percent markdowns now common in a price-driven retail environment).

- They fail to track expenses (for a large multi-site retailer, the launch and maintenance investment can easily reach $30 million in the first year).

- They are competing on unequal terms with the virtual world (dot coms with venture capital and an intense need to create buyer awareness commonly offer cash rebates of 5 percent and more – a level beyond the reach of most retailers).

The reality is that many of the loyalty cards now on offer are not about loyalty so much as price promotion, since they are available to anyone, regardless of how profitable that customer is to the organization, and simply incentivize customers to spend their money with the company offering the best discount (thinly disguised as points). Many customers now have wallets full of loyalty cards and simply use whichever one is most convenient or advantageous on any given day. Part of this apathy comes from the fact that few loyalty card holders fully understand the benefits their card is supposed to bestow. Research carried out by General Motors for its GM card found that only 32 percent of respondents knew the details of the perks offered by their card's loyalty scheme.[4]

The benefits of airline loyalty schemes are better known and therein lies their danger. One major airline calculated that if a competitor offered a frequent flyer program superior to its own, most of its customers would desert, because the underlying satisfaction levels were not enough to keep them loyal. Since then, it has placed much more emphasis on improving its customer experience, the key to creating true loyalty, and even going beyond it. This is well understood by the very profitable Midwest Express Airlines which operates commuter routes. The airline has created a loyal following of customers through a recipe of superior seating, food, and service. "Frequent flyer programs are a hook, but they're a meat hook," according to Cliff Van Leuven, the airline's director of customer service.

Likewise, Kevin Hawkins, communications director for the UK operation of Safeway, says: "Loyalty is not synonymous with having a loyalty card. Since we scrapped our ABC card we have gone on gaining customers – one million more customers have come to us over the past year. You can give them a point for every penny spent but it doesn't buy you loyalty. It's the fulfillment of the offer that transcends everything."

So are we against customer cards? The answer is no *if* they are used to gain insights about target customers and their needs and to shape the offer the organization makes to them. Their real value is in creating knowledge about the customer. As Ian Eldridge, group CEO of Pizza Express, puts it: "Our Pizza Express club has over 22,000 members who write to me, e-mail me, and phone me, on a very regular basis, with their experiences. Some executives may see this as a pain but I don't." It is then up to the organization to create a customer experience that earns real value. A card alone won't do it.

Loyalty requires an emotional engagement with the organization or product. This engagement comes from experiencing the brand or organization in a unique way that creates true value for the customer.

In an often quoted study, Xerox is said to have polled 480,000 customers for several years regarding product and service satisfaction using a five-point scale from 5 (high) to 1 (low). Until a few years ago Xerox's goal was to achieve 100 percent satisfaction – 4's (satisfied) and 5's (very satisfied) combined. But the company discovered that the relationship between loyalty and satisfaction differed depending on whether the rating was satisfied or very satisfied. In fact it found that those customers awarding a 5 were six times more likely to repurchase Xerox equipment.

In a survey conducted in 2001 by Forum with consumers in the US, Canada and the UK, 69 percent of customers who awarded top scores for satisfaction indicated their intention to be loyal to that organization. That figure dropped to just 19 percent for customers who were still satisfied but rated one box lower. The reason is that over the past ten years organizations have become increasingly aware of the need for customer focus and customer satisfaction. So much so that it is now the norm and the entry price for any organization wishing to be successful. As a result, differentiation on the basis of customer service has actually declined, price sensitivity has increased, and it now takes a unique customer experience, one which goes beyond satisfaction to create real value, for the company to regain the edge.

So is brand loyalty a thing of the past? Carlson Marketing Group's annual brand survey found that brand loyalty has decreased by 25 percent overall in the last year. The younger age groups seem particularly promiscuous, with 70 percent of under 35s professing only slight or no loyalty to their financial services provider. Marcus Evans, Chairman of the Carlson Marketing Group, said: "This is a real wake up call for the banking industry. It is clear that it has been guilty of over-promising and under-delivery." Yet the same survey found that those organizations that provided a good experience for their customers over multiple touch-points and over a variety of channels had loyalty levels 33 percent higher than the norm. A 30 percent higher retention rate translates into significant increases in profitability.[5] So what should we take from all of this?

The message is that satisfied customers are not necessarily loyal customers. Satisfaction is now expected, taken for granted. According to Forum research, 80 percent of customers who switch suppliers express

Many of the loyalty cards now on offer are not about loyalty so much as price promotion.

satisfaction with their previous supplier. They are pleased with the service they receive and yet they still head off to a competitor. Some companies might dismiss such customers as fickle or promiscuous and reflect that securing their loyalty is probably an impossible task. They are wrong. The challenge is to provide a customer experience that successfully differentiates the organization and drives brand loyalty – as many of the organizations we researched are proving.

Loyalty at work

Loyalty happens because it is worked at, invested in, considered, and pursued. Gaming company Harrah's Entertainment consistently delivers customer experiences in a number of ways. "We concentrate on building loyalty and value for our customers, shareholders, employees, business partners, and communities by being the most service-oriented, technology-driven, geographically diversified company in gaming," says the company. Harrah's CEO Philip Satre says that the company's strategy is built on the brand, service, focus, distribution, and loyalty.

Extensive customer research led to the company identifying five drivers of customer loyalty. From this it created what it calls the FOCUS strategy, which concentrates on those loyalty drivers. This strategy, and the value drivers themselves, are so intrinsic to the Harrah's experience that we are not at liberty to divulge them. How worried would you be if your competitors found out your brand values or customer service standards? If the answer is not very, then you have a long way to go in turning these into a Branded Customer Experience® that truly drives loyalty.

In itself this sounds like one of those cheesy but well-meaning initiatives companies are prone to announcing. But Harrah's used the examination of what customers value and the FOCUS strategy to completely realign its metrics to ensure delivery of the customer experience. Its employees were trained to deliver FOCUS at every customer touchpoint. Harrah's also developed a customer information system that tracks preferences and ensures a truly personalized experience.

In 1999, Harrah's launched a $10 million service initiative which included a Target Player Satisfaction Survey and a Performance Payout Incentive Plan which rewards employees for meeting customer experience goals. In the first year, the company paid out $7 million to employees for achieving improvements in service.

That's a lot of money, but Harrah's has benefitted. Its 2000 revenues were $3.5 billion, a record for the company and up 15 percent over the year.

Loyalty happens with products too. When Steve Jobs, the CEO of Apple, introduced the new PowerMac at the annual Apple convention the reaction of the audience was more akin to a revivalist religious meeting than a product launch. There is no doubt that many Apple Macintosh customers are passionate champions for their preferred brand in a way few other computer users are. Jobs has managed the company's rebirth by tapping into this rich source of support.

Or look at the car rental business. The deals offered by various rental companies are all much the same. There are differences, but they tend to be small and relatively unimportant. What truly differentiates is not whether you have a 1999 or a 2000 model; it is the experience. Does the experience provide you with the value you expect?

Avis thinks so. F. Robert Salerno, Avis president and COO, explains: "Avis has dedicated tremendous amounts of resources over the last several years to develop a process for managing the customer experience and to provide our employees with the tools for supporting our strategies of winning customer loyalty and service excellence. Customers are telling us that there is something special about Avis and the value we deliver that the others can't match."

According to a survey carried out by Brand Keys, Avis has the highest customer loyalty among rental car companies by some distance.[6] Indeed, Avis received the highest number of points for customer loyalty among all 129 companies in 24 industry categories. They found that rental car customers determine loyalty based on: pricing and options; convenience; safety of vehicles; customer service; and services in case of breakdown.

Avis scored best in the area of customer service – the very area where customer expectations are highest.

Look at another company, one which creates such loyalty among its customers that they subject themselves to pain in order to promote its products. Next time you meet a Harley-Davidson owner look out for the famous winged logo tattoo. The likelihood of a customer switching to a competitor's product after having your identity literally "branded" on their body is fairly remote.

Harley-Davidson really understands that its brand is much more than just its famous winged logo – it is a total ownership experience. This realization can be traced back to 1981, when a group of 13 senior Harley executives led by Vaughn Beals bought the company. They celebrated with a victory ride from the company's factory in York, Pennsylvania, to its headquarters in Milwaukee. The new owners started the Harley Owners Group to get customers more involved with the brand. The Group now has over 600,000 active members.

In 1993, the company celebrated its 90th anniversary with more than 100,000 Harley enthusiasts converging on Milwaukee and a drive - through parade featuring 60,000 Harley-Davidson machines. When Richard Teerlink took over as CEO, he continued to tap into Harley's greatest asset – the people who care about the Harley-Davidson brand. He opened a dialog outside the company with the loyal customer base and inside the company with its workforce. John Russell, President of Harley-Davidson Europe, sums it up: "Every company probably has their real brand enthusiasts, their loyalists, but I think what Harley has been able to achieve is that we've made it a very significant proportion of the ownership."

Loyalty colors the way people feel about organizations. John Lewis, the UK retail stores partnership, was one of the organizations identified in our research as offering a high-quality experience. A poll of 10,000 London residents conducted by recruitment firm TMP ranked 125 well-known organizations in terms of their desirability as employers. Respondents were asked to rate the extent to which the company was one they knew much about, would consider working for, had a good reputation, looked after its staff, was forward looking, had a name that would look good on a résumé, was to be trusted, and would make one proud if someone in the family worked for it. The organization voted favorite was John Lewis. When organizations provide a high-quality experience to customers they also become more attractive to prospective employees. This connection is clearly understood by the group chairman, Sir Stuart Hampson: "I want John Lewis to be two things in the future. The destination of choice for our customers and the employer of choice for people who want to work in retailing and have the creative and individual talents that would suit our business. I deliberately state both of those because I think unless you achieve both of them you won't achieve either of them."

From loyalty to advocacy

Revenue growth has everything to do with "advocacy," the readiness of customers to prefer a supplier and then refer friends, relatives, and colleagues. Advocacy is genuine, deeply felt, loyalty. The dictionary definition of "advocate" is "plead for, defend, champion, recommend, support." This is much more than customers who come back time and time again. Advocates are people who are prepared to argue your case. They are willing to offer their support as well as their business.

While we use the word advocate, others have their own vocabulary. Scott D. Cook of the software firm Intuit coined the term "apostles" to describe highly valuable customers. He should know. Intuit achieved sales of $30 million with just two field sales representatives by creating very high levels of customer satisfaction and word of mouth marketing for its Quicken personal financial software.

Sometimes, an organization can create such high levels of loyalty that the brand is accepted on trust by the market at large because of the positive word of mouth support of satisfied customers. Phil Dourado of www.ecustomerserviceworld.com tells the story of attending the annual CRM conference in Paris a couple of years ago when relationship marketing expert Professor Adrian Payne asked for a show of hands from those who considered themselves to be advocates of Virgin Atlantic. Around 50 hands went up out of the 300-odd people in the room. He then asked those with their hands up to put them down if they had flown with the airline. This left about ten hands up. "So, you are people who are advocates of Virgin Atlantic ... but have never flown with them?" Payne said to clarify. The hands stayed up.

How can an organization create advocacy without customers having a first-hand experience? By creating such a differentiated experience that customers become your best salespeople. Richard Branson launched Virgin Atlantic at a time when most airlines were still state-run and had a reputation for being operationally driven and rather boring. What Branson did was to create a proposition that matched the safety and procedural efficiency of competitors but created a new and exciting customer experience. He put the fun back into flying. His upper class was soon a big hit, essentially a first-class product at a business-class fare. The on-board bar, interactive entertainment system, in-flight massage, CD-quality music channels, and friendly and attractive cabin crew all created a customer experience that was new and different. When Virgin started flying the Hong Kong route using medium-range aircraft, it sometimes had to build in fuel stops because of strong head-winds. British Airways, on the other hand, was using its long-haul 747s that were easily able to carry the fuel to make the trip non-stop. Even so, many business passengers still preferred to risk the delay of the refueling stop for the sake of the unique on-board experience.

Business people soon started talking about Virgin and recommending it to others. "There is definitely a club feeling about Virgin Atlantic," said Steve Ridgeway, Virgin Atlantic's customer service director. "You feel it particularly among customers in our upper class. It comes across in a fierce loyalty – our loyalty levels are around 98 percent – and in a keen-ness to make word of mouth recommendations, coupled with a slight hesitancy, as if customers feel they don't want to let too many people in on a secret they've discovered."[7]

Loyalty makes the difference. What is striking about the examples we have cited is that they come from a huge range of industries and busi-nesses. Some are household names, others more obscure, but all have deliberately, creatively, and determinedly set out to build loyalty. Loyalty can be designed in as we shall see in Chapter 3.

Advocates on main street

In the spring of 2000, Forum partnered with Verdict, the retail research company, to survey 2,000 consumers in the UK market across five retail segments. Our purpose was to discover which large brands had the highest levels of customer advocacy. We asked customers to rate the quality of their experience on a ten-point scale of satisfaction, with ten being the highest score. We broke down the findings into three groups of consumers: the Advocates rating 9 or 10 for satisfaction, the Vulnerables rating between 5 and 8 as we know that merely satisfied customers are liable to switch supplier, and the Terrorists who give less than 4 for satisfaction and who are likely to tell others of their dissatisfaction. Table 2.1 shows the advocacy levels overall for the five segments we studied.

At the individual company level we found that William Morrison, the supermarket chain that is best known in the North of England, scored a mean of 8.42 out of 10. This may explain why William Morrison is one of the country's fastest growing supermarket chains.

Table 2.1   *Ratings of quality shopping experiences*

	1–4 – Terrorists	5–8 – Vulnerables	9–10 – Advocates
Food/Groceries	3%	71%	26%
DIY	4%	76%	20%
Electricals	4%	74%	22%
Personal Care	1%	70%	29%
Clothing	5%	74%	21%

On the other hand, Marks & Spencer, one of the UK's oldest and most revered retailers, scored a mean of 6.95. Quite similar results then with a difference of only 1.47 in the average satisfaction level. Clearly, both organizations have fairly satisfied customers, but could they justifiably take the view that no action was required? Not so.

We also calculated the percentage of those customers rating 9 or 10 (what we define as "advocates" since these are the customers most likely to recommend to others) and rank ordered the 31 organizations according to this measure. The results were fascinating. The average percentage of customers scoring 9 and 10 for the retail segment was 24 percent. The level of advocacy for Morrison was a massive 54 percent, whereas the percentage of Marks & Spencer customers rating 9 or 10 was just 12 percent. So Morrison enjoyed more than four times the advocacy of M&S. Perhaps this is why in the year following our survey Marks & Spencer's share price collapsed and rumors spread about its likely acquisition. As we were writing this book in the summer of 2001, Luc Vandevelde, the Marks & Spencer chairman and chief executive, announced 5,000 layoffs.

Marks & Spencer is now embarking on a brand reinvigoration program. Only time will tell if this is successful but our hunch is that if M&S focuses on what its target customers really value and then sets out to create a shopping experience to deliver this, it may turn the corner and, once again, attract customers and shareholders. Early indications are that this refocussing on the brand and customer experience is beginning to pay off.

Over this same period, William Morrison achieved the highest margins in its sector. In early 2001 the company announced its annual results – reporting a gain of 500,000 new customers and an increase in sales of 9.1 percent while pre-tax profits rose by 16 percent. It is one of the few retailers refusing to offer a loyalty card. Advocacy translates into retention, increased share of spend, and higher levels of acquisition.

Morrison's has continued to build its brand reporting the highest like-for-like sales growth in the industry over the Christmas period 2001/2002. So what is the secret of Morrison's success? In the words of John Dowd, the company's managing director: "We keep it simple; we give good service and value and this attracts people." This is an important point. Advocacy is not about "gold plated" service but about delivering a consistent and distinctive customer experience that creates value for your most profitable customer segments again and again.

Are you managing customer advocacy?

Consider your own company and ask yourself:

1 Do you know who your most profitable customers are?

2 How much are they worth to you compared with your average customers?

3 What are the three most important customer expectations that drive loyalty in your business?

4 What do your managers and employees believe customers expect?

5 How does your performance compare against your competitors in relation to the top three customer expectations?

6 To what extent do you consistently deliver a distinctive experience for your most profitable customers based around these expectations?

7 What would be the impact on customers' willingness to recommend you if you were to achieve top-ranking performance for these expectations?

8 What would be the impact on your market share growth and bottom line if you were to increase your advocacy rate (i.e. customers awarding a 9 or 10 rating) by 10 percent?

Notes

1 Dearlove, Des, "Loyalty Can Pay Dividends," *The Times*, September 13, 2001.

2 "The CEO Challenge: Top Marketplace and Management Issues 2001," The Conference Board 2001.

3 James Cigliano, Margaret Georgiadis, Darren Pleasance, and Susan Whalley, "The Price of Loyalty: Do You Know If Your Loyalty Program Is Working?", *McKinsey Quarterly*, 2000, No. 4.

4 *Loyalty Magazine*, Issue 4, 2001.

5 2001 Brand Loyalty Survey, Carlson Marketing Group.

6 Brand Keys 2001 Customer Loyalty Leader's Index.

7 *Loyalty Magazine*, 2001.

3

■■■■■■■■■■■■■■■■■■■■

Loyalty by design

Any damn fool can put on a deal but it takes genius, faith, and perseverance to create a brand

David Ogilvy

Intuit nurtured word of mouth referrals causing its customers to act as their sales force; First Direct intentionally wanted consumers to close their accounts with competitors; Harrah's wanted its target customers to spend more of their gambling budget with the organization; Harley-Davidson wanted its customers to buy more than just the bike.

These companies have made loyalty an integral part of their business models. They remain a minority. As customer loyalty has risen up the corporate agenda, responses have followed a conventional pattern. A great many companies jumped on the loyalty bandwagon and pro-claimed customer loyalty a key issue. Usually their initiatives offered lip service to meeting true customer needs. The retailer that installs a piano player on the mezzanine, or the financial services firm that spends millions on CRM systems are both likely to be disappointed in cust-omers' responses *unless* those elements are part of a well-conceived customer experience strategy that is consistent across all business channels. Good intentions only get you so far.

Others have pursued customer loyalty with greater commitment but similarly limited understanding of the dynamics which lie behind loyalty. The key questions often lie unanswered: How do you create a level of customer satisfaction that is so strong that customers become your best salespeople? How do you create advocates, true believers in a world of agnostics?

The answer lies in creating a customer experience that is so distinctive and valuable that it goes beyond satisfaction and even individual loyalty and becomes instead the primary engine for growth.

Jill Griffin, in her book *Customer Loyalty: How To Earn It, How To Keep It,* suggests a useful ladder of customer relationships:[1]

- **Stage 1 Suspect:** suspects include everyone who might possibly buy your product or service. We *suspect* they might buy; we do not know enough yet to be sure.

- **Stage 2 Prospect:** a prospect is someone who has a need for your product or service and has the ability to buy. Although a prospect has not yet purchased from you, he or she may have heard about you, read about you, or had someone recommend you to him or her. Prospects know who you are, where you are, and what you sell, but they still haven't bought from you.

- **Stage 3 Disqualified prospect:** these are prospects about whom you have learned enough to know that they do not need or do not have the ability to buy your products.

- **Stage 4 First-time customer:** first-time customers are those who have purchased from you once. They can be customers of yours and still be customers of your competitor as well.

- **Stage 5 Repeat customer:** they have purchased from you two or more times. They may have bought the same product twice or bought two different products or services on two or more occasions.

- **Stage 6 Client:** a client buys everything you have to sell that he or she can possibly use. This person purchases regularly. You have a strong, ongoing relationship that makes him or her immune to the pull of the competition.

- **Stage 7 Advocate:** like a client, an advocate buys everything you have to sell that he or she can possibly use and purchases regularly. In addition, an advocate encourages others to buy from you. An advocate talks about you, does your marketing for you, and brings customers to you.

If loyalty is seen as a process, an evolving relationship, then it is clear that it cannot be instantly introduced. Instead, loyalty needs to be built in a systematic way. Loyalty must be designed and created. The end result of designing customer loyalty into a business model is about building a brand and creating advocates for that brand. The customer's experience is the ultimate builder of a brand and the ultimate driver of brand loyalty. The experience and the brand, what the organization stands for, become so inter-twined that they can no longer be separated or torn apart by a competitor.

> **Loyalty must be designed and created.**

Creating loyalty is about being intentional, consistent, different, and creating value. The companies that succeed consistently in designing in loyalty follow these steps (see Fig. 3.1 also):

Define customer values

1 Identify target customer segments.
2 Define what target customers value and determine which values drive buying and loyalty behavior.
3 Create a differentiating brand promise.

Design the Branded Customer Experience®

4 Develop a profound understanding of the customer's experience.
5 Design critical touchpoints and employee behaviors to deliver the brand promise.
6 Develop a comprehensive change strategy to implement the new customer experience.

Equip people and deliver consistently

7 Prepare managers to lead the delivery of the customer experience.
8 Equip employees with the knowledge, skills, and tools needed to deliver the brand promise at every customer touchpoint.
9 Reinforce performance through leadership action and measurement.

Sustain and enhance performance

10 Use customer and employee feedback to maintain a line of sight to the customer and continuously enhance the customer experience.

11 Align business metrics, HR systems, and business processes with the delivery of the customer experience.

12 Continuously communicate progress and results to embed the Branded Customer Experience® as the way you do business.

We shall now look at each of these steps in considerably more detail.

Figure 3.1   *How to implement a Branded Customer Experience*®

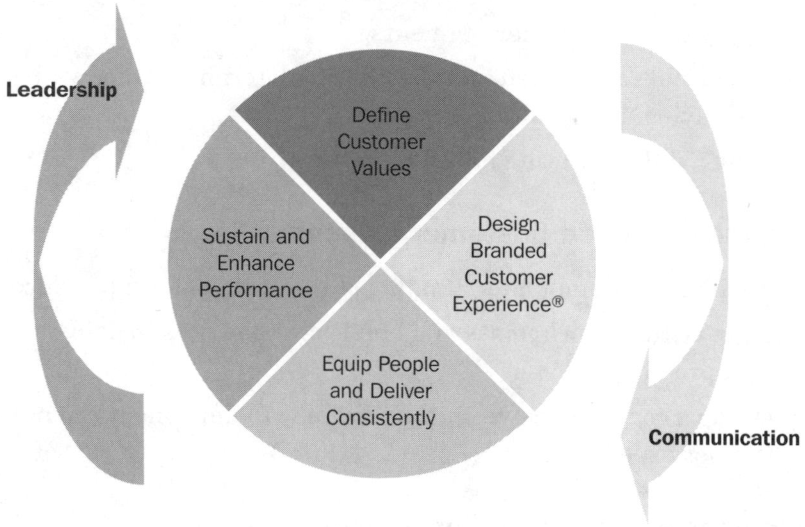

Define customer values

'The brand is all around the customer experience," says Scott Kisting, group executive vice-president of the commercial and retail banking arm of the California Federal Bank. "The product has to be competitive. Our home equity product was a mess when I got here. It was overpriced and undifferentiated. Everything about it was not very strong.

Not surprising, they were not selling it. First, we fixed the product. We made the price right. We made the underwriting correct. We did all those things. Then, we focussed on the two things that matter to customers. How long does it take to get an answer? How long does it take to get my money? We took out all the white space in between. We were doing 13 million a month in home equity, net; now, with the same amount of branches, same amount of people, we are doing 100 million a month."

To build a branded experience, companies must have absolute clarity about which customer segments are most profitable, what these best customers value, and how the organization can create and deliver on a brand promise which differentiates them from competitors.

Historically, companies have relied on demographics to segment their customer base. We find that segmenting customers by behavior creates a more useful focus – whether it's the small percentage of customers who generate the bulk of your revenue who have specific requirements, those customers whose lifestyle causes them to use your products and services in a particular way, or a potentially lucrative segment of the market with an unmet need. Stelios Haji-Ioannou, the chairman of easyGroup, applied this thinking to starting his rental car business: "Another Easy principle is we don't want to be all things to all men. We choose our target audiences and go for them. For instance, I find booking online highly convenient, I know people that hate it and will never do it. For them we are a nuisance because they can't rent our cars."

By focussing on delighting target customers, companies keep them loyal and eventually turn them into advocates who attract others who value the same things. Advocates are much more interested in product and service quality and significantly less interested in price. This results in higher margins and more resistance to the price promotions of competitors. Advocates buy more often, are prepared to pay more, and stay with you longer. They will also bring new customers to you. The strategy of focussing on your best customers – those who are most profitable – is not rocket science, yet it is surprising just how many organizations do not know who these customers are.

We were working with a major bank which comprised 14 major divisions covering credit cards, mortgages, etc., as well as the retail bank itself. Each division knew who its profitable customers were, but because the database was not integrated, the organization overall was unable to recognize its most important customers. This led to highly profitable mortgage customers being treated as new and, therefore, "high risk" by another division.

Many organizations seem to adopt the strange strategy of rewarding new customers rather than their most profitable customers. For example, some banks offer better rates of interest to prospective customers than existing clients. In supermarkets there are checkout lines reserved for those customers with "5 items or less." What about those customers spending $7,500 a year or more who are standing at the back of a 20-minute checkout line? A true reward for loyalty would be if these highly profitable customers were awarded a gold card and sped through special fast-track checkout lines. Let those customers only wishing to buy five items or less go elsewhere (unless they have a gold card allowing them to use the fast-track lines!).

Ashridge College's Tony Cram cites the example of a builders' merchant supplying house construction materials in the east of England. It analyzed its trade customers and discovered that the top 20 percent accounted for 80.2 percent of revenue. The tendency for a small number of people to account for the bulk of the value was first explored by the Italian sociologist and economist, Vilfredo Pareto (1843–1923). In his first work, "Cours d'economie politique" (1896/7), he observed that 80 percent of the wealth of Italy was owned by 20 percent of the population. With a complex mathematical formulation, he attempted to prove that income distribution is not random, and that a consistent 80/20 pattern appears throughout history.

The key to keeping your best customers is to know them.

Retailer Dayton Hudson chose to focus on its top customers. By this it meant not the top 25 percent, but the 2.5 percent who gen-erate the majority of sales. The retailer invested in a customer information system to track purchases and build relationships with this elite group. Dayton Hudson predicted that its "Great Rewards" program would enroll 3,000 top customers in year one. This objective was reached in the first month, a strong indication that these customers had been waiting for Dayton Hudson to recognize and reward their loyalty.

As Dayton Hudson vividly demonstrates, the key to keeping your best customers is to know them. Customer knowledge is the true benefit of a membership card program. As Sir David Putnam, the film producer, said: "The best and most effective brands in the future will be built around knowledge."

One such brand is Smarterkids, a successful e-business selling toys and educational software, based in Massachusetts. Smarterkids competes head-to-head with Toys Я Us and others but, instead of leading on price, it chooses to compete on knowledge. Its principal tool for this effort is a questionnaire that parents fill out for each of their children at the Smarterkids website. The resulting profile identifies the child's preferences, learning style, etc., and recommends toys that match these.

David Blohm, president and CEO of Smarterkids, says the company's objective is simple: "We help parents develop their kids." This is a straightforward statement, but one which goes to the heart of what the company's customers value and the commitment Smarterkids has made to deliver it.

Companies which succeed in creating loyal customers follow the same course. They pick their customers carefully and then they use a variety of methods to truly understand what these target customers value and which of these values will have the greatest impact on customer loyalty.

Customer research is about determining the precise expectations, experiences, and, most importantly, behavior of your most important customers and the extent to which you are meeting their needs. The result of this is an "expectations map," which identifies what customers expect in any interaction with the company. These interactions range from receiving a brochure in the mail to checking into a hotel, being greeted in a restaurant, buying a shirt, or taking out a mortgage. For each company there will be a distinct and unique "touchline" (comprising a series of touchpoints) that will map the experience the customer expects to have and actually has with your company (see Fig. 3.2). When working with clients we are amazed at how often we need to undertake expectation mapping because, although they have done extensive market research, the organization really does not know what its most profitable customers expect or currently experience in any meaningful detail.

Figure 3.2

Touchline map

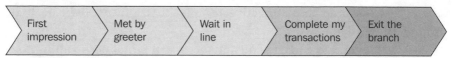

| First impression | Met by greeter | Wait in line | Complete my transactions | Exit the branch |

Customer expectations:

- Clear signage
- Clean surroundings
- Available staff
- Comfortable seating area
- Special area for premier customers
- etc.

As part of this process, there are two vital questions to keep in mind: What would make the interaction outstanding? And what goes wrong? Creative organizations open up the possibility of creating a very different customer experience by asking customers to relate their experiences, expectations, likes, and dislikes and then finding innovative ways to serve them. First Direct – on learning that its target customers most value speed, convenience, quality service, and value for money – responded by developing 24-hour telephone banking at a competitive price.

In one private client banking situation, relationship managers identified "assurance factors" as crucial, i.e. the bank's ability to inspire trust and confidence in customers. More specifically, they said, customers looked for peace of mind and reassurance after they had made decisions. They looked for knowledgeable, enthusiastic customer relationship personnel who also understood the need for confidentiality and discretion. When the bank tested a model based on the ability to deliver these consistently, it quickly identified opportunities to substantially increase business with existing clients. Having understood the expectations and current experience of target customers, the organization can now turn its attention to crafting the brand promise.

What is a brand promise? It is an articulation of what target customers can expect from their experience with an organization. It describes the proposition and the value that this represents to the customer.

- Carphone Warehouse, the UK retailer of mobile phones, promises "Simple – impartial – advice."
- Virgin Atlantic promises "To provide the highest quality of innovative service at excellent value for money for all classes of air travelers."
- Krispy Kreme, the US doughnut retailer, promises "To create Magic Moments."
- Midwest Express Airlines promises "The Best Care in the Air."
- First Direct bank promises "A bank designed around you, which doesn't expect you to fit around it."

Is that all an organization needs to do? Is creating a catchy promise that has appeal for target customers enough? Not quite. Now comes the hard part.

The brand promise represents the decisions made by managers about the value the company will deliver to its target customers in order to earn their loyalty. As with other statements of direction, management must create the brand promise, own the brand promise, and relentlessly drive it to completion. The brand promise drives all of the company's actions and investments in people, processes, products, technology, and delivery channels. It creates a laser beam focus that provides clarity and cohesion to the firm's many and disparate activities.

What does a brand promise look like in action?

Well, first of all it needs to be of value to target customers. Richard Branson believes the Virgin brand is based on five key factors: value for money, quality, reliability, innovation, and an indefinable, but nonetheless palpable, sense of fun. (Another, slightly snappier, version of the Virgin brand values is: genuine and fun, contemporary and different, consumers' champion, and first class at business-class price.[2])

Second, it must relate to one of Maslow's levels of need. Harley-Davidson promises "We Fulfill Dreams," which directly targets those seeking self-actualization.

Third, it must be actionable. A private banking group translated its brand promise into standards for each client interaction. A core value in their brand promise is to meet clients' needs and expectations on the client's terms, not the bank's. As a result, each relationship manager must understand how their customers want to be serviced, for example, at their place of business or at the bank. When presented with his employer's brand promise, a bank employee commented: "I like that it is so well defined. It does not only say that we provide the best service; it explains what providing the best service means and what it encompasses."

Fourth, the brand promise must be the focus and anchor for the organization. It serves as the promise made to customers, what the brand represents to customers and employees, and the internal values that are required to deliver it. In short, it replaces or aligns the numerous and disconnected missions, visions, values, brand values, and customer charters that we see in so many organizations that often are contradictory, confusing, and of little practical value in running the business.

Finally, the promise cannot be made lightly, it has to be delivered. In the words of Steve Jones, author and professor of genetics at Galton University: "The good opinion of the public will become increasingly important to big brand owners. If you've got a message, it has to have some truth in it or you'll be found out."

All of an organization's processes, products, and people must be designed to deliver the brand promise every day. The simple proposition of the coffee and sandwich chain Pret A Manger is that it is "Passionate About Food" and it promises not to compromise quality in any way. This is why Pret goes to the unusual lengths of using a four-foot wooden paddle to mix the ingredients for its fruit and oat slice (too pulpy otherwise). Pret has made a clear, unequivocal, and ultimately highly successful decision as to what it stands for. (That seems to be an appetizing proposition for McDonald's too. The hamburger empire has a 33 percent stake in Pret.)

The key to winning customer loyalty – and advocacy – with your brand promise is to meet or exceed the promise with every customer in every one of his or her interactions with your company.

One practical application of this tenet can be viewed at Disney parks, where customers in long lines for attractions see signs indicating they will board the ride "30 minutes from this point." In fact, these customers will reach the ride or attraction in 25 minutes. No wonder a Disney manager might tell you that his company "manages the customer's experience and manufactures profits!" Disney has an intimate under-standing of customers and is firmly in control of its promises.

While we're definitely not suggesting that you should set out to create 30-minute lines just so that you can over-deliver, the principle of inten-tionally and consistently delivering on your promises is critical: whether it is waiting no more than five minutes for a cashier, being able to return the product "no questions asked," or being able to get a good night's sleep in your hotel room.

Design the Branded Customer Experience®

As a result of its research and carefully thought-through customer promise, First Direct created a telephone experience that enables the customer to do all his or her banking transactions from the convenience of home. It supported the experience with state-of-the-art technology and a top-quality workforce. The result is that First Direct's customers are ten times more loyal than those of First Direct's closest competitor. First Direct is growing at an average of 10,000 new customers per month, one-third of whom come from referrals.

Designing the customer experience requires rigorous analysis and inspired creativity, attention to detail and holistic thinking, organiza-tional champions and cross-functional perspectives, up-front commit-ment and ongoing stewardship. Most of all, it requires customer empathy – seeing what the customer sees, feeling what the customer feels, and making it better.

According to Richard B. Chase and Sriram Dasu, both professors of operations management at the Marshall School of Business, University of Southern California, the underlying psychology of service encounters – the feelings that customers experience – remains comparatively unexplored.

Chase and Dasu suggest there are five operating principles that will produce better service management:[3]

1 **Finish strong**: the ending is far more important than the beginning of an encounter because it's what remains in the customer's memory. Chase and Dasu illustrate the point with the example of cruise lines, which end the experience with the

captain's dinner and the giving away of souvenirs on reaching the home port. In contrast, they found many website experiences end badly with difficulties exiting the site if a product is out of stock, canceling orders, and other problems.

2 **Get the bad experiences out of the way early**: in a series of events, people prefer to have undesirable events come first and to have desirable events come last. Here Chase and Dasu use the example of a pediatric dental hygienist cleaning a six-year-old's teeth. If the child experiences slight pain during the process, behaviorial science suggests it is better to complete the task, so that the child goes away with the idea that it "wasn't so bad," rather than leave the memory of the pain as the dominant impression.

3 **Segment the pleasure, combine the pain**: since experiences seem longer when they are broken into segments, it's best to combine all the boring or unpleasant steps of a process into one stage but keep the pleasant aspects spread throughout. For example, people would rather have one long wait in line than have to wait multiple times for a service. Disney theme parks have one long line but provide entertaining distractions for the people waiting, thereby making the wait more tolerable. On the other hand, gamblers would rather have two small wins of $5 than one larger one of $10.

4 **Build commitment through choice**: people are happier when they believe they have some control over a process, particularly an uncomfortable one. Chase and Dasu cite the example of a photocopying servicing company which countered complaints by allowing customers to have more choice over its servicing schedule, allowing them to determine the urgency of the problem. Customer satisfaction rose without the need to recruit more repair staff. In fact, fewer were required. In a similar vein, British Airways has totally transformed the way it thinks about in-flight service, so that it starts from the perspective of what the customer wants rather than what the airline offers. BA's "Raid the Larder" concept is an example whereby hungry passengers can help themselves to food and drink at any time of the night rather than waiting for the meal service.

5 **Give people rituals and stick to them**: most service encounter designers don't realize just how ritualistic people are. We are creatures of habit and what are habits but experiences we enjoy or find useful which we like to repeat?

Ultimately, only one thing really matters in a service encounter, conclude Chase and Dasu: the customer's perception of what occurred. "In any service encounter – from a simple pizza pickup to a complex long-term consulting engagement – perception is reality." In other words, what you get is what you see.

Designing the new Branded Customer Experience® to deliver the brand promise is part science, part art. The science part is described below.

> **Designing the new Branded Customer Experience to deliver the brand promise is part science, part art.**

Figure 3.3   *Designing the customer experience process*

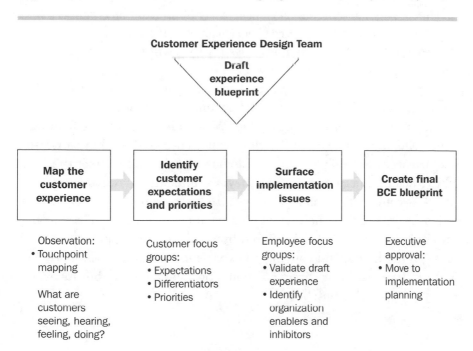

Customer Experience Design Team

Draft experience blueprint

Map the customer experience	Identify customer expectations and priorities	Surface implementation issues	Create final BCE blueprint

Observation:
• Touchpoint mapping

What are customers seeing, hearing, feeling, doing?

Customer focus groups:
• Expectations
• Differentiators
• Priorities

Employee focus groups:
• Validate draft experience
• Identify organization enablers and inhibitors

Executive approval:
• Move to implementation planning

The method we use when designing the customer experience is illustrated in Fig. 3.3. We gather together the key decision makers from marketing, operations, customer services, and HR along with the CEO, and over the course of two days we review customer expectations research, create a brand promise, review the current customer experience and then design a new branded customer experience to deliver the promise. This is where the art or creativity part comes in because it requires executives to think outside of the box, let go of established ways of doing things, and think the unthinkable. The new experience needs to not only meet core expectations, i.e. those expectations that customers demand from any provider, but also those which would differentiate the organization from competitors. This is exactly the kind of process Virgin uses when it enters a new market. One of the reasons that the Virgin brand has been so flexible is that while the markets in which it operates are so different, the values that it represents and its approach to customers is very consistent.

Finally the executives consider the enablers – the technology, processes, and training – that will enable the employees to deliver the promise and customer experience every day. Enablers can often be determined through employee observation and focus groups. This will in turn identify the implementation issues that will need to be addressed to successfully deliver the new experience. See Fig. 3.4.

A process such as this results from recognizing that each of an organization's interactions with its customers will either strengthen or weaken the relationship with them. What this suggests, we believe, is that companies have to take a whole experience view, so they can design experiences that deliver their customer promise. Of course, the great thing about experiences is that they are difficult – sometimes impossible – to copy. In the financial services industry, companies have become adept at introducing new products very quickly. A particular mortgage product can be copied and offered by a competitor within a matter of days, if not hours. But copying an experience is a great deal more difficult. In the UK, First Direct has had a host of emulators but its experience has yet to be matched.

Figure 3.4

Designing the new experience – bank example: routine transactions in branch

	First impression	Met by greeter	Wait in line	Complete my transactions	Exit the branch
Core	• Branch is clean, bright, safe, welcoming • Employees' appearance is professional	• Welcomes customer to branch, asks "May I help you?"	• Well communicated time for waiting	• Rep greets customers with "How can I help?" • Transaction completed accurately, quickly	• Rep asks "Is there anything more we can do for you today?" • Rep thanks customer using customer name
Differentiated	• Bank has comfortable coffee bar available • No admin tasks are visible to customers	• Greeter offers customer a beverage • Backup greeter always available	• No idle staff while customers are waiting • Roving teller helps customers in line prepare for transaction • Kiosk available to speed transactions	• Rep offers suggestions when appropriate • Customer never asked for same info twice	• Customers are provided with 800 number for feedback with an incentive to respond
Enablers	• New standards for housekeeping crews • Hire outside coffee service	• Process for backup greeter	• Line timing technology • Physical setting hides admin work • Process to ensure tellers always available	• Teller screen prompts cross sell opportunities • CRM is fully interactive across channels with customer info	• Process and technology for feedback capture • Teller knows which personal bankers are available

Experience Engineering

Customer experiences must be managed as a business strategy

Managing the customer experience is still often thought of as a marketing and services issue – or worse, creating entertainment.

The retailer that installs a piano player on the mezzanine, or the financial services firm that spends millions on CRM are both likely to be disappointed in customers' responses *unless* those elements are part of a well-conceived customer experience strategy that is consistent across all business channels.

You are already in the experience business

Experience is every firm's value proposition because no company can avoid delivering a total experience. A customer cannot *not* have one. However, most organizations do avoid managing them in a systematic way, in part because they don't realize the competitive potential, and also because managing experiences well is a complex undertaking which requires strategic commitment, new competencies, and management disciplines.

The composition of experiences

A managed total experience takes into account customers' rational *and* emotional expectations – an area most businesses overlook. Yet research confirms emotional connections are among the biggest drivers of repeat business.[4] As Harvard Business School Professor Gerald Zaltman says: "Consumer preferences and motivation are far less influenced by the functional attributes of products and services than the subconscious sensory and emotional elements derived by the total experience."[5]

Customers constantly filter a barrage of clues and organize them into a set of impressions – some of them rational, some emotional. Anything that can be perceived or sensed – or recognized by its absence – is an experience clue. If you can see it, it's a clue. If you can smell it, feel it, taste it, or hear it, it's a clue.

Products and services emit clues, as does the physical environment in which they are offered. The employees who assist customers are another source of experience clues. Each clue carries a message suggesting something to the customer. The composite of all these clues creates the total experience.

It is possible to positively manage the total experience by orchestrating the hundreds of clues customers sense as they interact with the organization. Conversely, when an experience is unmanaged, it is not uncommon for negative, unintended clues to cancel out even the most high-impact positive ones.

The need for an experience management system

All businesses are capable of delivering value-creating total experiences. A few, like Disney and Harley-Davidson, have been able to do it innately through the legacy of visionary leaders. Most, however, require a disciplined system that first establishes an experiential view across all business channels and touchpoints and then challenges the organization to move from random delivery of clues to more managed delivery.

For example, consider the impact of an automobile showroom designed to reflect the essence of the cars being sold. A Corvette showroom would have a distinctly different palette of experience clues than a showroom for Buick Park Avenues. Added to the environmental clues are those involving human interactions.

Imagine the potential for evoking positive and brand-distinct perceptions when the organization is attuned to the hundreds of clues throughout the entire experience – and seeks to manage them systematically.

Experience Engineering, a Minneapolis-based consultancy, has a Total Experience Management® methodology which takes an organization through the life cycle of the experiences they deliver every day. This rigorous audit develops insights into the subtleties of how customers feel about doing business with the company. The subsequent experience design that is created ensures that every clue throughout the experience is fashioned to register or reinforce a specific take-away impression and never detract from it. This then enables the organization to integrate these experience clues with people, product, and process changes to create a total customer experience. The outcome for customers is a far more aligned and brand-distinct experience due to the distinctive weave of clues that are embedded and repeated throughout the experience.

As an example of this approach at work, consider University Hospital's Emergency Services Department in Augusta, Georgia. One would assume that in a healthcare environment, caring and emotional connections would be par for the course. However, the emotional needs of customers – even in a highly emotional environment – are often systematically overlooked.

University Hospital implemented customer experience management for emergency services as a hedge against competition and to stem slowly declining customer satisfaction scores. The experience audit and discovery of the emotional strand for the ER revealed minimum recognition of the emotional needs of patients and even less for their families. The motif and clues that were subsequently designed focussed on creating a reassuring, empathetic connection with patients, family, and friends.

Over one hundred clues were created, starting from the beginning of the experience journey. They included:

- *Directional road signs* – additional signs were placed further out in all directions from the campus. "Hospital 3 miles" created reassurance further downstream in the experience, especially for newcomers to the area.

- *User-friendly entrances* – ironically a giant EMERGENCY sign and entrance that could easily be seen from the street was reserved for ambulances only. This left others perpetually confused as to which entrance to use and where to park. Repositioned and reworded signage addressed the problem.

- *Security guard turned greeter* – a stationary security guard, previously posted behind an imposing desk, became a roving ambassador to help people navigate the registration process.

- *User-friendly language* – "Care Points" were created to direct patients to where they needed to go. For example, "Triage Station," which appeared over the emergency room reception desk, was changed to "Care Point 1 – Reception." Most people had no idea what "triage" meant or what to do there. Pediatric Emergency became Care Point 3 and patients were directed to it by following a Popsicle icon.

- *Reconfigured furniture* – chairs arranged in the traditional straight rows were perceived as big "waiting" clues to patients and families. The chairs were rearranged into small circles with tables to moderate the perception of a long wait, to promote conversation and privacy, and to open up the area.

- *"Emergency room air traffic controller"* – once patients were admitted, registration staff and waiting family were cut off from their progress "inside." A new position was created to track patient charts and keep the family connected and informed.

No one set of clues provided the magic. The benefit came in the elimination of negatives, followed by the cumulative design and build of emotionally positive clues, all related to the motif. Once the UH experience task force began looking through the lens of an experience management system, "a huge revelation and transformation took place," according to George Ann Phillips, director of Emergency Services at University Hospital: "It was impossible to look at the world the same way again."

Some members of the experience project team – doctors, nurses, and administrative staff – were so motivated by the initial scanning for clues that they devoted part of a weekend to change the morgue experience. The morgue? What can it possibly mean to design the morgue experience from a customer perspective? Normal procedure was for a gurney with the body to simply be wheeled into a storage room where the family was left to spend time with each other and their loved one. In just one day, the group put up curtains to create privacy, disconnected harsh fluorescent lighting and brought in lamps, furnished the area with chairs, repainted the room, and even put up a wallpaper border.

Equip people and deliver consistently

Passion is one thing, proof another. The proof lies in the delivery of the Pret A Manger experience. Pret goes out of its way to ensure the ingredients it uses (and the ingredients in its ingredients) are as natural as possible. The shops and processes are designed to help customers find what they want and be served as quickly, efficiently, and in as friendly a manner as possible. Staff are hired for their personality under the motivational slogan of "Passion, creativity, development, and teamwork" and are trained in every aspect of their products and processes. Pret employees have to prove they're passionate about food every time they serve one of the customers.

What Pret understands is that you need to equip people with the tools to deliver the experience time and time again. The experience must happen. It must be real for customers.

And we are not just talking about people in the front line of customer service. At too many organizations, executives remain out of touch with the daily reality of customer experiences. It's almost always smart for senior executives to occasionally take a day and experience their company as their customers experience it. Then they should go on to experience their competitors and ask people about their experiences. Are they 100 percent enthusiastic? How loyal are they?

Consistently delivering such customer experiences requires companies to fully equip employees to deliver the customer promise, support the customer experience with technology and infrastructure improvements, and continually reinforce the importance of the experience and the need to measure performance.

Look at how Home Depot delivers an experience that connects to what its customers value. Its target audience is "do-it-yourselfers" looking for a combination of value, convenience, and advice. Home Depot employees are knowledgeable (often with building experience), are well trained, and are given responsibility to use their initiative to sort out any problems that may arise.

The emphasis is on using interactions with customers to develop relationships. Relationships are built through initiatives such as free design and decorating consultations, truck and tool rental, home delivery, and in-store clinics – given so that customers can develop their DIY skills. In a single year, nearly 50,000 customers honed their skills at Home Depot University, a four-week customer education program.

A customer experience of this kind requires employees to have more than just vanilla flavored service training. The fact is most organizations provide service training to their staff and yet few deliver any kind of Branded Customer Experience®. It is necessary to identify the practices or brand behaviors required to deliver the new experience and, in turn, design training which equips the employees with the knowledge, attitude, and skills to behave in this way. We call it *head, heart, and hands training*.

In order for employees to deliver a Branded Customer Experience® three faculties are involved – the head, the heart, and the hands:

- *The head* – employees must *know* what customers expect and what this requires of them.

- *The heart* – employees must *want* to provide that experience® on a continuing basis.

- *The hands* – employees must be *able* to deliver the experience both in terms of skills but also empowerment.

We will say more in a later chapter about how employees can be trained to deliver the Branded Customer Experience®. However, training is only one part of it. Equipping employees is also about giving them the tools and supporting processes to deliver the customer experience (see Fig. 3.5). All too many organizations rely on the heroics of their people to recover customers after poor processes or technology have failed to deliver. There is a place for heroics in exceptional circumstances but such behavior should not be relied upon. Similarly, gimmicks can never replace meeting customers' core expectations.

Gimmicks can never replace meeting customers' core expectations.

For example, while Disney can and does serve as a model for other companies – in exceeding its brand promise and a host of other aspects of superb business management and customer relations – such benchmarking can be carried too far. It's not that Disney has it wrong, but when non-entertainment companies make scouting trips to Disneyland

Figure 3.5

Defining the practices or brand behaviors

EXPERIENCE ATTRIBUTES

	Serviced promptly	Interaction handled correctly	Knowledge of products/ services	Know me and my relationship	Solutions to meet my needs	Deal with issues promptly	Professional, friendly, courteous, etc.
Account opening	Greet customer warmly and by name	Confirm customer info to ensure accuracy	Describe products and services clearly	Create a profile of customer's needs	Confirm solution fits customer's need	No more than one handoff to solve problem	Always thank customers for their business
Routine transactions							
Financial planning/advice							
Loan request							
Problem resolution							
Request for information							

CUSTOMER EXPERIENCES

PRACTICES AND BRAND BEHAVIORS

Technology HR Policies Processes	Customer friendly info screens	Online product knowledge training and reinforcement	Need online customer profiling tool			Problem resolution network	

ENABLERS

to seek answers for lagging customer loyalty, they may be looking in the wrong place.

For instance, Mickey and Donald have found the secret to keeping people docile in a 40-minute line for a 90-second ride. But in most businesses the goal must be to eliminate, not placate, the line. Several years ago one of us dialed tech support for a highly profitable software maker. Instead of the normal recorded "please hold for the next available agent" message, we were greeted by a disc jockey who told us to expect a 25-minute delay and to enjoy a few pop hits while we waited. He came on the air every few minutes with an updated report: "System admin callers, your wait is down to eight minutes. Let's listen to 'Allison' by Elvis Costello." It was a novel approach, but missed the point. If the company could hire a DJ and buy all the latest hits, why couldn't it hire another tech support person or two or, better yet, produce a manual that would allow customers to answer their own questions?

The lesson: not everything Disney (or any other company) does can be profitably transplanted to other companies in any industry. What we can and should learn from Disney, among other things, are the bottom-line benefits of paying close attention to customer experiences and exceeding brand promises. More broadly, we all have favorite stores, restaurants, airlines, dry cleaners, and florists. They know what matters to us and bend over backward to provide it. In return we come back again and again. If more companies would make that special relationship with customers a priority, perhaps at the expense of the costumes and explosions, we might all be a little less Grumpy and a lot more Happy.

Sustain and enhance performance

"Building a brand is about consistency. Every company, once it assumes a brand identity, has to live with the moral consequences of that identity. A brand is a promise and you have to keep your promises. There's no difference between what we sell and who we are," says Jim Taylor of Gateway 2000.[6]

Delivering a consistent customer experience is the not-so-secret of success for UK retailer Pizza Express. Founder Peter Boizot tried a variety of different ways of producing the pizzas he wanted to produce, and he ended up with a formula that is still used for today's menus. "We have really just stuck to what it was we started doing all that time ago," says UK managing director James Parsons. The formula seems to be working, with some 300 Pizza Express restaurants in the UK and other countries. The brand promise, according to Parsons, is "to consistently offer a good pizza, served by pleasant, well-trained staff in clean, well-presented restaurants."

Of course, it is also important to recognize that what customers value is not static. It changes over time and so, too, must the customer experience.

A company that learned this the hard way is Iceland. The British frozen foods retailer started to get to know its best customers in the late 1990s, when it was faced with falling operating profits, a plummeting share price, and the need to issue a profits warning. The *Financial Times* said that Iceland has "no viable business proposition." Despite cutting costs, investing continuously in "price watch" campaigns and tactical advertising, sales continued to fall.

At this point Iceland conducted research that clearly identified its most profitable customers and what it was they valued. Broadly, it came down to convenience, keen prices, quality products, and friendly service. Iceland then went on to implement its "Legendary Customer Service" program to focus on these important customers and to create a Branded Customer Experience® that would differentiate the store for these shoppers. A year later sales had grown by 17 percent, operating profit by 11 percent and earnings per share climbed 30 percent. Iceland was at the forefront of home delivery and led the way in the movement against genetically modified foods. The company grew strongly over the next two years and then in late 2000 forgot the lesson that it had learned: to stay in tune with the needs of your most profitable customers. Iceland's enthusiasm for the non-genetically modified food cause prompted it to take the bold decision to replace all of its produce with organic lines. However, Iceland's core customers, who above all want convenience and value, did not want this choice made for them and sales dropped. Iceland is now getting back in touch with its most profitable customers and realigning its offer with their needs.

Brands take their value from the perceptions of customers. In order to remain valuable, they must continue to provide a customer experience that continues to be valuable. This requires a continual focus on the brand and the experience to ensure that they are sustained and even reinvented as the needs of customers and the competitive landscape change. This is the task of leadership.

This is well understood by Scott Livengood of Krispy Kreme, who puts it this way: "To me, understanding the customer is our primary marketing imperative. We have a 1 percent of sales fund that all of our stores, company, or franchise, are required to contribute to, according to their franchise agreement. In most companies that fund is an advertising fund and goes into traditional media advertising. We call it a brand fund, because to me it's about how we increase our potential. How do we increase the potential of the brand? What advertising ultimately ought to be about is generating sales but in a sustainable way over the long term. The best way we can increase sales and increase our potential over the long term is to continue to fully understand how we connect with the customer and, on an emotional level, what our customers' expectations are – all the things that got us to where we are now."

E by E Bay/Satmetrix

The online auction leader eBay has made the user experience a top priority, and since 1999 has relied on a customer feedback system from Satmetrix Systems to measure, analyze, and improve customer satisfaction and loyalty in real time. eBay has consistently generated high customer loyalty index scores, putting it at the top of its class in the internet market space. It has done so by paying close attention to the expectations and perceptions of its customers, partners, and employees.

The eBay story is compelling because the company catapulted to the number one shopping site on the internet, as measured by total user minutes (119 minutes per user per month), and yet had no way to meet any of its nearly 30 million registered users face to face. As it implemented a real-time customer feedback system, eBay understood e-mail contact with each customer must address the heart of the customer's concern and make each customer feel a personal connection.

Using data extracted from its own customer support database, eBay e-mails about 50,000 survey invitations to a randomly selected percentage of customers who have received e-mail responses from eBay within the past 24 hours. Customers click on an embedded link to complete the survey. The company regularly receives a 31–33 percent response rate. All responses are analyzed, graphically reported, and updated in real time on the web. A high level of dissatisfaction instantly alerts eBay managers that corrective action is urgently needed.

eBay uses the real-time feedback to not only zero in on customer issues, but to uncover performance gaps of individual customer service representatives, to reward strong performance, and to project a continuously updated picture of how well the company is managing the customer experience at any given moment. By seeing what its customers think, eBay has steadily gained a more precise understanding of the wants, needs, and priorities of its divergent customer base – insights which enable it to adjust its services to rapidly adapt to customer wishes. With 600,000 customer touchpoints each month, eBay is now moving further to examine how it can use those touchpoints to truly deepen customer loyalty.

The loyalty by design self-assessment

So where is your organization? Use the self-assessment below to determine where your organization is currently. The remaining chapters of this book will delve into many of the key issues that are highlighted in the assessment. They will provide you with compelling examples of organizations that are getting it right, as well as some clear direction for your company in your quest to engineer the Branded Customer Experience®.

Branded Customer Experience Assessment®

Defining your customer values
Please rate the following questions on a 1–7 scale, where 1 = Not yet, 7 = Completely

A We have identitfied our target customer segments and the profit they represent to our company

1   2   3   4   5   6   7

B We have a factual understanding of what our most profitable customers expect and value from our company

1   2   3   4   5   6   7

C We know which customer expectations impact our target customers' intention to re-purchase and recommend us

1   2   3   4   5   6   7

D We have a factual understanding of how customers rate our performances vs our competitors against these loyalty drivers

1   2   3   4   5   6   7

E We have a compelling brand promise that clearly communicates what target customers can expect in their relationship with us

1   2   3   4   5   6   7

Our Score = [   ]

Scoring:
Complete your assessment for each item, total your score, and record it in the box at the bottom.

Scoring menu
5–10 Understanding who your most profitable target customers are should be your key priority.
11–20 You have an understanding of your target customers. The challenge now is to really gain an intimate understanding of what they expect and value.

21–30 Your focus should be on those few expectations that drive attraction, retention, and referral, and then building them into a compelling brand promise and customer experience.
31–35 You are making great progress in defining a brand promise that provides real value. The challenge is to constantly upgrade your knowledge of your most profitable customers, what they expect, and ensure that your promise is aligned with it.

Section 2: Designing Your Branded Customer Experience®
Please rate the following questions on a 1–7 scale, where 1= Not yet, 7= Completely

A We thoroughly understand the experience our customers currently have with us

1   2   3   4   5   6   7

B We have clearly identified the critical "touchpoints" which make up the customer experience touchline

1   2   3   4   5   6   7

C We have designed new service experiences which will deliver our customer promise in a way which is consistent, differentiated, and valuable to target customers

1   2   3   4   5   6   7

D We have defined the specific employee behaviour required to deliver the customer promise at each touchpoint

1   2   3   4   5   6   7

E We have developed a comprehensive and fully integrated change strategy to implement the new brand promise and experience

1   2   3   4   5   6   7

Our Score = [   ]

Scoring:
Complete your assessment for each item, total your score, and record it in the box at the bottom.

Scoring menu
5–10 Understanding the nature of the experience that your customers have of you should be your first priority.
11–20 You have a good understanding of what your customers experience. The challenge now is to clearly define the critical touchpoints from the customer perspective.

21–30 Your focus now should be on designing a customer experience which delivers your promise and efining how employees must deliver it.
31–35 It is all about execution now! Creating a fully integrated change strategy to align the organization will ensure your success.

Equipping people and delivering consistency
Please rate the following questions on a 1–7 scale, where 1= Not yet, 7= Completely

A We have an internal communications plan to build commitment, understanding, and clarity around implementing the brand experience

1   2   3   4   5   6   7

B Leaders at all levels of our organization understand their role as champions of our customer experience and are prepared for their role in leading its implementation

1   2   3   4   5   6   7

C Leaders have clearly communicated to our employees what our brand promise is and their important role in delivering it

1   2   3   4   5   6   7

D We have prepared our people with the skills and knowledge required to deliver our customer experience

1   2   3   4   5   6   7

E We are taking specific action to improve people, processes, and products, to deliver our branded customer experience

1   2   3   4   5   6   7

Our Score = [   ]

Scoring:
Complete your assessment for each item, total your score, and record it in the box at the bottom.

Scoring menu
5–10 The key to delivering the customer experience is communicating the promise throughout the organization and your people's role in keeping it.
11–20 You have begun to communicate the brand promise and new experience. The challenge is to equip leaders and employees with the skills to deliver it.

21–30 People are beginning to understand your brand promise and how it can be delivered. Your focus now should be on equipping people throughout the organization with the skills to deliver it consistently.
31–35 You are making great progress in delivering your customer experience. The challenge is to constantly upgrade your people, processes, and products to improve the delivery of your promise over time.

Sustaining and enhancing performance

Please rate the following questions on a 1–7 scale, where 1 = Not yet, 7 = Completely

A We have a formal process for continually collecting customer and employee feedback on our customer experience and how this can be improved

1   2   3   4   5   6   7

B We have a balanced set of performance metrics that provide executives with objective, timely feedback on how well we are delivering against our promise

1   2   3   4   5   6   7

C We have a reliable, effective training system that continuously builds our capability to deliver our customer experience

1   2   3   4   5   6   7

D We have performance management and HR systems aligned with and supporting the delivery of our customer experience

1   2   3   4   5   6   7

E We have an effective process for continually communicating to our people progress and results in delivering our customer experience

1   2   3   4   5   6   7

Our Score = [   ]

Scoring:
Complete your assessment for each item, total your score, and record it in the box at the bottom.

Scoring menu
5–10 Creating systems to gather customer and employee data should be an important focus for you.
11–20 You are collecting data but will need to ensure that this is communicated to executives in a way that creates action and improvement.

21–30 You are seeing results. The challenge is to sustain the effort and focus by recognizing and rewarding these results through your HR systems.
31–35 You are making great progress in delivering a customer experience that provides real value. The challenge now is to sustain and refresh this over time through ongoing communication and improvement activity.

Customer Experience Analysis: Summary

Scoring menu

20–35:   You are becoming increasingly aware of the need to understand your
         most profitable customers and how you can differentiate through
         offering them a Branded Customer Experience®. Awareness is the first
         step to your success.

36–70:   You have begun to understand how you can differentiate your customer
         experience and create value for target customers. The challenge now is
         to design the customer experience that delivers your brand promise.
         A comprehensive and integrated plan is key to your success.

71–104:   You have begun many of the activities necessary to implement a
         Branded Customer Experience® throughout your organization. The focus
         now should be on ensuring that your employee education, HR, and
         business systems support your people and their ability to deliver the
         promise. Consistent execution is now the key to success.

105–140: You are seeing results from your focus and improvement activity. You are
         delivering your customer experience and measuring performance against
         your promise. The challenge now is to refresh and upgrade the customer
         experience so as to build lasting loyalty and brand equity. Continual
         measurement, feedback, and improvement will ensure your long-term
         success.

Notes

1 Griffin, Jill, *Customer Loyalty: How To Earn It, How To Keep It*, Jossey Bass, 1997.

2 Campbell, Andrew and Sadtler, David, "Corporate Breakups", *Strategy & Business*, Third Quarter 1998.

3 Chase, Richard B. and Dasu, Sriram, "Want to Perfect Your Company's Service? Use Behavioral Science", *Harvard Business Review*, June 2001.

4 For a summary of some of this research see Gregory Zaltman and Kathryn Braun's "Mind of the Market: Introduction to Neuroscience" primer series published by Harvard Business School.

5 Zaltman, Gerald, "Lighting Up the Shadows", a presentation at Proctor & Gamble's Future Forces Conference, September 1997.

6 Coomber, Stephen, *Branding*, ExpressExec, 2002.

4

■■■■■■■■■■■■■■■■■■■■

A new brand of leadership

*People don't quit companies. They quit
their leaders*

Carolyn Clark vice-president, Human Resources,
Fairmont Hotels & Resorts

Loyalty from customers and employees is inspired from the top; branded customer experiences demand leadership of the highest order. But this is not leadership as it has been routinely understood in the corporate world over recent decades. This is a new brand of leadership.

To put it simply: the customer experience is a leadership issue.

"Find a way or make one," advised Hannibal as he led legions in his conquests of mountains, countries and armies. His admonition has stood the test of time. It embodies the fundamental spirit of leadership in setting a direction and challenging the troops during the conquest. A similar spirit of leadership is required in companies that set out to win customer loyalty. The commitment of leaders to the experience is central. They must be champions of the customer experience in order for it to succeed.

Truly understanding what customers value and then executing to deliver that value requires the courage of conviction. They may not need the physical resources required by Hannibal when he and his troops crossed the Alps, but today's business leaders need to draw on their courage to overcome the obstacles in the road to building a differentiated customer experience. Critical, also, is an ability to engage the troops to actually deliver the experience. It is up to the leader to unleash employee power to build and execute an experience that is untouchable by competitors. Leadership also needs to ensure that the infrastructure is in place to manage the customer experience. Just as an army marches on its stomach, the customer experience runs on a current and accurate supply of customer data that needs to be owned, managed, and communicated by leaders.

The challenge for many companies is to dramatically change their organizations into customer-focused enterprises. They must create an entirely different culture. This requires leadership of the highest order. And of the right sort.

Deserving to be followed

In the past, blind obedience to business leaders was commonplace. Not so any more. "Why should anyone follow you?" was the chilling headline of a recent article in the *Harvard Business Review*. Perhaps a better question would be "Why should anyone keep following you?"

It is also worth reminding yourself why leaders need followers. Leaders need followers in the same way as companies need loyal customers. Loyal followers are key to performance. Bain & Co's Frederick Reichheld looked at a number of different industries and consistently found a link between staff loyalty and business performance. Even the fast food business, with its prodigious employee turnover, shows the effects of relative employee loyalty. Reichheld found that stores with "low" employee turnover (100 percent on average) had profit margins 50 percent higher than stores with high employee turnover (averaging 150 percent).[1]

This improvement in margins is a function of a number of things – lower recruitment costs, greater knowledge of company processes and systems, efficiencies in the return on training, and, of course, the positive impact loyal staff can have in developing loyal customer relations. So how do you create an environment where staff remain loyal enough to carry on following you?

Look back at the leadership of Admiral Horatio Nelson. In an age when sailors had few rights, Nelson earned not only the loyalty but also the love of his men. There were numerous reports of tough, battle-hardened sailors weeping upon hearing about his death. But his greatest strength was in creating leaders further down the ranks. In a navy that was built upon discipline and a strict adherence to following orders, Nelson led by communicating his vision, aligning his captains and empowering them to take independent action.

Finally, his concern for the training and well-being of his men ensured that the front line were ready, able, and willing to execute his strategy.

Nelson is still regarded as one of the most successful exponents of creating and implementing strategy – indeed his tactics are studied at military academies to this day. In Nelson's time, navies used to fight battles by forming their fleets into long lines, sailing past the enemy line, and firing. However, the smoke from the cannon made effective signaling almost impossible and the damage to enemy vessels was frequently minimal due to the inaccuracy of the guns and the strong reinforcement of the sides of the ships.

> **Nelson led by communicating his vision, aligning his captains, and empowering them to take independent action.**

Nelson conceived a totally new and innovative strategy – to sail at right angles to the enemy line, pierce it in two places, and surround the middle. It required perfect execution and carried high risks, most particularly during the time that the fleet sailed directly toward the combined French and Spanish line, unable to return fire. To address these issues, he called together his captains (his "Band of Brothers") over a series of dinners and talked about his vision for the new strategy. Together, they planned the battle, using pepper pots and other tableware. Nelson engaged his leaders in discussion of the different scen-arios until they all fully understood the details of the proposed new approach.

He also told them that, if they could not see the signals from his flagship as they engaged the enemy, each of his captains could not go far wrong if he placed his ship alongside one of the enemy. He empowered independent action – unheard of in those days.

Nelson also cared for the main body of his men – what became known as the "Nelson touch." He knew by name all of those with whom he had sailed for years and he fought for improved welfare, pay, and conditions for the ordinary seaman under his command. He led from the front –

literally – and was fatally wounded early in the attack on the enemy line. However, such was the alignment that he had created and the loyalty that he had earned, the engagement continued and a resounding victory won that day at Cape Trafalgar.

As a leader, Nelson's example remains useful because he:

- conceived an innovative strategy, to beat the competition;
- aligned all his key leaders behind the strategy by involving them in designing the detailed execution;
- empowered his team, within a given framework, to react to changes in circumstances;
- had the common touch and demonstrated care for his employees;
- led from the front.

When Nelson was appointed as Admiral of the British Fleet tasked with finding and destroying the combined French and Spanish fleets, it was reported at the time that the confidence of the nation and the navy soared. Nelson was a brand in his own right, as is Jack Welch or Rudolph Giuliani today.

In fact there is evidence that one of the biggest influencers on the share price movement of companies is the movement of the CEOs leading them. The *Sunday Times* in the UK carries an annual performance review of the shares selected by its business reporters. In its December 30, 2001 edition, the newspaper reported that in a market that had bombed one of its youngest reporters, Lucinda Kemeny, had picked a stock that had soared more than 200 percent. She easily beat her more experienced colleagues in the quest to forecast winning stocks. Her secret? She chose the retailing group Arcadia because Stuart Rose, the chief executive, "had a solid record in turning round companies." The *Sunday Times* concluded: "No company has ever failed because of external competition. Internal weakness is what destroys shareholder value. Similarly, firms succeed because of great leadership."

So the leader is a brand and is responsible for the value of the brand that he or she leads.

Nelson was heroic but was also one of the first leaders to realize that leadership does not reside only at the top of the organization. One-dimensional heroic leaders are no longer appropriate. MIT's Peter Senge explains that the sort of leadership required today is that which is elicited and developed "throughout the organization." This stands in contrast, Senge asserts, to the heroic brand of leadership still aspired to in many organizations. "The new hero-CEO then pumps new life into the organization's suffering fortunes, typically by cutting costs (and usually people) and boosting productivity and profit," Senge writes, "But the improvements invariably do not last." A downward spiral of new crises addressed by new hero-leaders ensues, with "dramatic changes imposed from the top, increasing fear, and diminishing leadership within the organization, leading eventually to new crises and calls for more heroic leadership."[2]

So if a company is to embark successfully on the journey of leading the brand, what is the leadership road map? What are the key things leaders need to do if they are going to build customer loyalty through a Branded Customer Experience® delivered through their people?

Understand your customers

In 1995, Amazon.com set out to be the world's biggest bookstore. Today, it is rapidly becoming the world's biggest store of any kind. Given the fact that, in six short years, its sales have risen from zero to $3 billion, it would hardly be an overstatement to describe the growth of this world-renowned e-commerce company as meteoric.

Jeff Bezos, Amazon's founder and CEO, was as surprised by this phenomenal growth as anyone. "When we began in July of 1995 we were woefully unprepared," Bezos says candidly. "Our business plan called for us to grow incredibly slowly. We hung our shingle out on the World Wide Web of 1995, which was a very different place from today, and we didn't expect anybody to come. In the original business plan we thought it would take years and years before we had any substantial level of sales. That turned out not to be the case, and in the first 30 days we took orders from all 50 states and 45 different countries."

"Our mission is to be the earth's most customer-centered company," says Bezos and for him this means three things: listen, invent, and personalize. Just follow Bezos around for a day and find out for yourself whether this is a guy driven by a passion for the customer. For Bezos, the customer is at the center of the company, and he has bet the entire business proposition on the experience that Amazon.com customers get when they click into the Amazon world. With customary self-effacement, Bezos disclaims direct responsibility for his company's customer focus, saying it results more from hiring people based on very few criteria. "You had to be customer obsessed and you had to want to be part of a pioneering company," he says. "You had to want to work 60-plus hours a week. In a way, having just a few key things that you insist on leads to more diversity because you end up not caring at all about the other characteristics."

It is perhaps no coincidence that Bezos attended high school in Miami where he was a theme park enthusiast, a regular visitor to Disney World. For Bezos it was the sheer breadth of Disney's vision, rather than the rides, that was so impressive. He hasn't forgotten. "Cultures are incredibly stable," Bezos explains, "so one of the things that you find in companies is that once a culture is formed it takes nuclear weaponry to change it." Fortunately for Amazon.com, what Bezos refers to as "customer obsession" became central to its culture.

A perfect example of the impact that this "obsession" has had is that in the year 2000 Amazon shipped well in excess of 99 percent of all items ordered in time for them to arrive for the holidays. As David Risher, senior vice-president of marketing and merchandising explains: "In November and December of every year, 100 percent of the management team and 100 percent of the marketing boards spend at least five days working out of the distribution centers. Most spend closer to two weeks … It's not optional for the senior leaders because it's not optional for the junior people in the company. You can't very well expect people to mess around with their Christmas time unless you are willing to do the same thing." This holiday "tradition" demonstrates not only Amazon's commitment to the customer but also its leadership style and its teamwork.

Leaders understand – intuitively or otherwise – what customers are looking for. Remember that customers are already accomplished travelers on the road – seeking value wherever they can get it. So when Howard Schultz conceived the Starbucks experience as a cup of flavorful coffee, brewed just right, served by "barristas" who actually knew something about their product (and their customer), it is no wonder that people pulled off the road and lined up. They were already out there looking for more value. Did they know they wanted "Starbucks" before it existed? No, but they were ready for something more than what they were getting. The key to leapfrogging what currently exists in the competitive marketplace, as Starbucks did, is understanding thoroughly what customers value, single-mindedly focussing on it, and delivering on it with solutions that customers may not have even expected.

In another familiar example, customers in the recent past who were interested in buying books needed help on what they might enjoy reading and the ability to choose from a wide variety of books. They also wanted a retail store that was comfortable – maybe even a place where they could browse at leisure. Hence, Barnes & Noble bookstores. Throw in a means to get their desired book with minimal time investment, at a good price, delivered to their home, plus access to the entire world's published literature, and voila – Amazon.com.

If you had asked customers what they wanted before either of these two business concepts appeared, they would not have described the particular experiences that Barnes & Noble or Amazon.com now provide. But they would have told you their needs. They would have told you they wanted convenience, ease of book shopping, decent prices, help in finding the right book, and a comfortable, relaxed shopping environment. Perceiving these needs and then creatively converting them into an experience is what drives customer loyalty, and is the passion of the best leaders.

Bring the courage of conviction

Before even embarking on the journey, the leader must realize that there are many roads to a destination. And there will be wrong turns for any chosen route. The key is to recognize the wrong turn, adjust, and continue the journey. Charles Schwab has

The intuitive response to change is often negative.

mastered this with its entire approach to consumer services. It took many attempts and failures to reach where it is now – a leader in the online brokerage industry. Obstacles are seen as the stepping stones to future success for business executives who bring the required spirit of leadership.

The intuitive response to change is often negative. Naysayers and "I've seen it before" types quickly come out of the woodwork. They will clothe their objections in reasoned thought, but they will typically sound like "We're doing fine right now"; "We're already doing it"; or "How's this going to be different?" The leader's task is to expect these objections and enroll the objectors in the heat of the battle. There is no better way to win converts than to involve them actively, with responsibility and accountability, in the conversion process. Leaders must set the direction, maintain the line of sight to it (despite the naysayers), and hold steadfast to the courage of conviction.

The tests of this conviction come in many guises. When Harry Gambill, CEO of Trans Union, a major US-based credit reporting agency, suggested that the entire executive team spend two days per month getting the customer focus strategy in place, a few said they didn't have time. Harry looked at his diary and said: "I've got two days." End of debate; they all found time.

When one major European financial institution set out to differentiate through its customer experience, it crashed head-on into the wall of executive non-commitment. The business was performing well, but customers were complaining (a sign of bad times ahead). The CEO spoke of the need to focus on service, but when the time came for the board to commit to action, consensus decision making prevailed, with the CEO acting as facilitator. The board decided not to pursue efforts to transform the customer experience. The company has since been absorbed by another financial institution. These journeys require the Hannibal charge and conviction, not the consensus style.

Leaders do not discover what customers really value by sitting in their offices. At Pizza Express executives are put through the same training as everyone else in the company. UK managing director, James Parsons, went through this training even though he had already been in the catering service business for 16 or 17 years. "I had to go through a three-month program," he recounts. "I spent four weeks in the kitchen making the pizzas for the day, making the pizzas in the evenings, doing all the shifts, working as a cleaner, cleaning the kitchen, the toilets and the back of house areas, working on the restaurant floor, and working beside experienced people. I also spent some time running the restaurant as well, locking up at three in the morning and those kind of things."

"When it comes to leadership, there is a tendency to over-complicate what makes good leadership or what good leadership looks like," says Rick Leweke, executive vice-president for human resources at California Federal Bank. "There is no one on the senior management team who would ask an employee to do something that he or she wouldn't do himself or herself. Scott [Kisting] will get involved in a personnel issue. When he was in a branch and there was a teller with an issue, he would get personally involved. He won't say, 'Well, no, it's not my job.' He has shown the organization that he's willing to roll up his sleeves and get involved in customer issues or personnel issues, or to try and solve somebody's problem, or get involved and fix it. I try to do the same thing with my team. And that attitude is fairly pervasive at the management level."

On any journey, energy will wane at some point. When it does, what do true leaders do? They reach down into their own reserves and tap energy to share with others. They stand by the courage of their conviction and win converts along the way, involving people at each step to build enthusiasm, accountability, and responsibility. And, if they had no conviction at the outset, then they will surely fall off the journey along the way.

Unleash the power of people

"In the late eighties ... one appointed chairman was not a hotel person but he did understand quality and service, and he understood the rich history of the assets and our custodial responsibility for these assets. He put in place what at that time would have been described as a very sophisticated human resource management philosophy. No one got hired without going through a standard interview process ... from the dishwasher to the president everyone started that way. He recognized very early on that everything related to the employee: the business drivers, the assets, and all the rest of it. This was kind of unusual for a company so rich in (physical) assets," says Chris Cahill, COO of Fairmont Hotels.

Leaders unleash the power of people. Len Schlesinger, while a professor at Harvard Business School, noted: "Strategy only exists in the behavior of the company's leaders." And, we would add, when it exists in the behavior of everyone then it becomes an unbeatable advantage. All employees need to get it. They need to understand their role as ambassadors for the brand. Unleashing the power of the company's employees is the most essential component in determining whether customers return or go to the competition.

Central to unleashing this employee power is the leader who can point the way to the destination and do it in a way that enrolls the troops. How do they do it? What would you do to convince anyone to go on an uncertain journey? You'd paint a picture of what it could be like to go – and not to go. Paul LaPerriere is executive vice-president of the Affluent Personal Insurance Business at Fireman's Fund Insurance Company (FFIC), the property and casualty insurer, part of the German Allianz group. When Paul embarked on his journey, he put it simply to his executive team and to all his employees: "If we don't change, we'll lose." (His group was already the most profitable group within FFIC.) Paul then went on to describe the strategy for winning and engaged all his senior team in the leadership challenge of making it happen.

Leo Burnett's Hong Kong operation began evaluating its strategy for the future in the midst of disappointing business results. It resolved to change. Allen Chichester, former managing director for Leo Burnett Greater China, painted this picture: "Here's what we'll face if we don't do this: dissatisfied clients, eroding market share, and declining earnings. But here is what it could be like if we work together – delighted clients, expanding business, and record profits. With your help, I am confident we can achieve this – are you with me?" There was not much argument. Leo Burnett increased client retention by 25 percentage points and new account profitability by 63 percent. The agency rose to the number one ranking in the People's Republic of China, reduced employee turnover by more than 40 percent and was named by *Media* magazine as "Agency of the Year" at the Asia Ad Awards the following year.

Customers buy because they expect to receive a benefit – a promise made by the organization that they will receive value. Leaders know that the brand promise is made or broken based on the interaction customers have with the company. The brand of the company embraces all of its products, the processes that deliver value to the customer, and the company's employees. What the customer experiences is the proof statement that must follow any promises by advertising and communications.

Leaders must therefore engage all employees as ambassadors for the brand – everyone must understand how his or her work impacts the customer experience. (This is discussed in detail in Chapter 6.)

In these companies, leaders create brand ambassadors throughout the organization and at the same time never relinquish responsibility as the ultimate guardians of the brand. These leaders articulate the company's brand strategy and consistently demonstrate commitment to the Branded Customer Experience® by investing the time and resources required to make good things happen. Delivering a Branded Customer Experience® is a strategy that, in most cases, requires leaders throughout the organization and significant organizational change. Without informed and inspired leadership, the strategy will fail.

In North America, Coastal Mart is a convenience store/gas station firm that trained all of its employees on what it meant to serve customers. One day, an assistant manager gave a friendly hello to a regular customer. The customer didn't respond in his normal cheerful way and acted a bit strangely in the store. The assistant manager said to her clerk: "You watch the store, I'm going to follow Mr 'Smith' home to make sure he arrives safely." Upon arriving at home (and not knowing the assistant manager was close behind), the customer walked up to his front door and collapsed from a heart attack. The assistant manager called emergency help and literally saved the customer's life.

This story may sound like heroics, but it really isn't. This is about people doing things for customers as a result of working in an environment where, through determined leadership and good training, everyone knows what is important and focuses on it – the customer. Such people come from cultures where leaders have brought their employees along with them on their journey – where customer-focussed values matter and leaders have set a climate that unleashes the power of the employees – and given them the tools to do the job, like skills in customer interactions.

To build this environment, leaders must first be what they want to see. Their own behavior in installing this shift is critical. When Lord Marshall, the then CEO of British Airways, wanted the culture to change, he was the one who changed first. He was the one seen numerous times greeting the arriving flight at 5:00 a.m. and asking customers how their flight was. Do you think employees might have got the message of what was important?

This sort of leadership by example is institutionalized in a variety of ways at a number of progressive companies. In one global, high-tech company, the board takes its approach to the customer so seriously as a competitive differentiator that it requires every corporate officer, including the CEO, to spend one day at regular intervals handling customer calls. This direct contact with customers not only provides a shining example to the rest of the organization but it has been an invaluable tool in helping shape the company's overall customer focus and sharpen the corporate response to customer needs. A similar approach was adopted by MBNA America Bank, the highly successful credit card issuer, which requires each officer to spend four hours a month listening to customer phone interactions.

> **Nobody leaps out of bed saying I want to create shareholder value this morning.**

Pret A Manger takes leadership involvement in daily operations yet another step further. Each person in Pret's head office is assigned a "buddy shop" with which he or she will be closely involved on an ongoing basis. And everyone who goes to work at Pret at any level of the organization is first sent to work at his or her buddy store for a two-week period.

An alternative take on keeping close to the front line comes from Julian Richer, chairman of Richer Sounds, the UK hi-fi retailer. When Richer bought a jet he decided to have a "no empty seat" policy. It's an eight-seater, and whenever he goes on a business trip seven of the seats go to colleagues. "So the irony is," he says, "I've got to keep sober because I'm on a business trip, while they're all getting smashed from the chairman's bar and having a wild time."

Manage the business from the customer experience

"Most organizations have some form of customer satisfaction measurement, and in most cases it is close to useless. It is not timely, does not link back to practical results and to the people who have to take action to achieve those results, and does not link to the financial bottom line. You have to have a loop," observes Fred Reichheld.[3]

On any strategic journey, essential building blocks must be put in place: a road map, resources, and so on. Key building blocks on the customer experience journey not only include these but, in addition, a means of measuring progress along the way. Leaders focus on what they can control as progress is made, before they get the financial results.

Instead of focussing on financial results alone, leaders need to focus on things they can control upstream. We call these factors *leading indicators*. If lagging indicators are the financial results (that is, they lag behind action that has already occurred), then leading indicators are the actions that people in the organization take every day to create a customer experience that in turn drives customer loyalty and the consequent financial results. (See Fig. 4.1.)

Figure 4.1   *Measuring the Branded Customer Experience®*

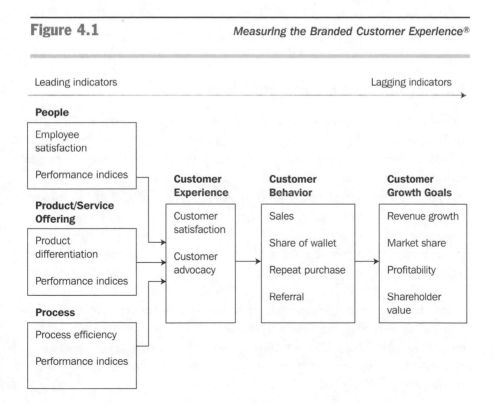

"If you say our objective is to drive this business to profit, then you're looking in the wrong direction," says Sir Stuart Hampson of the UK retailer John Lewis. "First of all, nobody leaps out of bed saying I want to create shareholder value this morning. Even if it motivates *me*, it certainly doesn't motivate the people who will make a difference; that is, the people on the selling floor … If all you're doing is saying I'm here to make more profit and to do that I'm going to reduce my pay costs, then there will be fewer people on the selling floor to offer service and more stressed staff who are feeling that they can't deliver service. As a result, the customer says it isn't much fun shopping here and goes off shopping elsewhere."

Sears is one organization that has focussed on the sources of growth rather than just profit. It has statistically determined that a 5-unit increase in just 10 employee satisfaction measures will result in a 1.3-unit increase in customer satisfaction and a 0.5 percent increase in store revenue growth. Now store managers can focus very clearly on the things they can control that will make a real, measurable difference in the net profit of the store.[4]

Measuring employee satisfaction

Some years ago Shaun Smith created a survey that set out to measure the extent to which employees were aligned internally with organizational strategy. Recently, the survey was subjected to a very thorough validation by David Matsumoto, of San Francisco State University. Responses were correlated from over 23,000 Organizational Alignment Survey® respondents from 52 companies representing a variety of industries and across 20 countries. The 60 statements of the survey were correlated against six business results areas namely, customer service, employee retention, sales growth, meeting agency requirements, competitive performance, and profitability. Finally the dimensions were correlated against all six business results areas overall. The results support what we found in our interviews and in the themes discussed in this book. The employee responses which correlated most closely with the improved business results achieved by these companies were:

1 We are a highly successful organization.

2 We have a well-defined strategy to overcome competitors.

3 We match the claims made through our advertising and promotion.

4 Employees are well trained to meet the performance standards required by their jobs.

5 We measure our quality/service performance against the world's best organizations in our field.

6 Managers meet with customers and consumer groups on a regular basis.

7 We carefully monitor the product/service quality of our suppliers, distributors, and agents.

8 Employees are regularly briefed on departmental and organizational performance.

9 There is good cooperation among all departments in my organization.

10 Performance targets that my department sets are realistic and consistent with our organizational vision/mission.

David Matsumoto concluded: "All of the correlations are statistically significant and seem to predict the desired business results."[5]

Measurement is not simply about tracking results from the customer experience; it is also about installing and communicating a way to run the business, a way that sometimes completely shifts the mental model of how leaders have traditionally managed to create business results.

With a customer experience-based scorecard, one financial services company has found that the entire agenda for business meetings has changed. Where business reviews used to be strictly about the numbers – forecasts, current sales, and so on – they are now about what customers are saying, what is happening with customer retention, and – oh, yes – what the numbers are as a result. The impact is both dramatic and subtle. The entire approach to measuring and managing the business has changed. Leadership conversations have also changed. The questions leaders ask have shifted to focus on what can be done to boost customer value, satisfaction, and loyalty. But none of this would have happened without the top executive team committing to this scorecard as the way to run the business. The analogy is a simple one: if you want to improve your golf game focus on your swing, not reading your handicap.

When the business is measured in this way, investing in improving the customer experience becomes a business decision like any other; what will we get and what will it cost us to get it?

Applying this model allows organizations to calculate the costs of training, improving products and services, or introducing more efficient processes and compare this with the benefits to business results. The likely ROI determines if the improvement is justified in terms of customer satisfaction and their subsequent behavior. (See Fig. 4.2.)

One organization that thought very carefully about investing in the customer experience is Harrah's Entertainment, the largest gaming company in the United States and the second largest in the world. At the time Forum was asked to work with Harrah's in 1997/8, the company employed 35,000 employees. Harrah's objective was simple: to improve the customer experience so that target customers would return again and again. Much of what was done is covered in the "Entertainment Company" case study in Chapter 12, but suffice to say that Kathy Wade-Yacoubian, the corporate director of human resource development at Harrah's, estimated that the entire cost of the program was "conservatively, $10 million." In terms of the results, the key metric was that same-store gaming revenues in 1999 grew by 15 percent over the previous year to a record $814.1 million. This same-store growth was considered to be a direct result of the brand promise development and training. In terms of leading indicators, there was a 31 percent drop in employee turnover and a 22 percent increase in customer satisfaction leading to a 17 percent increase in target customer spend.

Taking a disciplined approach to improving the customer experience is a sensible business approach and yet it amazes us how many leaders will happily spend millions on a new CRM system, or better in-flight entertainment, or new rolling stock, or 24-hour business centers in hotels without much pause for thought and yet will balk at spending money on upgrading their people or service when this will realize a much greater return on their investment in terms of customer loyalty and retention.

Figure 4.2

Delivering the brand promise – the business case

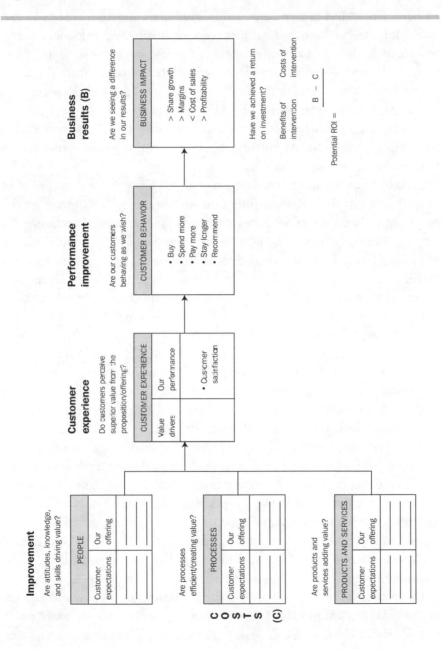

Business results (B)

Are we seeing a difference in our results?

BUSINESS IMPACT

> Share growth
> Margins
< Cost of sales
> Profitability

Have we achieved a return on investment?

Benefits of intervention   Costs of intervention

Potential ROI = $\dfrac{B - C}{}$

Performance improvement

Are our customers behaving as we wish?

CUSTOMER BEHAVIOR

• Buy
• Spend more
• Pay more
• Stay longer
• Recommend

Customer experience

Do customers perceive superior value from the proposition/offering?

CUSTOMER EXPERIENCE

Value drivers	Our performance
	• Customer satisfaction

Improvement

Are attitudes, knowledge, and skills driving value?

PEOPLE

Customer expectations	Our offering

Are processes efficient/creating value?

PROCESSES

Customer expectations	Our offering

C O S T S (C)

Are products and services adding value?

PRODUCTS AND SERVICES

Customer expectations	Our offering

Create leaders at every level

In companies that are truly great at implementing the Branded Customer Experience®, we find not just leaders at the top but leaders everywhere, at all levels of the organization. One of the key elements of our work at Harrah's was the development of a training program for 1,044 managers in how to lead and deliver the Branded Customer Experience®.

The Carphone Warehouse, the UK retailer of cellular phones, has created a huge following of enthusiastic customers and has managed to successfully maintain its culture through various acquisitions. It is a leadership-driven organization.

"You have to try and break down hierarchy. Everybody must feel that everybody's got their sleeves rolled up and everyone is fighting for the same thing," says Charles Dunstone, CEO of Carphone Warehouse. "It was fascinating when we bought Tandy; you could not have picked two organizations that were more different in their cultures. We merged our warehouse into their warehouse in Birmingham just before Christmas … and it was a disaster; it just didn't work and there was chaos. They sat behind reports and people were saying these figures can't be right. No one ever drove to the warehouse and looked round it. The view was it would be better by Easter, and this was October – we couldn't afford to wait until then. So we said there's no point in managing stores if the stores don't get the right stock. So some of the directors, area managers; and heads of sales went to Birmingham and ran the warehouse. The people that worked in the warehouse, who worked for Tandy, could not believe that the bosses were coming in and were driving pallets around the place and shifting phones and packing them up and making the whole thing work. And through this attitude of "it's got to be fixed, we've got to make it work," we solved the problem. We didn't really realize how much we needed to do it at the time but we completely won over all the people that worked in that side of the business. It's this thing I come back to again and again; we're all in it together, we've got to do it for the customers."

But getting to this point requires the commitment, vision, and passion of the boss. It all starts there. Grassroots approaches simply won't work. Ask Marty McGuinn, CEO of Mellon Financial Corporation, the financial services institution based in Pittsburgh, Pennsylvania. He has personally led the charge for nearly two years on his journey. He has trained his own direct reports and holds them accountable for the behaviors that everyone in the organization needs to demonstrate to live their brand promise, each and every day. The results? Dramatic improvements in employee connectedness to the strategy – a 40 to 50 percent increase in employee satisfaction and dramatic increases in benchmark numbers on how employees feel about the strategy of the firm.

> **Leadership is the number one key to successfully changing an organization into one that delivers a Branded Customer Experience.®**

This connection between leaders and learning is not new. John F. Kennedy said: "Leadership and learning are indispensable to each other." Leadership is the number one key to successfully changing an organization into one that delivers a Branded Customer Experience® and, in its absence, it is the number one reason why companies will fail.

Notes

1 Reichheld, Frederick, *The Loyalty Effect*, Harvard Business School Press, 1996.

2 Hesselbein, Frances, Goldsmith, Marshall, and Somerville, Iain (eds), *Leading Beyond the Walls*, Jossey Bass, 2001.

3 www.ecustomerserviceworld.com

4 "The Employee Profit Chain at Sears," *Harvard Business Review*, Jan–Feb 1998.

5 Smith, Shaun, "Organizational Alignment Survey®." The results of this research are the intellectual property of Pearson International, Inc.

5

■■■■■■■■■■■■■■■■■■■

Creating triad power

In principle, business functions should mesh harmoniously to achieve the firm's overall objectives; in practice, departmental relations are often characterized by deep rivalries and misunderstandings

Philip Kotler

A top American Express executive told his employees: "Each and every one of you will make or break the promise our brand makes to our customers." He was right. To deliver your brand promise, you must have the right people, in the right place, doing the right things, all the time, throughout every operation. Developing that mindset and skill set throughout your business is a major challenge; the brand promise cannot be delivered by your marketing department alone. Nor is it the responsibility of HR or of operations. Each department has a role to play.

Some years ago the term "triad power" was coined to describe the need for organizations to operate across geographic boundaries and market in Asia, Europe, and the US to be fully effective. The new triad power is less global in reach but equally important to organizations.

The new triad power refers to marketing, HR, and operations or customer services working together as agents for change in order to deliver the promise. "I've never viewed HR as an island unto itself. I have always felt that if we didn't understand our connection to the customer, we were missing something. This is fundamental in terms of how I encourage my team to look at their roles in the organization," says Rick Leweke, executive vice-president for human resources at California Federal Bank.

Creating and implementing a strategic agenda in the new economy requires executives to work across functional boundaries not just geographic ones. Creating and delivering Branded Customer Experiences comes as a result of aligning the whole organization behind the customer proposition, and as a result of key executives combining resources, budgets, and competencies to implement organizational transformation. We believe this notion is far more powerful and likely to create value than the old concept of "internal customers." We are asked our view about the importance of internal customers at so many conferences and our answer is always the same: there is only one customer and that is the person who is paying for your product or service. Focussing on the needs of colleagues is a dangerous route to take since it is all too easy to end up focussing on improvements that make life easier for colleagues but that have little or no benefit to customers. That is not to say we advocate ignoring the needs of colleagues. We use the term "line of sight" to suggest that by working back from the desired customer experience, each department can examine how it creates value for customers and how other functions can best support the creation of that value.

Great experiences are a trans-functional issue as Bill Fatt, CEO of Fairmont Hotels, makes clear: "We have a team that is focussed on making sure that our employees are properly positioned to be able to provide these guest experiences. Certainly this is so in the HR area, which Carolyn Clark heads up. She is a very important person in our group. We frequently talk about her as being the

> **Great experiences are a trans-functional issue.**

person who embodies the heart and soul of the company. She is front and center in terms of motivating employees, training them, making sure that we have the best employees to begin with, and recognizing employees who go above and beyond the normal call of duty. But the service culture and the focus on making sure that the guest has a positive experience runs throughout the team. Everything that we do has to be measured against whether or not it's going to enhance the guest experience and Chris Cahill our CEO is responsible for that."

Fairmont's CEO goes on to say: "Marketing has to make sure that what we are saying about our properties and our services is consistent with our ability to deliver. This is so when guests read about our promises and then arrive at our properties, they know what to expect and they're fully satisfied with what we are able to offer them."

Bill Fatt's description of these roles closely mirrors the way we think about triad power. Marketing, HR, and operations (which includes customer services) have a collective role in defining the desired customer experience and determining a process for implementing this throughout the organization. (See Fig. 5.1.)

Each of the functions in the triad has a role to play in addressing the three faculties of the head, the heart and the hands.

The role of marketing in the triad

Marketing is responsible for being clear about who the most profitable target customers are, what they value, and then defining a brand or customer promise to attract them. Marketing then has primary responsibility to communicate this to employees and the marketplace.

Brian Richardson, vice-president of marketing at Fairmont Hotels, puts it this way: "We want employees to think about their role in enriching the experience of the guests in our hotel who are visitors to our city. That means doing little things that don't cost anything but mean so much. That means making sure that all the guests' needs are met. We want our colleagues to think about this notion of fabric of community,

---

Figure 5.1   *Triad power*

and we want them to go beyond thinking about the experience as starting and ending at our door. So the positioning statement, communications, the employee covenant are all tied into the brand. It needs to affect communications, it needs to affect employee behavior, it needs to literally affect what we do on-site from an operational perspective."

Having defined the target customers, clarified what they value and created a clear brand promise and experience to deliver that value, it is marketing's role to specify that to the organization. It falls to HR and the training function to turn that into a profile for the people of the organization and align HR processes with it.

HR's real potential

HR is responsible for defining the skills, knowledge, and attitudes of the people required to deliver that promise. How do they need to behave and how will they be rewarded for doing so? How can they be found and what training is required to get them to behave in a way that is consistent with the desired customer experience? HR is responsible for communicating the customer promise internally.

For example, Carolyn Clark, vice-president of human resources at Fairmont Hotels, says: "With our recent re branding and our HR strategy, we're really, really excited. I think this will position us in terms of delivering the brand experience. We know that marketing and sales will bring our guests to the brand the first time, but it's the service that they receive that will keep them coming back. And our people have to deliver the brand promise." So she and her colleagues went on to develop a complete HR process to achieve just that, "we developed an integrated human resource strategy which we call 'Service Plus.' It has four components: select, lead, train, and reward." Service Plus is a totally integrated process for finding the right people, leading them in the right way so that they stay, training them in the right behaviors, and rewarding them for doing the right things.

The onus is also on the HR department to know more, to look beyond traditional departmental boundaries. Human resources must partner with marketing, sales, and operations to identify the innermost elements of the relationship between employees and customers. HR must understand the corporate DNA and from it create and sustain a culture that is reinforced throughout the organization.

In the 1980s, what was then known as the personnel department in British Airways completely managed cabin crew recruitment. At that time the airline had a reputation for employing well-educated but rather aloof flight attendants. As a result, the personnel department (now human resources) combined forces with the operations department to identify the most customer-focussed flight attendants and then trained a specially selected group of them as assessors in a new recruitment process. The attitudes of the new recruits were markedly different and much closer to the brand values of the airline. Just two years later BA won an industry award for Best Cabin Crew.

Over the last decades of rapid change and the outsourcing of some of its traditional functions, HR has been trying to prove itself as a business partner to those whose job it is to deliver on promises made to customers and shareholders. Highly complex metrics were constructed by research organizations like the Saratoga Institute to attempt to quantify the impact of HR. Balanced scorecards, including "people" measures such as employee satisfaction and retention, were established and business plans included people development objectives based on standards for training investment per employee. Titles were changed to monikers such as "Chief People Officer" to reflect the importance of people in fulfilling newly articulated mission and vision statements.

All of these tactics have certainly helped to *position* HR as a partner in the drive to reduce expenses and increase productivity. But, however poised and ready it has been, HR has generally failed as a community of practice to demonstrate and consistently realize its true partnership value: the ability to impact on customer value and drive revenue growth – to be a growth gene in the corporate DNA.

With today's me first generation, HR has an important role to fulfill. Unfortunately, this is because excellent interpersonal relations and orientation toward service to others are skills no longer acquired through upbringing and life experience – they must be learned and encouraged. From hiring to retiring, each process the HR function owns either enables or inhibits the customer-focussed organization to deliver its promises. Of all HR roles, however, it is that of educator that, arguably, will have the greatest impact. After hiring the right people, providing continuous education in a variety of ways is the one HR process that builds capital – *intellectual capital* – and that capital, like any other, can be quantified.

Good intentions and communication plans are not enough. The goal of educating people should not merely be to inform them of what customers expect, but to change behaviors to those valued by customers. Forum's research shows that the "experience" factor is the one with which customers are least consistently satisfied and companies invest in the least, yet the Accenture-Montgomery study referred to earlier found that investing in the customer experience provided the best returns.

So companies make explicit and implicit promises to customers through their branding, marketing, and service efforts. And it is on the basis of efforts by employees on the front lines – on their each and every customer interaction – that the company will succeed or fail in delivering on its promises. Whether or not success in the eyes of the customer is a random experience is largely driven by three factors: competence, confidence, and commitment.

Smooth operators

Operations or customer services is responsible for: creating the processes and environment whereby employees can deliver the customer experience; leading them in a way such that they want to; empowering them to act in the interests of the customer; and recognizing good and bad performance. Finally, operations in conjunction with marketing needs to measure the customer experience, compare this to what is promised, and then feed this back to the front line. In the case of Fairmont Hotels, Chris Cahill, president and CEO, ensures delivery of the promise in this way: "I believe that employees interpret the brand based on everything from the imaging and the new human resource language, the words we use and how we've adjusted the mission statement vision and values. They're 'getting it,' and it's permeating through the company. But, I think as with any organization that's been around a long time, you get people's view of what the brand means as opposed to what it actually *does* mean. So one of the things we've also done is to align our performance management process and goals and targets to drive the behavior that we expect out of the brand."

Partnership behaviors

If the triad is to be realized, partnership behaviors must become a reality rather than, as they are now in many organizations, a pipe dream. If any of the elements of the triad are to fulfill their potential as business partners, they must start doing just that – partnering with other functions that may have a clearer line of sight to customers and help them deliver value.

Many programs, for example, are developed by specialists and are based on "best practice" research. However, you get what you ask for, and most HR surveys are targeted to other HR functions. As a result, learning and development programs get built from the inside out, focussing on optimizing individual and team skill sets to better deliver against corporate expectations.

Strategic learning requires that the functions step out of their respective boxes and start to build knowledge about what customers want and expect; to find out which corporate behaviors throughout the organization consistently result in customer value and satisfaction so that education is built around consistently delivering an experience that exceeds customer expectations.

The potential for partnerships is immense. Some examples:

- *HR & Sales* – ensure that the sales force is delivering a differentiated experience that demonstrates enhanced value on the front end of the customer relationship. This may include sales force development initiatives, 360-degree feedback and assessment designed specifically for sales professionals, and sales compensation and incentive review.

- *Customer Service & HR* – ensure that service personnel know what critical behaviors must be demonstrated at every customer interaction. This may include programs designed to define and achieve service excellence, showing how cross-selling is enabled through service and change management support for CRM implementations.

- *HR & Strategic Planning* – ensure people understand the strategic intent of the business and have the skills to execute strategic imperatives. This may include programs to build business literacy throughout the organization and to build customer-centered development planning and budgeting into the corporate business planning cycle.

- *Marketing & HR* – ensure people know who the most valuable customers are and what they value the most. This may include working with marketing to define behaviors that support brand positioning and to define and track behavioral indicators in annual customer surveys.

- *HR & Finance* – ensure people know what customer and employee behaviors are the most profitable. This may help bring HR and finance together to help define the value of changes in employee and customer behaviors and to include behavioral metrics in balanced scorecards and performance measurement tools.

- *HR & Operations* – ensure people know how to do the basics consistently well, so they can focus on "enhancers." This may include working with operations and support functions to define and remove obstacles to delivering consistently on promises made implicitly or explicitly to customers.

A glimpse of partnership in action can be seen at Krispy Kreme, where HR chief Barbara Thornton gives the company's communications department a lot of credit, especially for the video work that they do which, she feels, "resonates in some pretty special ways" with the employees. She believes that one of

> **Ensure people know who the most valuable customers are and what they value the most.**

Krispy Kreme's strongest attributes is its increasing ability to communicate through all levels of the organization, whether it be through newsletters like "The Hot Doughnut News," meetings, newsreels, or simply by sharing stories of magic moments. Also, communication is not just from the top down at Krispy Kreme. "It is becoming more prevalent to have people talking about what they want to do with their careers at Krispy Kreme," says Thornton. "There is an openness about that, set at the top, that creates an expectation that people will have career opportunities."

Thornton's last remark correctly implies that neither HR nor any other department can form the partnerships required to reliably deliver Branded Customer Experiences without strong, continuous, and tangible support from the top of the organization. The organization – starting with its executive offices – must be clear about the forces at work within it that enable employees to deliver: Are those involved in delivering service to customers getting the support they need from management? Are there organizational issues that get in the way? How do metrics and measures that shape employee behavior affect their interaction with customers? How consistent is delivery across all the company's operations?

Achieving the engagement of every employee and every department further entails significant investment in education and training, effective teamwork, performance management, communications, and technology. These will provide the skills and information everyone will need to succeed. They are required to gain the essential organization-wide alignment that delivers what customers perceive as seamless branded experiences.

Significant change and hard work is required from everyone in the organization to synchronize numerous experience elements into a well-orchestrated set of clues that resonate with customers. Most organizations are accustomed to dealing with customer experiences in a disconnected manner. The barriers, political and otherwise, separating sales, marketing, operations, and the financial functions in companies are often so wide that an experiential abyss is created. Frequently, the reality of what a customer experiences and what advertising portrays aren't even close.

Experience management systems (as opposed to fragmented single department efforts) have the potential to focus different parts of an organization on the common goal of creating an integrated, aligned customer experience. They offer a means for breaking down organizational barriers, they form a foundation for creating distinctive customer value through experiences. But they can't happen without a cross-functional organizational perspective.

How is your triad power?

Ask yourself the following questions, better still meet with your colleagues in each function of the triad to debate them together:

1 Does the brand promise and customer experience form the basis for the annual strategic planning and budgeting cycle?

2 To what extent are individual departmental agendas and budgets driven by shared strategic goals?

3 Are Marketing, Operations or Customer Service, and HR tasked with working together to deliver the brand promise and customer experience?

4 How often do the three functions formally meet together to align activities and monitor progress?

5 To what extent do performance management systems reward cross-functional collaboration?

6 Do career development paths span functions or promote people within narrow silos?

6

■■■■■■■■■■■■■■■■■■■

People first

*We have about 3,500 secrets to success,
and they are the terrific people who make
up our team*

Tim Hoeksema, CEO, Midwest Airlines

Manchester United Football Club is one of the most successful sports teams of all time. It is also a brand that is recognized around the world. The leadership of the club has long known that the secret of their success is putting the people first. Paddy Crerand, a former player, remembers it this way: "Manchester United has always had its own way of doing things. For example, everything was done for the players – all you had to do was perform. You worked hard in training but there was nothing behind the scenes that wasn't done to support you. All you had to do was turn up!" This story sums up the culture required to deliver a great customer experience. If you concentrate on creating a great environment for your employees, they will focus on creating a great experience for your customers.

People make the difference. They create the experience, time and time again. In a survey of several thousand customers for a variety of products and services, our research found that personal contact with company employees – whether in person or over the phone – typically has a demonstrably greater impact on customer loyalty than does the company's advertising. Manchester United clearly understands this. David Beckham, one of their star players, recently concluded a new contract with the club that now makes him the world's highest-paid soccer player. His contract is believed to involve a $112,000 a week salary but a further $22,000 a week for "image rights." His personal "brand" is so powerful and so closely identified with Manchester United that the club is willing to pay extra for it.

Forum asked consumers to rate the extent to which a number of different attributes create a customer experience that drives loyalty. This was the rank order of importance we discovered:

1 People

2 Product and service delivery

3 Place (convenience)

4 Product features

5 Price

6 Policies and procedures

7 Promotion and advertising

These findings echo similar results in a Gallup survey of 6,000 consumers.[1] Gallup also found that the fifth "P" of the marketing mix, *people,* is by far the most important determinant of customer loyalty to brands. In motor retailing, Gallup found that customers who feel their dealer representatives "stand out from all others" were ten to fifteen times more likely to choose that same make of vehicle for their next purchase. This same ratio held true for the airline industry, while in the banking sector the influence of people is even greater with customers saying they were ten to twenty times more likely to repurchase from organizations with outstanding employees. Even in telecommunications, employees are three to four times as important in driving loyalty as other factors. Dr Bill McEwen of Gallup summed this up: "It's the people, stupid."[2]

While this realization is not revolutionary, making it work continues to be a surprise. Indeed, it is sometimes newsworthy. For example, an account executive for the Menasha Corporation had a long day of internal flights. He flew from St Louis to Milwaukee on one airline, and from Milwaukee up to Appleton, Wisconsin by Midwest Express. The only problem was that when he landed he couldn't find his luggage. The Midwest Express agent, Brad Braine, looked all over, made some calls, and sent messages and telexes and faxes but couldn't find the missing luggage anywhere.

Dejected and annoyed, the man from Menasha got in his rent-a-car, went downtown, and checked into the Paper Valley Hotel, and then got back in his car to drive around looking for a men's clothing store. He wanted to find a white shirt, a tie, and a sport coat, something suitable for his meeting on the next day with the president of the company and the senior VP of sales. He came back to the hotel thoroughly despondent. All the stores were closed. But, when he walked into his room, he found a suit and two ties on his bed. He called the front desk, and asked what was going on. They told him: "Somebody by the name of Brad Braine from Midwest Express just stopped by the desk, and asked if we could deliver this to your room."

The Midwest agent had noticed that he and the luggageless executive were about the same size. He closed down the station and drove home to La Peer, a 25-minute drive from Appleton. He got one of his own suits and a couple of ties, drove back to Appleton, and dropped them off at the hotel. The suit fitted and the meeting went well.

> **Organizations that deliver their brand promise through their people reap benefits that directly impact customer loyalty, market share, and profitability.**

A corporate myth? If you've flown with Midwest, it may come as no surprise that its staff should be so committed and willing to solve problems. A small airline with a penchant for winning big awards, Midwest has earned a reputation for doing just what its slogan claims, providing "the best care in the air." Against all odds, Midwest has found a way to offer luxury service at competitive or discount rates and still make a profit.

All this being said, it is not surprising then that employees are hired and treated with a "best care" approach too. According to Cliff Van Leuven, management at Midwest goes through "a lot of angst" about trying to find the right people. "You've got to have the right energy," he says. "I call it *oomph*."

Companies like Midwest manage to harness the full potential of people power day in, day out. They need to. Battles for customer loyalty and profits are won and lost not by product or service quality but by people. Organizations that deliver their brand promise through their people reap benefits that directly impact customer loyalty, market share, and profitability. The Brad Braines of the world make a real difference. Indeed, often, they *are* the difference.

The good thing is that there's nothing particularly magical in providing superior customer service. Nor is it a matter of providing breathtaking, legendary customer service. Instead, it is providing an experience that matches or exceeds the expectations and desires of the target customers (see Fig. 6.1). Is the service of Midwest Express the same as the service of Virgin or easyJet? Of course not. Yet their customers are advocates of these airlines. It is about being something special to somebody special. (In fact we argue that the litmus test of a Branded Customer Experience® is that it will *not* appeal to a number of consumers.)

So, how can you electrify and energize the people in your organization? What are the secrets to delivering your brand promise through your people? As we have seen, knowing what customers expect is the starting point for the creation of any worthwhile customer experience. "Sixty-six percent of customer loss is through failure in customer service," says Richard Forsyth, founder of the CRM Forum. "But, that does not mean the winner in any sector is the one who offers the BEST customer service. It means you need to be sure you create a proposition that the customer understands and buys into. It's not the absolute value

---

Figure 6.1 *How people impact the customer experience*

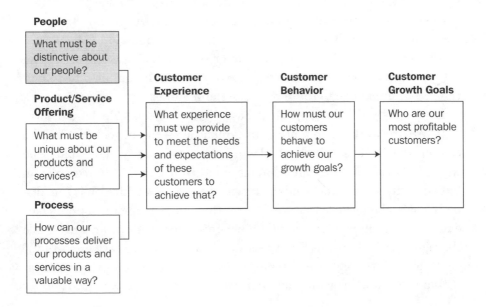

of the service that counts, but whether it's relevant and appropriate and what the customer expected."

Four things are essential if you are to harness people power:

- Hire people with competencies to satisfy customer expectations.
- Train employees to deliver experiences that uniquely fit your brand promise.
- Reward them for the right behaviors.
- Most importantly, drive the behaviors from the very top of the organization.

Hire people with the attributes to satisfy

You have to get people with service in their souls.

Chris Stone vice-president of human resources, Midwest Airlines

Once you know and understand customer expectations, you can move on and create an organization with the culture and the people to deliver on these expectations. This means identifying the fundamental behavior your brand requires and the values which are integral to the brand. This is the essence of the organization, the company DNA.

The obvious corollary of this is that those behaviors and values must be placed at the center of your hiring criteria. It is little use espousing certain behaviors and values while hiring people ill-equipped to deliver them. You must hire to those behaviors and values.

Increasingly this is happening. Says Krispy Kreme's Barbara Thornton: "We are working on a pre-employment assessment tool that will be customized for Krispy Kreme and will help us to identify individuals who would be a good fit with our organization. I can't say that it's completed, but what drives our work and the target that we're working on is the ultimate goal of being sure that we are creating magic moments for our customer. To do that, you have to find the right people and they have to have the right fit which means that the culture piece becomes very important."

People set the culture. People with ingrained habits which do not match your culture or the customer experience you are trying to deliver will find changing their habits a challenging task. Better, then, to hire people without such habits in the first place. First Direct hired people with top notch communication skills rather than experience in financial services.

At Pret A Manger, it is restaurant employees who make the hiring decisions about which candidates will join their work team. Employees must have the right attitude to fit into the Pret culture. "We've got some amazing people who work for us," says Pret's Andrew Rolfe. "There are a couple of things that allow us to have these people working for us. One is the way in which we recruit. Only 5 percent of people that apply for jobs at Pret get accepted. Candidates have an interview, they then get sent to their closest shop to have an interview with the general manager, after which they are brought back to work in the shop for a Pret experience day. After that the shop team vote and if the team doesn't vote for you, you don't get the job. So already we're creating this team atmosphere."

People matter, but the right people matter even more. Tesco, the UK's largest supermarket chain in number of stores and market share, has shaped its employee hiring and development processes to attract and retain people who are most likely to own and live the company's values. Those values are both clearly articulated and widely disseminated. "Treat people how we would like to be treated" and "Give support to each other and praise more than criticize" are examples. When Tesco's values are spelled out in Tesco's advertisements, they serve as a powerful attraction to those who appreciate them. The values in their entirety make up the culture of the business.

Recruitment has to be followed by retention – as Frederick Reichheld puts it in *The Loyalty Effect*: "If you wonder what getting and keeping the right employees has to do with getting and keeping the right customers, the answer is *everything*."[3]

One can see all of these principles in action at Pizza Express where, for example, rising through the ranks is not that unusual. In fact the chairman started out in the company washing dishes. UK managing director James Parsons cites his own boss as a typical example. "My boss started off as a company secretary, a secretary on clerical duties." He goes on to say: "Not everyone wants to go on and be the chairman or area manager of whatever, but for those that do there are great opportunities."

Not surprisingly in light of this policy, Pizza Express experiences relatively low turnover of managers and staff and so, rather than a lot of time and effort being spent on training new people, the existing staff can be "nurtured," as Parsons puts it. Staff members are considered to be the essential components of the customer experience, and they are treated as such. "The people on the restaurant floor earn good money," Parsons says, "they get well looked after and, if they want it, there is career progression.' Pizza Express group chief executive Ian Eldridge sums up the company's approach: "We're not in the customer retention business, we're in the good staff retention business."

Train employees to deliver experiences

*Attention to detail isn't written in our training
manuals, it's in our DNA.*

ANA advertisement

In a detailed study of brand sales effectiveness, Gallup found that people with a high natural degree of personal "sales talent" sold, on average, 9 percent more brand volume than the norm. Those with additional "brand talent" profiles outsold the rest by 21 percent. They defined people with "brand talent" as those really owning and living the values and behaviors that align with the brand personality and positioning. These people are a living extension of the brand, bringing the values to life, and delivering them direct to customers.

Employees do not instantly walk through your door and utilize their attitudes, skills, and intelligence in a manner best suited to deliver great customer experiences. Nor can existing employees be expected to transform themselves instantly and alone. Not everyone has the luxury of starting with zero employees and hiring to clearly identified behavioral models. (And even if they do, training is still required. Hiring people with good phone skills is one thing, teaching them the First Direct way of handling customers is a better thing.)

The question for many companies is what do you do with existing employees? And how do you develop people so that they have the requisite core behaviors and values? How do you train people to do it "your way?"

The best route is to first map the core behaviors against the customer touchline maps. You can then identify specific behaviors and standards along the touchlines that demonstrate the brand values. These specific behaviors and standards can then be tested against the brand promise.

On the training front, you need to develop training that teaches employees not just what the core behaviors are, but HOW to live them for customers. "We're very well trained in knowing what the customer wants, making that link to the employees so that they can make their own decisions when something isn't programmed, and they'll choose the right way," observes Marilyn Winn, senior vice-president of human resources at Harrah's.

The employee-owned John Lewis Partnership puts a lot of effort into training. But chairman Sir Stuart Hampson admits that it's much easier to train people around product knowledge than it is to find people who are passionate, confident, and keen to sell. "That's something we look very hard for," he says. "There is a lot of passion in our business, and I wish we had more."

Giving people the skills is vital but insufficient. Employees also need permission to act in the best interests of the customer – as demonstrated by an experience Sir Stuart had when visiting one of the company's Waitrose grocery stores. He was being shown around by one of the store assistants when she excused herself in order to talk to an elderly customer. She asked: "I'm sorry to bother you, but I just wanted to check if your husband is all right. I usually see the two of you shopping together but I noticed last week you were on your own, and again today." The customer thanked her for her inquiry and explained that her husband had been in hospital for a minor operation and was now recovering well. The shop assistant returned to her chairman, apologizing for having abandoned him. Needless to say, his reaction was one of delight that the instinctive attitude of the employee was that the customer comes ahead of a head office visitor.

Sir Stuart Hampson notes that employee turnover is not much different from that of competitors for relatively new workers, but is markedly better for staff with two to five years with the company. "We have in the business, very considerable numbers of people who've been with us 25, 30 years and we value them enormously," he says. "They are the bedrock of the business. Anyone who has been with the business for 25 years gets a six-month sabbatical on full pay."

Training can be bolstered by the use of customer experience success stories to help communicate desired behaviors. At Midwest Airlines, everyone has heard Brad Braine's story. It makes an impact.

Spontaneity needs to be enabled by training. There needs to be a balance between the human and the mechanical. This is something Disney has long proved adept at. Its employees – cast members – tend to be genial conversationalists rather than automatons. At the Disney World parking lot each section is differentiated by a Disney cartoon character. But it's the awning-striped tram that arrives to give you a lift and the driver who spontaneously strikes up a conversation about your home town that turns acres of asphalt into a means of connecting with guests.

> **Spontaneity needs to be enabled by training.**

The "State of the Industry" report issued by the American Society for Training and Development (ASTD) highlights the value of investing in people.[4] For example, companies spending at the higher end of training per employee outperformed those at the lower end on each of three key business measures:

- net sales per employee + 57%
- gross profits per employee + 37%
- "market to book" shareholder value + 20%

Given the frequency of the "People are our most valuable assets" call, perhaps this data comes as little surprise. Yet the ASTD research found wide variation in the extent to which organizations made investment in their people a priority. Leading edge companies spent 3.4 percent of payroll on training while average performers invested only 1.5 percent. Similarly, leading edge companies trained an average of 8.6 percent of their employees against the average of 6.9 percent.[4]

One such leading company is Carphone Warehouse. "We invest four times the average amount on training compared to any other retailer. There is a lot of emphasis placed on induction training and equipping you with the knowledge and skills you require. The fact is that you cannot even serve the customer or greet the customer until you've been through two weeks of intensive training and been assessed and passed that strict assessment. Then there is ongoing support and training that enables you to learn in store via the company intranet," says Simon Nicholas.

Carphone Warehouse's commitment to training employees in delivering all aspects of customer service is a vital part of their success, but so is the value-based approach that they take. Simon again, "It's not about telling people what to do, but encouraging people what to do. So training courses are more like workshops," Nicholas recounts, "What we wanted to do was create boundaries within which we expect people to operate, but allow people to have the personality to do it their way."

Pret A Manger also subscribes to this approach. "What is important is the way in which we treat and develop our people once they are here," says CEO Andrew Rolfe. When he is asked how Pret trains its team members in customer service, his answer is simply, "We don't." Yes, Pret employees are scrupulously taught such tasks as how to use the cash register and how to make sandwiches and coffee. However, the only guidelines Pret gives them about customer service are, in Rolfe's words, "to greet the customers when they arrive; look them in the eye when you put the money in their hand; make sure you say something when they leave; but more than anything else, be yourself."

It is the critical degree of latitude in behavior allowed by companies such as Carphone Warehouse and Pret that in turn allows employees to deliver customer experiences that precisely align with company values. But it does require a very clear understanding of what customers value, what the promise is, how to deliver it, and the style of leadership that encourages employees to do so. Most companies have a very "loose" understanding of their brand promise and values and yet attempt to keep a very "tight" control over how employees behave. Companies like Pret do just the opposite. They have an extremely "tight" understanding of what customers value and their brand promise and so can afford to be "loose" in the instructions they give their people. All of these ingredients can be built into an integrated communications and training plan like the example for a bank shown in Fig. 6.2.

Experiences and the training in delivering those experiences must be inclusive. Professor Paul Nutt's recent research on different styles used to implement strategies vindicates this approach. He studied over 350 strategic implementations and compared them both for style of

Figure 6.2

Branded Customer Experience® training plan

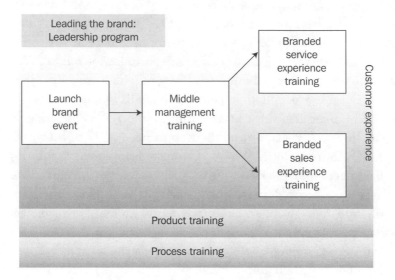

implementation and success rate in terms of sustained adoption. He looked at four different styles, which he characterized as:

1 **Tell:** leader announces decision and tells people what they are expected to do.

2 **Persuade:** leader sells decision as a way to realize an important goal – often supported by expert opinion or research – then waits to gain sufficient support.

3 **Participate:** leader stipulates what is needed then delegates action to a task force and awaits recommendations.

4 **Engage:** leader creates awareness of the need for action by bringing to life the gap between current and desired state; leader outlines some options for people to consider as examples of how to overcome current problems.

Nutt's findings are conclusive. "Tell" and "persuade" were the most commonly used methods for introducing new strategies, largely because they take less management time. However, by far the greatest success rates came from those strategies introduced through a more engaging process – virtually all were still effective two years after introduction, compared to less than half of those introduced through "telling."

Tesco went through a concerted effort in the 1990s that, in effect, transformed the company from one that largely trained by telling to one that encourages engaging. The initiative was launched when all 12,000 Tesco managers took part in a massive retraining program, primarily designed to provide them with new skills in communications, teamwork, and planning. Retail director David Potts explains that previously Tesco was much more rigorous about the specific training given to staff; even down to saying "please" and "thank you." Today, that's changed, he comments: "We say that as long as we've hired the right person, and we have broadly explained what we want them to do, they should just be able to get on and do it. People in Tesco are more confident with the customer and with being themselves with the customer."

The lesson for aligning and developing people? You can't "tell" employees what to do to be the best – you have to use more innovative, engaging approaches.

Increasingly, successful organizations are using tools such as story telling to win the hearts and minds of their employees. In a recent training session with a leading food retailer, a store manager was seeking to inspire his colleagues to create exceptional customer service. Historically, these sessions had concentrated on the hard, more tangible aspects of service – line length, signage, availability of product, shopping carts, etc. This manager recognized that these were generic to all grocery stores – the "price of entry," not a differentiator. He wanted colleagues to deliver something more and to help bring his vision to life he told stories he had heard of inspiring service – service where an employee created a truly exceptional experience for a customer. He asked his staff to share their stories and soon colleagues were beginning to suggest new ways in which they could use some of the lessons to develop the service they provided in their own store.

The power of the story – like those of Nelson and Brad Braine – is that people remember them. The texture of the story helps to provide context and meaning for the learning; it allows people's imaginations to have free rein; it appeals to the emotions. Above all, the stories of what the "best" have achieved are infinitely more memorable to the "rest" than a set of bullet points on a slide.

Krispy Kreme human resources vice-president Barbara Thornton refers to the power of stories when noting that the allure of customer experiences in the company's shops has been described as "a hot doughnut theater," where the company is in the business of creating magic moments through people, places, and product. It is in the relating of these magic moments that employees gain "a huge amount of guidance," Thornton observes. So she sees it as a principal mission of her department to help find the right people to create those magic moments for customers, helping them to develop their strengths and talents so that they can grow in the company, and create magic moments within the company.

Reward the right behaviors

> Great leaders spend 20 percent of their time talking about what they want people to do and 80 percent of the time talking about why.

Recruiting and retaining talent does not happen accidentally. It has to be planned for and systematized. There has to be a process. Organizations have to have systems to retain the best people.

"We really worked hard in the middle '80s to leverage the loyalty that has been built over years and years. We just about bankrupted customer patience and loyalty and had to earn it back. We had to get back in the marketplace," says Scott Kisting, of his experience running commerical banking at another major bank prior to joining California Federal. "What I have found is that there are behaviors that you have to understand, your behaviors and how your behaviors impact customers. Most companies measure results. I guess, at that time, I figured out that unless I changed the behaviors I wasn't going to change the results."

At Cal Fed one initiative involves the use of mentoring. This began when the company did some analysis of performances to see who was really doing well. The company had an incentive plan through which it measures results. Star performers are recognized through a "Circle of Excellence" process. Further analysis revealed that there was a group of bank managers that was doing particularly well on customer service and sales results.

"We looked at it closely, and we found that there were about 50 bank managers who did extremely well on customer service, cross-selling, doing all of the things that we consistently discussed," says Rick Leweke, executive vice-president for human resources at the bank. "Our challenge was to determine what these people were doing, and how do we get them to share their experiences with everybody else?"

The result was the Power of Partnerships, a mentoring program. People from lower performing groups become the mentees of people in the highest performing groups for a week. The mentees are shown how the best practice team handles things and put together an action plan on what they are going to do when they return to their branch. When the mentees return they are accompanied by their mentors who help them to install the measurement systems and best practices they had determined would improve results. The mentees then present their action plan to regional managers who will monitor its progress.

While this is a simple enough idea, Scott Kisting points out that sharing knowledge and best practice does not come easily. "This has huge potential for our company and nobody has ever fully implemented best practices," he says. "We were 1.73 sales per FTE (full time equivalent – a measure of productivity) per day, which would make us pretty good in the industry. I said, 'But there's a man sitting in this room among you – and we publish this data every day to all the branches – who has been 3.0 for the last year.' I said, 'Pablo, stand up.' I said, 'Anybody in this room ever call Pablo?' Nobody ever called. We had a lady who had the best existing customer cross-sell. And anybody ever call her? But you all know what her numbers are, right? Yeah, we've seen her numbers. They all, for the life of me, couldn't figure out why they didn't call."

To concentrate the minds of mentors and mentees, Kisting suggested that the mentors consider their reaction if the mentee were to take over their branch and the mentor's bonuses were still tied to the branch's performance. Would they be comfortable? "Because if you're not comfortable with them doing that, then don't send them back to their branch because they're not ready," Kisting explains. "Keep them the second week. I don't care. I'm willing to invest in people because we need to have them go back and not just institute the practices but understand the reasons behind the practices. Great leaders spend 20 percent of their time talking about what they want people to do and 80 percent of the time talking about why. Let's go back and spend the majority of the week on why this worked, why you did it this way, and why you think this is what we ought to do."

From an HR point of view, Rick Leweke regards the mentoring program as an opportunity to improve the performance of the bottom half or bottom third of the organization – "That's the magic of it, getting everyone to emulate these best practices or adopt some of them, then execute quickly. It is a very simple process when you think about it. It's very powerful, and it has an immediate impact."

To Scott Kisting, such mentoring is a powerful adjunct to the company's training programs – "The difference between the mentoring and the classroom training is the visual learning, the experience of seeing a top producer do it."

What is interesting about Cal Fed's experiences is that systems which some would see as intrusive are actually welcomed by employees who are fully committed to delivering a great experience for customers. Take the company's monitoring of the performance of its call center staff. "We created a quality assurance organization in the telephone channel," says Elvis Schmiedekamp, director of customer service. "This group monitors calls and scores them utilizing a quality scorecard. They review the quality scores with the Customer Service Representative's supervisor for coaching purposes, reinforcement, and for recognition. When you say – 'We're going to monitor your calls and we're going to score the quality components, not how long you talk to the customer. We're going to be concerned that you're in compliance with regulations and so forth, but we're not going to be so concerned about how long you're taking to handle the customer as long as you're delivering the experience and providing intelligent responses to customer issues and you're enhancing the relationship with our customer. The quality scores will reflect how you perform against that criteria' – employees say, 'It feels good. It's what I'm all about. It's what you hired me to do. It's what my personality and instincts tell me to do.' They embraced it. It was like a breath of fresh air for them."

Once people have the skills and understand customer expectations, their performance needs to be evaluated against the right behaviors. The soft stuff needs a hard side. People power requires that you also develop metrics for evaluating the use and impact of core and specific brand behaviors. Reward and recognition systems need to be aligned with these metrics.

Julian Richer of Richer Sounds has an unusual approach to developing systems to reward the right behaviors. He is very precise about what he wants. "It's quite clear to me what the Richer brand stands for. That is value for money in parallel with great customer service," and how he will recognize it. "We have the Richer league which is a service-based measurement scheme and each month we have three winners, who each get the choice of a prize including the use of a Bentley. These are inner city kids who have never been in a Bentley in their lives. They can use it to visit their old school friends, or go down to the pub or take their mother-in-law out for tea; they have lots of fun with it." Richer is as focused on creating an experience for his employees as his customers. "If you're employing teenagers you've got to focus on your target audience," he says.

The basic style and philosophy at Richer Sounds is caring management. For Richer, that means being "a caring benevolent employer who is driving and demanding but also very loyal to his or her employees. That's exactly what I'm trying to do, warts and all, and I guess I am like that. That's what I grew up on and I've seen it work. It did work and it does work. The challenge is to be professional about it and systemize it … I make sure that anyone who does anything good gets a letter."

To the casual observer, the largesse of benefits at Richer Sounds might seem enormously expensive. However, Richer claims that all these things cost very little relative to "the phenomenal cost of having disgruntled or demotivated employees"; for example, the cost of absenteeism, labor turnover, theft, and bad customer service.

The philosophy evidently works. According to the *Guinness Book of Records*, Richer Sounds achieved the highest sales per square foot of any retailer in the world for six straight years.

At Tesco, Terry Leahy led the way in reshaping how the company managed and treated its employees. "What of course becomes quickly apparent in a service business is that the only way you can do anything for the customer is by looking after the staff,' says Leahy. "No manager or management team can possibly create the shopping experience for 12 million customers, but a quarter of a million staff can… We've had to revolutionize, to change completely the way we manage. We've changed out of all recognition."

As a result, over the past ten years there has been a significant pay increase for all Tesco employees plus an increase in benefits. Profit sharing was introduced to 80,000 long-term staff, and this has had a powerful influence on people's sense of involvement and ownership of the business. A "Save as You Earn scheme" has increased the personal wealth of Tesco's staff. The result of all this is an important alignment of the business interests, the shareholders' interests, and the employees' interests.

Drive the behaviors from the top

The final piece in the people power jigsaw is that senior managers set the tone and the example. The way they treat people is reflective of how people will treat customers. Organizations that treat employees the way they treat customers understand what the customer experience and people power are all about.

Perhaps the best-known example of this is Southwest Airlines. Its mission statement reads: "Southwest Airlines is dedicated to the highest quality of Customer Service delivered with a sense of warmth, friendliness, individual pride, and Company Spirit. We are committed to provide our Employees a stable work environment with equal opportunity for learning and personal growth. Creativity and innovation are encouraged for improving the effectiveness of Southwest Airlines. Above all, Employees will be provided the same concern, respect, and caring attitude within the Organization that they are expected to share externally with every Southwest Customer." The great success of Southwest lies in the fact that everyone in the company lives the mission and delivers the mission.

> Leaders must communicate a sense of purpose and constantly reinforce the values of the organization.

Jack McAleer, executive vice-president, notes that Krispy Kreme's leadership has historically been "almost paternal" and that founder Vernon Rudolph was "nurturing in that regard." Today, Krispy Kreme is still taking care of its employees in ways that range from creating a comfortable environment, complete with reading material and videos, where they can take breaks, to arranging for special travel such as a trip to the New York Stock Exchange. Having recently gone public, the company has also put a stock ownership plan in place for all full-time employees with a year's service.

People power cannot be delegated. Leaders must communicate a sense of purpose and constantly reinforce the values of the organization. They must exhibit the core brand behaviors, leading by example, walking the talk. The message must be clear. When Richard Branson took over part of the old British Rail network and started Virgin Rail he found that the people power had been neglected. "I remember going to a back room at Euston where the train drivers and people meet while they're waiting for their trains. It was the most despicable thing; British Rail had given them a horrible place, a hovel of a place. I decided to spend some money on giving them television to watch whilst they waited for the trains, games to play; again, treating people as human beings and encouraging them to keep in touch."

At Hewlett-Packard, the vice-president of total customer experience sets the goals against which all of the company's executives are compensated. "In the customer economy, your executives' and employees' performance-based pay is based on customer metrics – how you're doing in meeting customer satisfaction and customer loyalty goals," says Patricia Seybold.[5]

Another vital part of the leader's role is to acknowledge achievements, to provide motivational feedback to accelerate progress. Good leaders habitually catch people "doing things right" and publicly recognize their achievements. They link training and coaching to strategic issues. They remember the connection between what customers want and what colleagues want. Above all, they treat colleagues the way they want them to treat customers and encourage them to observe and challenge the organization through the customer's eyes.

One way to look at this is to consider the extent to which your organization balances making the numbers with living the values. Jack Welch is credited with the thinking that lies behind the grid shown in Fig. 6.3, looking at the variety of behaviors you can encounter.

For the best companies, people in box D are the role models – the high performers who act out the organization's values. Those in box C are the targets for development – can your high performers coach them to meet the quantitative goals?

Figure 6.3

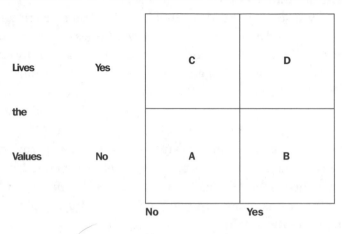

Lives   Yes

the

Values   No

No   Yes

Makes the Numbers

The challenge is box B – people who hit the numbers but reject the organization's values. Jack Welch himself is quoted as saying: "Making your numbers but not demonstrating our values is grounds for dismissal." One of our colleagues describes a situation in his former company where the highest performing store manager, in terms of sales and profit growth, was dismissed because his behavior toward employees and attitude to customers was "off message." The impact? The entire organization knew that the leadership was serious about implementing the new customer-focussed strategy – the ultimate support needed for the rest to become as good as the best.

High fliers

While traditional airlines struggle from crisis to crisis, the airline industry also has some outstanding performers. UK-based easyJet, with its no-frills proposition, improved profits by 94 percent from 1999 to 2000 and is receiving numerous awards as the best low-cost airline. It is not yet as consistent as it needs to be in its delivery, but there is no doubt that it is creating an enthusiastic response from the market. Midwest Express and Jet Blue airlines joined Continental in receiving top customer service honors in a Zagat survey of 150,000 voters. Virgin Atlantic won the coveted Airline of the Year award from subscribers to *Official Airline Guide* (OAG) in 2001. According to the OAG, Virgin Atlantic staff go "above and beyond the call of duty."

So what makes the difference between those airlines whose customers are calling for a legislated Bill of Rights and others whose customers are enthusiastically advocating the experience? All are struggling with the basic issues of on-time performance and mishandled baggage, but those who are winning go beyond basic service requirements and realize that their people are the key to differentiation and true customer advocacy. It's not coincidental that both Southwest and Continental are prominent in *Fortune* magazine's best companies to work for list, with Southwest achieving the #1 position.

A study of over 6,000 consumers by the Gallup Organization found that in the airline industry outstanding people are more important than schedule convenience and *three to four times* more important than brand advertising in building airline loyalty. Customers who report an airline's employees as outstanding are *15 times* more likely to fly again with that airline. According to a J.D. Powers study, the success of Continental in creating high levels of satisfaction is due in large part to "the performance of its employees in the air and on the ground. Southwest had the highest ranking in the flight attendant factor. Continental also received high marks for courtesy, responsiveness, and helpfulness of its attendants. In addition, Continental received high marks for the helpfulness and concern of its ticket counter and gate staffs."

In a world of product and service parity, people can and do make the difference. Perhaps the answer for the airline industry is to realize that bigger is not necessarily better. Do they need to fix on-time performance and baggage handling? Absolutely. But sustained profitability will come when customers become true advocates, not merely hostages to their frequent flyer programs. At the end of the day, it is people who make or break the experience.

People first with Fairmont

An employee at Fairmont Hotels heard two guests in a restaurant arguing about which one of them had locked the keys in the car. Unbeknown to the guests, this trainee called a towing service to retrieve the keys, which were then served to the guests under a silver dome as the chef's "special dessert."

"Three basic factors that will ensure success for a hotel company are location, product, and service," Fairmont CEO Bill Fatt explains. "Because we're an old company with heritage assets, we tend to have very good locations. We've spent a lot of money on the product and our various partners have spent a lot of money upgrading the product, so we are quite proud of our assets. But service delivery is really the key. The people working within the hotels are the ones who have the face-to-face contact with the customers, and they are the most important part of the overall equation of meeting the promise that the overall brand represents."

Although the company invested $750m in its properties in 1988, it became clear then that if there wasn't just as much emphasis put on service delivery and the people side of the business then there wouldn't be sufficient return on the investment. A correlation study of the guest and employee surveys led to an important discovery: the hotels with the highest employee satisfaction scores also had the most satisfied guests.

Fairmont uses an integrated human resource strategy called Service Plus that has its roots in an earlier performance management approach. It has four components: select, lead, train, and reward.

Selecting the best is the first component, and a lot of time and effort goes into each hiring decision. Every new hire, from room attendant up to executive vice-president, goes through a structured interview that has been developed by studying profiles of the top service providers in the company. The process identifies those with a natural service orientation.

Then, because Fairmont understands that people usually quit leaders rather than companies, another structured interview process is used to select leaders. As a result, fully 70 percent of all promotions come from within the company. Leaders are given the training and tools to support those who have the day-to-day interactions with the guests.

Extensive and intensive training is given to every employee, and this includes everything from teaching required tasks to teaching empathy. Every hotel has a learning coach, and programs run the gamut from a Leadership 2000 program to allowing employees paid days off to investigate interesting aspects of their community to tell guests about later.

Reward, the final component in Fairmont's performance management approach, is carried out through many recognition and award programs, and employee satisfaction surveys are used extensively to monitor improvement. Not surprisingly, Fairmont has been cited as one of the 35 best employers to work for in Canada.

Ask yourself

To help you make the rest as good as the best, ask yourself the following:

1 Are you consciously recruiting against the brand values AND seeking a good fit for your culture?

2 Is your investment in training and developing people at the leading edge end of your industry?

3 Is your training designed to help people understand how they must behave to deliver your brand?

4 Are you using involving, engaging processes to earn the right to staff loyalty?

5 Are you treating people as you would wish them to treat your customers?

6 Are you using your own people to help develop their colleagues?

7 Are you actively demonstrating your support for the best by recognizing and rewarding them?

8 Are you dealing with nonconformance?

Notes

1 *Sunday Times*, May 12, 2002.

2 McEwen, Bill, "All Brands are the Same," www.gallup.com/poll/managing/mr010115.asp

3 Reichheld, Frederick, *The Loyalty Effect*, Harvard Business School Press, 1996.

4 "State of the Industry," American Society for Training & Development, 1998.

5 Dearlove, Des, "When the Customer Clicks, Jump," *The Times*, June 30, 2001.

7

■■■■■■■■■■■■■■■■■■■

The Branded Sales Experience

It's the sales effectiveness piece that is the engine that makes it all run

Anne Lockie executive vice-president for marketing and sales, Royal Bank of Canada

Without question, delivering a Branded Customer Experience® would not be complete without considering the Branded Sales Experience. This is exactly the same concept applied to how your organization sells as opposed to how it provides service. In our view, they are opposite sides of the same coin and must be driven off the brand promise together. If you wish to penetrate a new market or drive up sales, it is vital to create a sales experience that causes prospects to choose you over competitors.

This was exactly the strategy used by GM when launching the Saturn brand. The Saturn was launched in 1990 and was GM's first new nameplate since Chevrolet. GM knew that the product alone was insufficient to take market share from Japanese competitors, so Saturn created a distinctive sales and after-sales experience which was very different, created high levels of satisfaction, and quickly took Saturn to the number two position in the market.

GM realized that car buyers were fed up with buying from car salesmen and the poor service of many dealerships. Saturn created its own dealer network and, as a result, increased repeat purchases and customer satisfaction dramatically. Rather than view the car narrowly as a product, the new approach recognized that customers wanted a bundle of transportation services. Saturn's brand development focussed on the buying experience, service and support, rather than being narrowly focussed on the product. For Saturn the experience was the brand.

The Saturn experience is laid out in what GM calls its "pricing principles": "No hassle" means Saturn Retailers are up-front about all elements of a vehicle's price. No last minute add-ons or hidden charges. Nothing up our sleeves. "No haggle" means the retailer should stick to whatever price it sets. Horse trading and dickering don't fit with Saturn's philosophy: "No Customer should ever wonder whether the Retailer's next Customer will get a better price by driving a harder bargain." The feel-good factor with Saturn is such that customers even gave Saturn high marks on the service they received when their cars were recalled.

Companies like Saturn, Amazon.com, Royal Bank of Canada, California Federal Bank, and Carphone Warehouse have created experiences which make it easy and enjoyable for customers to purchase and use their products. Part of that customer experience includes a sales process that creates value for customers and the brand.

Creating a sales process that adds value to the customer experience has several common denominators:

- start with segmentation, but drive to personalization;
- design a sales process that creates value for customers;
- align the sales process with the total organization;
- train, coach, and reward the desired sales behaviors;
- manage the sales process to deliver a Branded Customer Experience®.

We shall now look at each of these factors in detail.

Start with segmentation, but drive to personalization

Segmentation is not new. Certainly it is fundamental to any sales or marketing strategy and there are as many approaches to segmentation as there are customer groups to segment. Traditionally, requirements for effective segmentation include:

1 **Adequate size:** sufficient potential customers in each segment. Involves trade-off between consumer homogeneity and scale effects.

2 **Measurability:** use of measurable variables as bases for segmentation. Need for combination of concrete (e.g. age) and abstract descriptors.

3 **Accessibility:** segments defined to facilitate targeting and marketing efforts. Segmentation variables must identify members in ways that facilitate their contact.

4 **Different response:** segments must respond differently to one or more marketing variables. Segmentation variables must maximize behavioral differences between segments.[1]

So much for the textbook. Companies that are passionate about delivering a Branded Customer Experience® drive segmentation to new levels of personalization in order to fully understand how to tailor the selling process to every individual customer.

Perhaps the most promising path to achieving such levels of personalization is through a Customer Relationship Management (CRM) system. Although the current business and marketing journals are full of tales of CRM implementations that never delivered what they promised, others have had significant impact. The difference lies in the extent to which CRM has been fully integrated with the customer experience. "CRM has really become a part of our business model. It's not a project, it's the way we do things around here," says Judith Hatley, vice-president, marketing, and customer management at Royal Bank of Canada. She should know. Back in 1992, RBC launched a program that segmented their customers based on monthly net income after tax. The objective was to retain and grow their most profitable customers and to "really get our arms around them." Unfortunately, they found that people in the branches were so bogged down with operations and other tasks that relationship building with their most important customers was not as high on their agenda as it should have been.

In response, RBC launched an effort to deliver a Branded Sales Experience that would touch literally every part of the bank. A new role was created – customer segment manager – responsible for driving the strategy for a group of customers and with bottom-line accountability for the organization for the profitability of those customers. They were the catalysts for bringing together all of the resources of the organization including marketing, product, and operations. CRM was at the center of it. "In the old days we would do direct mail to anybody and maybe it was for a product that they already had," says Judith Hatley. "Now, we are able to identify needs and goals for specific customers whether it is through contact or direct mail. We are building something called customer preference and choice. We are actually building capability so that we can find out personal information from you that you want us to know. For example, 'Don't ever call me up after 7:00 o'clock,' or 'Don't ever mention my business to my wife!'."

As a result, RBC has been able to free branch staff to focus on customers rather than administration. "We want to make them the most amazing salespeople we can make them," says Anne Lockie, executive vice-president for marketing and sales. "We need to take all the clutter away, as much as we can, from the front line so they can focus on a couple of things. They can focus on providing the four essentials of customer care and they can be proactive in terms of their contact and in providing advice."

Design a sales process that creates value for customers

World-class companies define a sales process that will ensure the delivery of a customer experience that is consistent, intentional, differentiated and valuable.

Once the value drivers of what targeted customers are looking for are clearly understood, world-class companies define a sales process that will ensure the delivery of a customer experience that is consistent, intentional, differentiated, and valuable. Anne Lockie, puts it simply: "We have a sales process that everyone in the organization follows – from me to every individual salesperson. We all do the same goal setting and reviews." The results of this dedication to the delivery of a consistent sales process have been impressive. Earnings growth is 25 percent, ROE is getting close to 25 percent and revenue growth is 8 to 10 percent.

Results such as these require that organizations really spend time defining the sales process from the customer's, rather than the organization's, point of view. For example, California Federal Bank determined that when most people walk into a bank branch to open a new account, most bank employees think that their primary job is to get the customer out of there as quickly at they can. They ask questions such as "How many checks do you write?" and "What kind of an average balance to you carry?". "That's about them. That's not about you, the customer," says Scott Kisting who set about changing things. "Now walk into our branch. If you sit down and say, 'I'd like to open a checking account' we have trained our people to say, 'I want to make sure you have the right checking account. Can I ask you a few questions.' We ask you questions about you. It's a program we call 30/30. We try to earn up to 30 minutes of your time. We are trying to tell you up front that I want to earn the right to become your personal banker. I know you probably don't believe banks do that, but we do."

Developing a real understanding of how customers want to buy is far more important than defining how you want your products to be sold. It gets to the core of the experience you are trying to create for customers and defining that early in the sales process communicates an important message to potential customers: this is going to be a different buying *and* ownership experience.

Making sure that the buying experience is differentiated doesn't happen by just asking the sales organization to figure it out. It requires the alignment and involvement of all parts of the organization. The key is in the integration of people and processes that may not have worked as closely together in the past.

Align the sales process with the total organization

The sales function alone cannot possibly hope to deliver a buying experience to the customer without partnering with other parts of the organization. Jim Rager, who leads RBC's Personal and Commercial Bank, understands this intimately. "The biggest differentiator we have is what we call our 'sales management wheel.' This is a continuum of things related to training, professional designations, technology, rewards, and recognition. Whenever we want to change something, whether it be goals, an approach, or going into a different market segment that we have ignored, we immediately create a total alignment of all of these things. You have to think about change in a very integrated, aligned way, otherwise you get the wrong behaviors."

One of the largest consumer products companies in the world took this so seriously that it spent several months developing a proprietary selling process that would deliver differentiated value and competitive advantage at the customer interface. This strategic imperative was nothing less than the reinvention of its approach to selling. Grounded in the principles of value-based selling, this initiative was a mission critical response to dramatic shifts in the business, including customer consolidation and increased pressure from key competitors.

The Forum team conducted in-depth client research, and defined the client's customer's value in relationship management. These value drivers formed the core of the Branded Sales Experience for the client that was then integrated with the client's relationship management process. The joint Forum and client team then spent several months developing competencies (for entry-level salespeople all the way through to strategic account managers), sales management tasks, the learning strategy and curriculum that would transform their sales force through learning, performance support tools, and performance metrics linked to their customers' key value drivers.

A key success factor was that Forum and the client team worked with several executive-level decision-making groups, including a cross-organizational executive committee and a Customer Management Council. These groups were instrumental in building cross-organizational alignment and collaboration, enabling them to bring their vision and the initiative to life at the customer interface.

This initiative is now seen as one of the few real change efforts to build alignment and unparalleled collaboration across the organization to differentiate the company with customers. It has produced significant results including close to double-digit growth in key markets. The company has also been able to institute a significant price increase with its key customers, an almost unheard of increase in their industry.

So it is not enough to simply design a sales process that is differentiated and extends the total value of the customer experience. To ensure its reliability you have to develop it in a way that involves other parts of the organization. One area top companies focus on is identifying the actual sales behaviors that shape a superior customer buying experience – and connecting them to their desired sales results.

Train, coach, and reward the desired sales behaviors

Perhaps this is a "no-brainer." That is, ensuring that the sales behaviors that your people demonstrate every day to customers are consistent with the unique, differentiated service experience you are trying to create for them. But we found very few organizations that were good – let alone great at it. Some stand out, especially those that represent a relatively complex or broad range of product offerings.

"I've coined a phrase here that great companies measure and coach behaviors. They expect to make their numbers," so remarks CalFed's Scott Kisting. "You are always investing in observing, coaching, and reinforcing the behaviors, because you know that is what leads to results. But first, you have to understand which behaviors make a difference. To do that, you have to look at the business through the eyes of the customer and ask, 'Why would I choose to bank there versus with somebody who has a brand that is more identifiable?' Scott's experience has led him to create and measure what are called minimum standards about how many prospects a person ought to have, how many calls a person has to make, what are the best amenities of an effective call. All the things that are the behaviors that create the results."

In other parts of the book, we argue that world-class companies invest more in training than their industry followers. This relates specifically to the sales process, as training is an essential component for shaping and reinforcing the desired sales behaviors. As referenced previously, Simon Nicholas, Training and Development Manager of Carphone Warehouse, states: "We invest four times the average amount on training compared to any other retailer."

At Harrah's Entertainment, an investment in training that was directly tied to performance standards aimed at delivering a Branded Sales Experience really paid off. Beside other results, gross revenues increased by 15 percent and average spend per customer increased by 17 percent. One of the things attributed to these results was the impact from the learning system that went across the organization.

When it really works, learning becomes embedded in the work process and, as performance standards are improved, the learning system adapts to support employees in achieving even higher standards of performance. Organizations that excel at providing a differentiated sales process understand that learning is not a one-time event or solved by installing a sales learning portal. It is a process that is central to the success of the business and represents a key opportunity to support the integrated delivery of a Branded Customer Experience®.

Drawing a clear line of sight between the sales behaviors that shape a Branded Sales Experience and the results they are expected to create is a triumph of common sense over common practice. But companies that dedicate themselves to this endeavor are reaping significant rewards.

Manage the sales process to deliver a Branded Customer Experience®

Managing an effective sales process is a daily, weekly, and monthly management task. It begins with setting goals and measuring performance that not only drives sales, but reinforces the desired behaviors that will deliver the Branded Customer Experience®. "I said from day one that we are not going to only be measuring how many products you sell," says Scott Kisting. "We're going to be measuring how many people you help every day." Does CalFed measure things like average cross-sell performance? Absolutely, but more importantly it measures the sales activities that drive those results.

To that end, the sales management task is an essential success factor. And what do the best sales managers do? Simply stated, they manage their sales force in the same way that good salespeople manage their customers. They focus on acquiring, retaining, and growing their salespeople:

- They look to acquire talented salespeople who have the attitudes and skills necessary to differentiate themselves with customers and deliver the Branded Sales Experience.
- Sales managers reward behaviors as well as results and ensure that compensation is aligned with desired behaviors and results.

- Top-performing sales managers understand that nothing is more important than the continuous growth and development of the sales force. They take the reins for leading learning to grow the capability of their salespeople. They view sales force development as an everyday activity, not as a two-hour motivational speech at the annual sales meeting.

> **Top sales managers view sales force development as an everyday activity, not as a two-hour motivational speech at the annual sales meeting.**

The sales manager has three critical roles to play in managing the sales process:

- *Be the example (but not the whole story)* – sales managers send a loud and clear message to their salespeople when they personally model the skills they expect their salespeople to exhibit with their customers. Conversely, credibility can be lost rapidly when salespeople witness a "do as I say, not as I do" approach.
- *Coach and motivator* – high-performing sales managers make time for coaching every day. They exhibit strong communication and people skills, and have the ability to assess sales skills and respond accordingly.
- *Crafter of strategy* – the ability to translate the brand promise into a sales force strategy, and then into what each salesperson should be doing differently on a daily basis, is critical to survival.

Managing the sales process to support the Branded Customer Experience® is part art (ongoing coaching and training to reward the right sales behaviors) and part science (centralized customer databases, setting goals and measuring performance against goals, etc.). The organizations that are successful in aligning their sales process with delivering a Branded Customer Experience® understand one fundamental truth above all others: it is not about selling products; it's about delivering more value to customers. As Anne Lockie of RBC told us: "When I hear someone tell me stories about how a Royal Banker called them [*a customer*] because we thought they were paying too much in service charges and could we get their permission to change their account and they ended up buying three more products from us and were happy about the entire experience, I think, yes, it's working!"

When organizations see the sale as the beginning of a lifetime relationship rather than the end of a transaction, then you know that the customer experience is well and truly on the management agenda. For example, Carphone Warehouse refunded $15 million to customers because the price of their mobile phone had fallen *after* they had purchased it. This is a rare example of putting the values of the brand and the customer experience ahead of the bottom line. Interestingly, CEO Charles Dunstone has reflected that the company has been even more profitable since implementing that policy.

The hard sell

In developing your Branded Sales Experience, do you:

1 Drive from customer segmentation to customer personalization?

2 Design a sales process that delivers value to customers?

3 Align the sales process with the BCE and total organization?

4 Train, coach, and reward the desired sales behaviors required to achieve the results?

5 Manage the sales process to deliver the Branded Customer Experience®?

Notes   1   Boyd, Harper W. Jr. and Walker, Orville C. Jr., *Marketing*, Pitman Publishing, 1994.

8

■ ■ ■ ■ ■ ■ ■ ■ ■ ■ ■ ■ ■ ■ ■ ■ ■ ■ ■

Putting the "e"
in experience

Price does not rule the web; trust does ...
Without the glue of loyalty, even the
best-designed e-business model will
collapse ... Acquiring customers on the
internet is enormously expensive, and unless
those customers stick around and make lots of
repeat purchases over the years, then profits
will remain elusive

Frederick Reichheld and Phil Schefter Bain & Co

First there was the Industrial Revolution. Then came the Technological Revolution, followed by the advent of the internet. While it took more than 100 years for the Industrial Revolution to take hold and some 22 years for the fax to reach 10 million people, the world wide web reached 10 million people in just two years. Little wonder that, downturn or not, organizations are still stampeding to go online. However, being on the web is not a guarantee of success. This chapter explores the secrets of organizations whose brands dominate the world of e-commerce.

A recent *Business Week*/Harris poll found that 57 percent of internet users visit the same sites again and again (rather than look for new sites). What causes this "stickiness?" In a word: brand. In a world of almost infinite choice, consumers want to know what an organization stands for, and they expect it to deliver. Strong e-commerce brands are built not by creating cool websites but by creating a customer experience that delivers the proposition again and again through processes and people. Some organizations are leading the way in successfully blending

Figure 8.1   *How processes impact the customer experience*

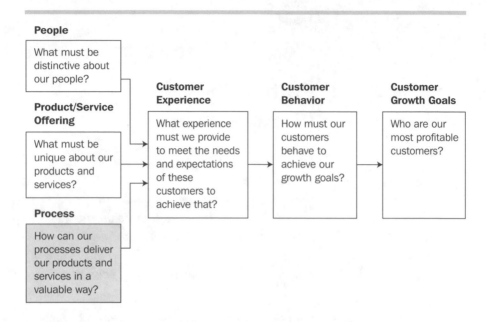

"high-tech and high-touch" to deliver high-quality customer experiences that become synonymous with their brand. Think of Amazon.com, eBay, Smarterkids.com, First Direct, L.L.Bean, Tesco, Egg, Dell, and many others. They blend technology and people to put the "e" into experience.

High-touch high-tech can be seen at work at Hallmark Cards, which has created something called the Hallmark Idea Exchange, an online community of 200 consumers who share their experiences, celebrations, and much more with the company. The sharing is such that Hallmark calculates it has generated new product ideas in less than half the time normally required and saved one-third the cost of traditional market research.

Connectivity+Content+Culture=Innovation/Learning suggests Thomas Brailsford, Hallmark's manager of knowledge leadership. "Research on communities suggests that once community membership exceeds 100–150, the sense of community cannot be maintained," he explains. "Obviously, there were some who wanted us to make the community bigger. Some online research companies boast of having hundreds of thousands of consumers in their online panels. We specifically wanted to foster a sense of community and so kept the group small. The issue was neither representative of the sample nor sample size. Our focus was to provide a more qualitative look into consumer's lives."

Building customer confidence

Thanks to technology, customers are more footloose and fancy-free than ever before. Yet many are reluctant to trust online brands. Why? According-ing to a recent survey, "The Direct Market-ing Industry Online: Perspectives on 2001," the top five reasons why people do not buy online are: worry about fly-by-night retail-ers; not wanting to deal with the hassles of returning goods; worry about using a credit card online; worry that they are opening themselves up to receiving junk mail; and a preference to see and touch what they buy.

> **The realization that high technology alone is insufficient became blindingly obvious at the time of the dot com crash.**

As these reasons suggest, technology alone only gets you so far. The realization that high technology alone is insufficient became blindingly obvious at the time of the dot com crash. While the web was still in its infancy, people involved in it were sure that business would be conducted in a new way, that the old certainties of brand building in a bricks and mortar environment were gone. The online revolution would mean that brands could be built and maintained in a totally different way.

The rationale behind this assumption was tantalizingly convincing: the dot com brand-to-customer relationship would be seen as a gen-uinely two-way marketing dialog between the individual customer and the site. Many also envisaged that the very lure of the site would be enough to build a long-term relationship between visitor and provider; customer loyalty to e-business was somehow going to be uniquely binding. Time and dot com failures running into billions of dollars have proved this wishful thinking – the e-commerce utopia hasn't quite arrived yet.

Now the signs are that traditional companies such as Barnes & Noble, The Gap, and Tesco are fighting back, using their skills in serving customers to create assurance, value, and follow-up that "pure" web-based companies find hard to compete against. The success of some bricks and mortar companies in developing their web presence shows that customers want choice and flexibility in interfacing with their chosen suppliers in a variety of ways.

This does not mean that these organizations are invulnerable to attack. A report from Warburg Dillon Read suggests that the average customer return rate is much higher in the case of goods bought over the web from bricks and mortar companies than over the web from pure online businesses.[1]

One reason for this may be that bricks and mortar web companies" stock delivery systems are just not geared to doing web business. Also, it is vital to look at e-business as a dynamic process – the IT infrastructure underpinning online business must be taken as seriously as any other management function.

One reason for the disappointment felt by some businesses is that customers visiting online sites tend, at best, to be fickle and mercurial. A generation brought up on armchair channel flicking is not going to be persuaded to stay online, onsite, and "on-message" just because of a few pretty graphics and animations. A study carried out by Dr Robert Passikoff, president of Brand Keys, a New York-based brand loyalty consulting and research company, found that nearly 70 percent of respondents indicated that they were visiting more sites than they had in the previous quarter. They were spending significantly less time on each site visited.

Most worryingly for online brand builders, 48 percent of those questioned in the survey said that the sites didn't hold their attention. Yet the *Business Week*/Harris poll found that online customers are increasingly returning to the same trusted sites. The reality is that these two findings are compatible; both are true. The explosion in online sites has created greater "promiscuity" but also greater loyalty to a few trusted brands.

In a report published by Neaman Bond Associates, branding was a top management concern for 91 percent of dot coms, whereas 71 percent of bricks and mortar companies cited profitability as their single biggest concern. The proper integration of the high-touch and high-tech worlds begins to answer both of these concerns. This is the point at which the processes and channels that deliver service need to be examined.

We live in a multi-channel world

Online communities have to be built around a deep understanding of customers and how they prefer to do business. The real revolution is how the new media has enabled a vast array of new potential customer channels and touchpoints. Customers can access the web in kiosks, via interactive TV, through their mobile phones, or by using broadband access. If they wish to communicate with their suppliers, they can call, text, write, fax, or e-mail them. As we have said, customers want choice and flexibility in interfacing with their chosen suppliers. This want to connect any time, anywhere, any way, any how.

A McKinsey research study concluded: "The more a person uses the community features of a site, the more that person tends to visit it and to make purchases there. Users who contribute product reviews or post messages visit sites more than nine times as often as non-users do, remain twice as loyal, buy almost twice as often."[2]

A key lesson for the future is that companies should recognize the profusion of new access points (as well as already existing channels) and try to reach the customer wherever he or she happens to be, in a way that is consistent, intentional, differentiated, and valuable – the four characteristics that form the Branded Customer Experience®. Even in today's high-tech, multi-channel world, these simple characteristics remain the cornerstones of brand delivery, ensuring that organizations realize a healthy return on their substantial technology investments.

The challenge for organizations is to find ways of delivering a consistent, intentional, differentiated, and valuable experience of their brands across multiple channels (that is, the web, customer service centers, branches, and so on). However, it would be wrong to make the assumption that all products and services can and should be delivered across all channels – that would not be integration. True integration comes from recognizing the opportunities (and disadvantages) a particular channel offers for customer service and mapping them onto brand and business objectives.

All too often we see examples of websites in which development has taken place in isolation from other communication channels and, indeed, from the brand proposition itself. As customers move beyond the superficial layer of an aesthetically pleasing website and discover that follow-up service is almost non-existent, they can be left wondering why a site was developed in the first place.

All of this will get worse. If companies cannot get web development right, what chance have they when even less well-understood media such as interactive TV and mobile telephony become more widely available?

Blending high-tech with high-touch

It is important for companies to realize that different mediums should offer different experiences and satisfy different needs. One is not simply a substitute for the other. For example , Rich D'Amico, head of new business development at IKEA, says that loyalists consider IKEA stores to be "a form of entertainment ... we don't want to disappoint people. Shoppers are used to seeing everything under one roof – from the kitchen sink to the soup bowl." IKEA realizes that the store provides a high-touch environment that satisfies a different requirement from websites.

The battle between the human touch and the technological touch is increasingly complex, but increasingly important. "There is an increasing degree of fuzziness between what is real and what is fake," observes the futurist John Naisbitt in his book *High Tech High Touch*. "The authenticity of a company's product or service is now all important. They need to establish intimacy with consumers." Some companies have already reintroduced people answering their telephones rather than having automated systems. The cold mechanical hand of technology will only get you so far. The warm hand of humanity is required to maximize the business potential of technology. "It is embracing technology that preserves our humanness and rejecting technology that intrudes upon it," says Naisbitt. "Companies feel pressured into keeping up with technology because they fear falling behind their competitors. They feel they have to be on the internet so move as fast as they can to make the internet their strategy. In effect the promise of the internet is running their businesses."

Organizations are faced with three key challenges when they bring together technology with customer service:

- Matching best practice in terms of integrating the human and system sides of service.

- Designing service experiences that are seamless and that deliver the same brand proposition and values across channels.

- Emulating best practices in web design to make e-tailing easy, enjoyable, and interactive.

Integrating the human and system sides of a business requires collaboration within organizations – the collaboration of marketing, operations, and human resources described in Chapter 5. In the case of e-commerce, not only must the triad work closely together, close co-operation with IT must also be ensured. The whole organization must work as one in breathing life into the brand. The website should be thought of as a window that allows customers a clear view of the brand proposition and the organization working seamlessly to deliver it. There should be no difference in the nature or quality of the Branded Customer Experience® that is offered online or in-store. They should deliver the same promise and the same value. All that is different is that they satisfy different buying requirements. This requires a better understanding of what the web can do and what it cannot.

In thinking about best practice in web design and development, it is helpful to look at the medium's strengths and weaknesses – discussed in more detail on pp. 146–8.

Though aesthetics are important, the starting point for any successful website should be a thorough understanding of its purpose and its target audience. Websites should be intentional: the right customers should go to the right places and do the right things. Intentional websites ensure that the customers" experience is meaningful.

> **The starting point for any successful website should be a thorough understanding of its purpose and its target audience.**

Companies can tackle the challenge of creating intentional websites first of all by understanding the current customer experience through observation and research (we call this touchline mapping), then by defining the desired experience through focus groups, and finally by designing a new customer experience that delivers the brand proposition and is aligned with brand values. Web specialists can create a website that replicates the customer experience online, using these values.

A good example of an organization creating an intentional website is Priceline.com, the "set your own price" website – still one of the most recognized brands on the web. A recent McKinsey analysis found that Priceline had reached the magic $100 million in sales only 1.7 years from start-up. Until the dot com crash of 2001, it was the fastest growing of any of the dot coms; it has moved at the speed of light compared to most traditional companies.

How did Priceline do it? By being very intentional about creating its proposition and customer experience. Priceline went through a rigorous three-step process:

- It first identified 27 different touchpoints at which customers come into contact with their travel supplier.
- It then analyzed each of these touchpoints to identify barriers and customer dissatisfiers.
- It finally identified ways to remove the barriers and create a smooth value-added customer experience. In the words of Priceline's Earl Quenzel: "We knew we had to offer a compelling brand, rooted in a shared definition of customer value."

Getting it wrong

Is your organization guilty of any of the following IT weaknesses?

1 IT departments driving web development.
2 Marketers lacking fundamental knowledge and experience of customer service delivery.
3 A lack of purpose; companies wanting a site because everybody else has one.
4 Shoehorning existing products and services onto the web.
5 An assumption that the brand proposition will automatically be of value to customers accessing other channels.

Aligning the inside and the outside

Building a strong online brand shares a requirement of building a traditional marketplace brand: the need for alignment inside and outside.

Organizations need to ensure that their internal values and organization mirror the brand values and the customer proposition that they wish to deliver.

A good case in point is easyJet.com, which relies on customers booking directly online in order to avoid agency commissions. In a recent interview, Stelios Haji-Ioannou said: "The first thing I did was walk the talk; I took my tie off, started dressing down. I worked from an office in Luton. All of that was part of a plan to create a culture which keeps cost down. At the end of the day, branding is not only for the customers but also for the employees."

Organizations do not always grasp the operational impact that a website can make. Call center operatives, for example, are not always properly trained to deal with basic internet-related inquiries.

New channels, such as the internet or mobile telephony, should be viewed as opportunities to create new value for customers. Creating new value for customers requires a precise understanding of what customers value and how it can be delivered from the CEO downward. Amazon.com is the 57th most valuable brand in the world, according to Interbrand, and it is the most widely recognized e-commerce company in the US, with 60 percent of the population knowing what the brand stands for. It has attracted 23 million customers and achieved more than $2 billion in sales in just five years. Amazon.com was launched in July 1995 with the proposition of making book buying a "fast, easy, enjoyable experience." The company's mission was achieved by focussing the whole organization on the proposition. In the words of company founder Jeff Bezos: "Our secret is that we have not been competitor obsessed. We have been customer obsessed, while our competitors have been Amazon.com obsessed."

That obsession has paid off for Amazon. In the spring of 1997, some experts said the company would become "Amazon.toast" when the big, well-established traditional retailers started coming online. What saved it? Bezos believes that the Amazon.com culture is self-reinforcing. At that time there were some 250 people working at Amazon, and they doggedly put the customer first. Says Bezos: "That's also the way that you pull together in times of adversity. You focus on that thing that's shared. It's worked extremely well for us." Amazon.com has recently declared its first profitable quarter ahead of analysts forecasts.

Online in practice

Let us look at some examples, both good and bad, of each of the characteristics of the Branded Customer Experience® in practice:

1 **Consistent ... reliable and trustworthy delivery of the customer experience across channels:** while other banks hurried to get online, First Direct decided to wait until the time was right. It now has a quality internet presence that is totally consistent with its brand proposition and the excellent reputation it has acquired through its call centers.

   First Direct's site is unmistakably branded: it employs a simple but characteristic color scheme and intuitive navigation. It conveys a modern quality image and offers easy access to online banking services. The tone of the site matches the enthusiasm of the company's call center operatives. The site also provides clear evidence of First Direct's conscious decision to use technology to provide high-touch services that provide convenience and build lasting customer relationships.

   Barclays, on the other hand, offers its customers an excellent call center experience through its Barclaycall service, but its website is difficult to navigate. For instance, if the customer inadvertently clicks the "proceed" button twice, the system will terminate the transaction and the customer will have to log in all over again.

2 **Intentional ... using new mediums to create new value:** Tesco, the UK's leading supermarket, achieved success through relentlessly focussing on the customer and intentionally creating a culture that, in the words of Tim Mason, Tesco's head of marketing, "focuses on creating value for customers so that we earn their lifetime loyalty."

   Tesco.com is the largest online supermarket in the world. It was designed to make the shopping experience quick and simple. With rather more than 400,000 visitors to date, Tesco.com has managed to prove that an online offering can be a viable extension of the main brand and channel. Tesco.com's strengths include:

- A truly consistent high-tech site that creates the feel of an actual Tesco store.
- Easy navigation and a highly reliable interface.
- Customer knowledge; the more customers use the site, the more the site remembers their favorite items and displays them first.
- A high-touch home delivery service that is convenient and friendly. (Interestingly, the quality of the service customers receive from the home delivery staff often exceeds the quality of the service customers receive in-store.)

In creating Tesco.com, the company saw delivery as essential to providing a seamless customer experience. Delivery involves customers logging on to the service, ordering goods, and receiving goods at their homes. The company also saw delivering the Tesco promise as a critical success factor – since Tesco's brand was already focussed on customer service. Tesco's $7.50 delivery charge has not been a barrier to its growth. The company has reported weekly revenues in the order of $4.5 million. It seems that people are prepared to pay for convenience.

Not all brand extensions from one channel to another are successful. Consider WH Smith, the stationery, video, and books company. Building on its successful web store, WH Smith moved quickly into digital TV, but it failed to understand the relationship between its brand and its content (and failed to understand how they related to the new medium).

WH Smith has simply put existing web-based content live on the Interactive TV service. The problem is that watching TV and using the web are two very different activities; simply putting existing web-based content live on the Interactive TV service does not add value or satisfy customer expectations. It merely requires customers to scroll through pages of re-purposed web material.

3 **Differentiated ... uniquely offering a customer experience that is different from the ones that competitors offer:** in the late 1990s, the Prudential realized that financial services needed to attract a younger, more affluent type of customer. So it launched a new internet-focussed brand: Egg. Egg brings a fresh image while enjoying its parent's values of trust and security – which are essential for any successful financial services brand.

The Egg site itself has a very contemporary feel, much more akin to that of, say, the Apple.com site than to any other conservative financial services site. The contemporary feel has appealed to the audience Egg targeted.

Egg has also sold on price (passing on cost savings achieved by automated distribution) and has focussed on providing added value through partnership relationships that cannot be achieved in any other channel than a website. The Egg shopping mall, for example, gives the Egg customer access to online discounts with the Egg credit card – and it is a mere click away from the customer's statement.

In contrast, HSBC, another financial services provider, has created an online service with existing products and services and traditional brand identity guidelines – but the online service provides no real added value in relation to that which can be obtained in branches and through telephone banking. The HSBC site looks conservative and its functionality is basic. It is as if the bank has tried to create a Branded Customer Experience® by sticking rigidly to a formulaic brand rulebook rather than by understanding its customers and their needs and seeking to meet them in new ways.

4 **Valuable ... creating new value in new ways:** the BBC has developed a web presence that not only supports its brand and provides information about TV programs but also delivers real value that is not available through other channels. The Teletubbies online page, for example, is colorful and simple to navigate, and its well-designed multimedia games and activities keep its target audience entertained and informed.

Perhaps no company has so successfully created value in new ways via the web as has Smarterkids.com. The Smarterkids website invites parents to complete a short on-screen questionnaire to profile their child. This profile identifies the child's preferences, describes the most effective learning style, and makes a solid basis for recommending toys matched to these preferences. Thus the parents receive a valuable assessment of their child plus recommendations for toys and games that the child will enjoy and learn from. Recommendations are age-based and range across the whole price spectrum.

CEO David Blohm says that customers who profile their children using the web questionnaire are worth 200 percent of non-profilers. Around 14,000 customers – 20 percent of the total – have filled out profiles; they account for more than 40 percent of revenue. They spend more and buy more frequently because, thanks to the recommendations, the children like the toys. Customer satisfaction results and they come back for more. Says Blohm: "The more you know us, the more you love us." The experience for parents and children is very positive.

The slogan on the Smarterkids website is "Learn, Discover, Grow." This applies to the company as well as its customers. The company learns and discovers by staying closely connected with its customers. There are frequent focus groups, and a panel of 1,000 parents is e-mailed regularly for advice and comments on new products, services, or systems. To support parents, Smarterkids provides tips for school success and invites questions on any educational topic; they're answered by seven qualified teachers employed by the company. The teachers also provide reviews of every item stocked by Smarterkids to aid selection.

The lessons are clear: organizations that can successfully create customer service experiences that are seamless and branded regardless of the channel in which they are delivered will be the most successful. Customers want choice and flexibility in the way they interface with their suppliers – but they also want to build trust with suppliers.

> **At its heart, e-business is not about computers or glitzy design, but about people.**

Living in a multi-channel world, it is ever more important that we focus on the customer experience and the service we provide through our processes and people. For this reason, brands that are built in the bricks domain and those that have a strong legacy of customer focus stand every chance of successfully competing with the new high-tech upstarts.

At its heart, e-business is not about computers or glitzy design, but about people. In the words of Jeff Bezos, CEO of Amazon.com: "Customer service is a critical success factor in any retail business. But it's absolutely critical online."

The web experience

Over the last decade, there have been tremendous developments in the technologies that enable the online experience. We have seen the birth, explosion, and near-death encounter of the entire new media design industry. We have also seen an array of uninspiring online experiences. There are only a few shining examples of organizations that have managed to create powerful online experiences.

Even so, the internet has clearly emerged as a channel which is becoming an essential part of people's everyday lives. More and more people are starting to use the internet to communicate, research, buy, and provide service. This audience is media savvy. They understand brands and they understand how these are communicated, through print, the TV, the in-store experience, and so on. They also have an expectation of how it should work online. In fact, it seems people are much more demanding online. If the experience isn't right, people simply click and move to somewhere where it is right.

There is a gulf in perspective between technologists and marketers. But this is not the only impediment to creating powerful online experiences. The industry has suffered from isolationism. All too often the development of websites takes place in isolation from other communication channels. This results in inconsistencies – between basic aesthetics, for example. Customers can be left wondering why a site was developed in the first place.

Web design should be driven by objectives. You should be able to understand a business's key drivers by looking at the site.

As a starting point websites need a well-defined purpose. This purpose is driven by an understanding of the business, what it is trying to achieve, and the fundamentals of the brand. You need to look very closely at the vision, mission, values, and the spirit of an organization and how these can be represented online.

Part of this process is understanding the end user – at both a demographic and behavioral level.

Additionally, organizations need to understand what the web is good at and its limitations.

What the web is good at:

- it is a functional medium (great for tools and data manipulation)
- it is interactive and user driven (i.e. a dynamic medium)
- it provides seamless links between information sources.

What the web is not good at:

- creating deep emotional, human, tactile experiences
- passive information gathering.

The knowledge gained through this process means that the web design process has key underlying guiding principles which in turn drive the core components that create the online brand. These components are the customer experience and the customer journey. Heath Wallace, a consultancy specializing in online experience design, uses the following approach.

The customer experience is created through a combination of design, copy, and functionality. The final design of a site needs to capture the essence of the brand identity to ensure consistency with other channels. Additionally, it needs to convey purpose so users will understand what the site is for and it needs to convey value so that they will see what they can get from it.

Best practice web design principles that underpin this process are that the site should be simple, clear, and straightforward. Among other things, this enables a benchmark of things like the screen size and the target base browsers.

The raw ingredients for creating the final look include imagery, typography, space, navigation, copy, and colors. Generally if it is a bricks and clicks site, the style is taken from existing brand guideline material.

- *Imagery* – as with all marketing communications, imagery should be used to reinforce a key message. Online, the additional requirement of ensuring that pages download quickly means that images have to be optimized.

- *Typography* – ensures that the user can immediately see key elements on a page, i.e. call to action, key selling points, and so on.

- *Space* – as used on a page can be used to reinforce key aspects. For example, content surrounded by white space will mean that the eye is drawn immediately to that part of the page.

- *Navigation* – should be presented in a way that enables the customer to identify what they need from a site and be able to get there quickly and simply. In a matter of a couple of clicks, users should reach the content they require.

- *Colors* – are used to reinforce the corporate identity. Usability rules dictate that certain colors should not be used as background colors and that the visual basics are still relevant online.

- *Copy* – is a key aspect of the final site. Many companies simply take existing literature and re-purpose it for a website. This is a bad mistake as the key driver for the copy should be the purpose of the site with the tone (identified in the brand guidelines) driving the style. This means that fresh content is often required for the website.

Additionally, having identified a purpose, it is necessary to consider the functionality on the page. The designer needs to ensure that the functionality is a seamless part of the page and that the technology is hidden. People use telephones but they don't know how and why they work. The same principle should apply online. Too often you see people using technology (e.g. Flash and Shockwave) for the sake of it.

The customer journey is an essential part of the final site. Through a process called information architecture, the purpose of the site is interpreted into a site schematic to ensure that only pages relevant to that purpose are created. Each page is identified as a separate entity and the key intent behind each explicitly stated. The outcome of this process is that the content for each page is identified and the navigational needs of the site are flushed out.

David Wallace of Heath Wallace

Branding e-commerce experiences

Organizations wishing to develop a strong e-commerce brand should ask themselves four key questions:

1 How can our organizational values support and strengthen our web presence?

2 What internal messages do we need to send to employees to support the external messages we send to customers?

3 How can we align our people and processes to deliver our brand promise seamlessly over the web as well as through our people?

4 What kind of cultural change across the organization may be necessary?

We have spoken about people, processes, and channels so now let's turn our attention to products.

Notes

1 Warburg Dillon Read report.

2 Brown, Shona L., Tilton, Andrew, and Woodside, Dennis, "The Case for Online Communities," *McKinsey Quarterly*, 2002 No 1.

9

■■■■■■■■■■■■■■■■■■■■

The Branded Product Experience: more than a doughnut

The secret to our enduring brand lies in delivering an experience rather than just a collection of products and services

Harley-Davidson annual report

Branded Product
Experiences bring
product and service
together to create
real value for
customers.

One distinction that is often made between a product and a service is that the customer is actively engaged in experiencing a service but only acquires and uses a product. A customer experiences a restaurant but cannot take it home. A customer buys a doughnut and consumes it, but the doughnut does not provide a service.

Things change and the world of neat definitions also changes. Branded Product Experiences bring product and service together to create real value for customers. The sales and service experience provided by Krispy Kreme, is as important as the product itself and totally integrated with it. Scott Livengood, the company's president, puts it this way: "We view the experience of a Krispy Kreme store as the defining element of the brand. We see the experience of the store as a multi-sensory experience and pay attention to each one of those elements as we look at how to express Krispy Kreme."

Take Harley-Davidson, the motorcycle company. Harley's mission statement is "We Fulfill Dreams." "Fulfilling dreams for people from all walks of life who cherish the common values of freedom, adventure, and individual expression, involves much more than building and selling motorcycles," pronounced the company's 1999 annual report. Unless you think that this is just a PR spin, the active members of the Harley Owners Group (now numbering over 600,000) typically spend 30 percent more than Harley owners who are non-members. This increased expenditure is on clothing, holidays, and events. In September 2001, 25,000 members from all over Europe met in Austria for a weekend of partying and riding. Harley-Davidson management refers to these events as "super-engagement" because the Harley-Davidson leaders are all active partici-pants in the HOG activities.

Harley's bundling of customer experiences with product and direct involvement with customers has led to 14 straight years of financial growth and a 50 percent share of the big bike market. A shareholder who invested $10,000 when the organization went public in 1986 would now be a millionaire.

Harley has redefined itself. When you think of Harley-Davidson, do you think of a very young, hippie Peter Fonda in *Easy Rider*? How about grizzly, tattooed middle-aged Hell's Angels? Think again. Harley recently launched its "Riders Edge" program, a motorcycling safety course designed to attract new riders to the burgeoning group of Harley owners. Of the 4,000 people who went through the program in 2000, nearly 45 percent were female and half of those were under 35. J.D. Power and Associates puts the median income of American motorcyclists at $67,000. The reality is a Harley-Davidson is much more likely to be ridden by a professional female than a young tearaway. Still, the old rebel image lingers. "Owning a Harley allows a middle-aged accountant to ride into town and have people be very afraid," observed one writer. A Harley-Davidson comes bundled with a Branded Experience that no other motorcycle manufacturer can match.

Figure 9.1   *How products and services impact the customer experience*

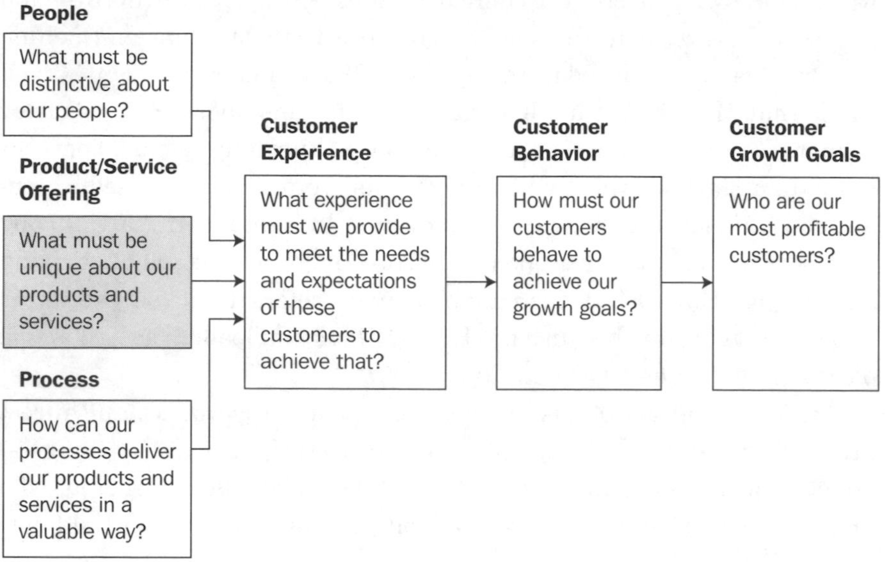

People

What must be distinctive about our people?

Product/Service Offering

What must be unique about our products and services?

Process

How can our processes deliver our products and services in a valuable way?

Customer Experience

What experience must we provide to meet the needs and expectations of these customers to achieve that?

Customer Behavior

How must our customers behave to achieve our growth goals?

Customer Growth Goals

Who are our most profitable customers?

Experiencing the bear

Product experiences are not limited to the adults. Even children are getting in on the act. If you have a child aged anywhere between 3 and 13 the chances are that you have heard, or will be hearing, about Build-A-Bear. This is a shop where children build and dress their own bears or other stuffed animals. Here is how it works. The Guest Bear Builder (yes, really) starts at the "Choose Me" station where they select the skin that will become the bear, monkey, or whatever. They then move on to the "Hear Me" station where they choose sounds to be installed in the animal. These can be pre-recorded or personalized. From there they move through "Stuff Me," "Fluff Me," "Name Me," "Dress Me," and, ultimately, "Take Me Home." Of course this process would not be complete without the fitting of the animal's heart accompanied by much hugging.

The toys range in price from $10 to $25 but most buyers spend much more than this on accessories and clothing. Perhaps this is why the stores average $700 per square foot compared with a national US average of $350 and the 70 Build-A-Bear stores in the US are bringing in close to $100 million in revenue. The concept has recently crossed over to the UK in the form of The Bear Factory and is gaining the same kind of foothold.

A friend recently took his small daughter and spent a Saturday morning purchasing a bear for several times the amount he would have spent in Toys Я Us. He said it was the most fun he had ever had shopping. The fun would also seem to extend to the company's employees too. In a little over three years, the CEO (sorry, Chief Executive Bear) Maxine Clark has taken this organization from one store in St Louis to 70 stores nationwide and a thriving Build-A-Bear Workshop business over the web. Clark attributes her success to the employees. She says: "We've got a big-company mentality and a small company heart."

The affluentials

From toys for children to toys for grown ups. A recent Barclays Bank survey in the UK identified a segment of the population it calls "affluentials." These are people who earn $100,000 and spend $22,000 of it having fun. But fun for the affluentials is about shopping for experiences rather than brand labels. They are more interested in lifestyle experiences and gadgets than designer brands; more Patagonia than Prada. When they buy gifts they are more likely to buy their partner a 747 flight simulator experience than a new sweater. They do not consider themselves rich and so are unlikely to be seen driving around in a Ferrari or sporting a Rolex. But riding a Harley-Davidson and wearing a state-of-the-art dive watch is an entirely different proposition. A significant part of their annual budget is spent on vacations but, once again, they are more likely to be hiking in the Himalayas than posing on Palm Beach. But above all, the affluentials love products and gadgets that enrich their lifestyles. So be it a Patagonian smock, Nokia Communicator, Sony Playstation2, or Gilera DNA Scooter, they are attracted to products that open up new experiences. Products plus.

Affluentials, not surprisingly, expect their employers to embrace some of their attitudes and values. And, they do. Patagonia is a $180 million turnover company that allows its employees to stop work and head for the beach when the surf is over six feet. It is a company whose founder and chief executive sometimes conducts job interviews while surfing; where the 11 times world freestyle Frisbee champion Chip Bell is the main receptionist; that publishes a collection of customer and employee stories about using its products called "Patagonia's Notes From The Field." Patagonia's products and the experience of using them are so inextricably connected that the clothing, the brand, the employees, and customers share a common bond. Unlike a number of designer sports-wear companies that have been criticized for their third world factories, Patagonia lives its brand values. For example, it is passionate about environmentalism and puts this principle before profit. So rather than building in obsolescence or encouraging customers to buy this year's range, it actively encourages customers to send in their clothing for repair if damaged – usually for free.

However, Patagonia's mission to make clothing that lasts created a dilemma. The high-tech expensive garments that it makes use carbon-based non-renewable petrochemicals. So the company was torn between using materials that create a long-lasting garment or low-tech materials that require replacing every year. Rather than solve it internally Patagonia raised the issue on its web page and asked its customers what they should do. The answer was to go for a ten-year plus life rather than produce a cheap annual fashion range.

The most noticeable thing about Patagonia is that it is almost impossible to distinguish the employees from the customers. In his book *Living The Brand*, Nichlas Ind quotes Hal Arneson of Patagonia: "Most of the people here are risk athletes. They're outdoor people working in an indoor environment that allows them to work here because it respects that about them. People are passionate about their sports and they bring that into the workplace. People spend time here agonizing over whether what they do has meaning."

The true Branded Product Experience is one that brings alive the product values in a way that becomes integral to the way in which the product is used. Customer focus becomes a much easier philosophy when customers and employees are often the same people.

Jack Daniels, the Tennessee-based whiskey distiller, applied its imagination to creating a customer experience around its product. Jack Daniels' customers are famously loyal. But, recounts Fred Newell in *Loyalty.com*, the distiller came up with another way to strengthen the bonds between itself and its hardcore fans by creating an amusing interactive experience. One day, in the mail, thousands of Jack Daniels' customers received a land deed. It told them they were the proud owner of one square inch of the land around the Williamsburg distillery where Jack Daniels is made. Thousands of those customers framed the deed, hung it on the wall, and told all their friends. But, it didn't stop there. Six weeks later, each customer received another envelope. This time it was a genuine tax bill for their land along with a note saying: "This is just for information. You don't have to pay. Your friends at Jack Daniels have taken care of it already." Another six weeks passed. Another brown envelope landed on the mats of the targeted customers. This one was a handwritten note. It said: "I was driving by your property the other day when I noticed it was looking kind of overgrown. I'm a gardener, so I cleared away the weeds for you. I hope you don't mind. There's no charge. Your friends at Jack Daniels took care of it for you."

This is a great story and an innovative piece of marketing. But, it is not a Branded Product Experience in the way that we define it because the experience did not create any lasting value for the customers nor was it intrinsic to the use of the product, unlike the Patagonia example.

The last of the real sports cars

Product experiences are not all about being high-tech. Nestled in the UK's Worcestershire hills in a village called Malvern Link lies one of the world's oldest car factories. The Morgan Motor Company was formed in 1909 and since then has continued to produce handcrafted sports cars which have changed little in appearance since the first Morgan 4-4 was produced in the 1930s. The current Morgan +8 is promoted as "The Last Of The Real Sports Cars" and costs about the same as a Porsche Boxster. The difference is that the Morgan will be slower point-to-point and less comfortable than the Porsche. Morgan owners used to joke that the suspension is so hard that if they ran over a coin in the road they could tell if it was facing up heads or tails. The car is still built from hand-beaten aluminium panels fixed to a wooden frame.

Until recent changes were made to the Morgan production process, the aspiring owner could wait for up to seven years for their car to be delivered due to the strong demand and limited supply of these handmade cars. So the question is: why would anyone spend so much and wait so long for a car that is, by any rational analysis, hopelessly outdated?

> **Branded Customer Experiences are at their most powerful when they are designed to meet the needs of clearly identified target groups.**

The answer is simple: because of the experience. What other sports car brand allows you to wander around the factory unescorted and speak to the craftsman hand beating the panels for your car (and you know it is your car because the tag attached to the chassis has all your details recorded); or chat with the lady who is sewing the leather panels for your seat; or, when your car is finally finished after about three months, visit the factory again to take personal delivery from Charles Morgan, the owner and grandson of the founder, and be presented with a photographic record of each stage of the build? Owning a Morgan is more about the ownership experience than the product in a way that a modern sports car driver might find hard to understand.

This raises an important point. Branded Customer Experiences are at their most powerful when they are designed to meet the needs of clearly identified target groups. The fact is, the Porsche and Morgan owners are likely to value very different things from their automotive experiences. Because of quality improvements and the huge costs of development, cars are becoming increasingly alike. We are fast approaching the point when the only true brand differentiation will be the ownership experience. Brands like Saturn, Lexus and Subaru are leading the way in this.

Branded Customer Experiences become all the more memorable when they combine elements of product, process, and people into one seamless experience. One of the most upmarket and respected hotel companies in Asia is The Banyan Tree Hotels and Resorts. This chain has become famous for its exotic locations and the way that the hotel environment has been transformed into a complete guest experience. In a recent interview for our book, *Uncommon Practice: People who deliver a great brand experience*, Ho Kwon Ping, the CEO, spoke of the Banyan Tree's approach to creating a branded experience. "What are the key steps involved in creating a great customer experience? For us, the physical design is very important – we have evolved so much in terms of what the latest Banyan Tree villa should be."

The Banyan Tree complements physical design with wonderfully creative service experiences but, for the moment, let's concentrate on their tangible offer. Mr Ho conveys his passion for the physical product: "We're just introducing a spa and pool villa concept in 156, which includes a special pavilion within your villa compound in which you can have your spa massage or other spa experiences. In this villa, the bedroom is set amidst a lotus pond and is fully enclosed by glass without columns. It has electrically controlled curtains, so that you can close it off if you want to. But the bed is not even a bed! It is basically a beautiful platform in the middle of the room, a perfect square. Traditional hoteliers would say that beds must be accompanied with strong reading lights, as found in every major hotel. In the Banyan Tree, we have created other spaces for guests to read within their villa. To us, the bed should be more like an altar. The bed is made like the Thai 'Dan.' In the day, beautiful cushions and a wooden server adorn the platform, so that you can relax and eat or drink there. At night, we turn it into a very romantic bed overlooking the lotus pond." The Banyan Tree believes that the physical product must be in absolute harmony with the service provided through its people and processes.

Multi-sensory experience or doughnut?

In a world of increasing uniformity, some companies stand out for their individuality and their passionate pursuit of creating brand experiences that go far beyond the product itself. In each sector there are product brands that differentiate themselves and attract a loyal, and in some cases, evangelical following of customers. Sometimes this is because the product is perceived to perform better – look at Dyson vacuum cleaners – sometimes it is because the product is enjoyable to use or cool – think of the Apple iMac – sometimes it is because the buying or ownership experience creates entertainment value – Build-A-Bear – and sometimes it is because the brand provides a desired lifestyle – Harley-Davidson.

However, many organizations fall back on advertising and promotion gimmicks to create interest for their brands. A case in point was Pepsi's Project Blue some years ago. In an effort to combat Coca-Cola, Pepsi re-branded its cola with a new blue identity. To promote this it launched its "Pepsi blue" day which saw the front pages of national newspapers printed with a blue banner, the supersonic Concorde repainted with a blue livery, and extensive media advertising. Despite spending many millions of dollars, the campaign failed to achieve its objectives. Wrapping advertising and promotion around a product alone is unlikely to have a lasting impact on customer loyalty.

How do organizations create brand loyalty by wrapping an experience around their products? By really understanding the individual needs of their chosen target customers and being prepared to create products and associated services that engage customers in the usage of their products.

Listen to the story of Krispy Kreme. "There are not many companies out there that are in the early stages of their growth (and) that also have artifacts in the Smithsonian Museum," says CEO Scott Livengood. Founded in 1937 and with a strong history in the southeast, this rapidly expanding manufacturer of premium quality doughnuts has only recently gone public. The company now has about 185 stores in 29 states with plans to enter Canada.

In addition to selling wholesale, Krispy Kreme also makes a variety of doughnuts in its 1950s-styled coffee shops where customers can watch the doughnut makers at work. Although it doesn't advertise, the company has a large, devoted following and, whenever a new store opens, people wait in line for hours and even camp out in order to get their hot glazed doughnuts and enjoy the overall experience.

It seems that the people of Krispy Kreme were almost the last to realize that Krispy Kreme is actually far more than a manufacturer of doughnuts, and it was their customers who showed them this. As Steve Anderson, the company's director of customer experience, puts it: "Our customers had to beat us over the head and explain our brand to us." As a result, Krispy Kreme has evolved away from being "just a doughnut company" to thinking of itself as more of an experience, one that is multi-sensory and interactive and that involves people, product, and place.

Certainly the doughnut itself is the most sought after part of the experience. It is truly an attracting force, and Anderson tells this story about it. "When Vernon Rudolph founded the company, it was totally wholesale. He would make doughnuts, throw them in the back of his Pontiac, and go to the local corner grocery. Then he would put the doughnuts out there, and the stores would sell them and pay him. But the smell experience people were having caused them to rap on his door and say, 'Would you sell me some of these?'"

What the customers have said over and over again, however, is that Krispy Kreme is really a total experience and it is an experience that drives many to a deeply emotional connection to the brand. People get a dreamy look in their eyes when they talk about Krispy Kremes.

Simply put, the brand promises magic moments. "Speaking as a Krispy Kremer," says Scott Livengood, "when people find out that you are with the company, almost invariably they have a story. They say, "I have to tell you about …" and "Let me tell you my story." They talk about their experiences as a child with their parent or grandparent and how it involved the store, what the use of the store was, their impression of the company, the business, and the brand."

Stan Parker, senior vice-president of marketing, explains that Krispy Kreme does not actually define magic moments for customers "because we've learned from them that magic moments come in all shapes and sizes … I think any attempt to define a magic moment would fall short. We just want the right elements to be in place for magic moments to happen, and every day brings a little different twist. We receive about 5,000 e-mails a month from folks, and a lot of them are sending us their stories, their testimonies, photographs, even a love letter. We post and rotate them – they represent many different magic moments."

"The experience in the store is inherently a magic moment," Livengood believes. "Customers are able to come in and see, almost literally, magic. Eighty percent of our doughnuts are yeast raised as opposed to most folks who sell cake doughnuts. Our dough-nuts, when we extrude them go through this proof box, and if you have ever seen bread made, the yeast bread rises. So you can see these little teeny doughnuts get bigger. There's magic to that, especially if you're a kid. The doughnuts

Every day smells like Christmas at Terminal One.

are little here, they are big at the end, and they go through this trans-formation from white dough to gold – cooked to a golden finish. Then, they go through a glaze. It's like the curtain going up as they come out. There's a lot of magic inherent in that."

Sensory marketing may be marketing's new frontier. Smells are being marketed as integral parts of the consumer experience. The logic is simple. If you walk past a baker's shop you will be enticed by the smell of freshly baked bread. Suddenly, you will feel the need to purchase a warm loaf. The power of air is nothing new. On board planes air is warmed up to encourage passengers to sleep and the air in first class is reputedly of a purer, less recycled variety, than that breathed in economy. Similarly, if you are trying to sell your house, filling it with the aroma of fresh coffee is advised.

Smell is particularly important in the car industry. Cars may end up smelling of a combination of gasoline, old boots, pets, mouldy food, and children, but they begin life smelling attractively and persuasively. Companies go to great lengths to ensure that their cars smell of nothing in particular or something vaguely pleasant rather than fabric, rubber, and freshly manufactured plastic.

The scent of pine needles is sprayed around the terminals at London's Heathrow Airport. For most people, forests have strong associations with vacations, weekend walks, and childhood. Every day smells like Christmas at Terminal One.

The importance of sensory experiences helps explain how some organizations can charge a premium for their products. One example is Maggie Moo's, the ice cream franchise. Richard Sharoff, the Chairman, is very emphatic about this: "If you look at the market, there's a variety of different brands across the category, and, for the most part, the common denominator is: you walk into a store, you get an ice cream cone, you stand in line, and you walk out." He continues, "The stores are dirty. There is no branded experience, *per se*, and they're not very well executed. Product quality is variable. It's not, generally, a good experience." Ken Rowland, President and COO, describes the Maggie Moo's experience in sensory terms: "I walk through the door and enter a store that's clean, colorful, it's got the 'Tail of Maggie' that I can see clearly. The store is structured such that I can flow through quickly in terms of speed of service. I'm greeted by a smiling associate who says, 'Hi. How are you today?' Or, 'Hi. Welcome to Maggie Moo's, have you ever been to Maggie Moo's before? You haven't? Well, let me tell you about our concept. First, we make all 24 of these flavors, right here in this store. Let me let you sample "Utterly Cream." Let me let you sample "Cinnamon." Let me let you sample 'Espresso Bean'." Not, 'Do you want samples?'"

"The customer chooses a flavor, and we take them to the next station, which is the frozen table. We say, "At this table, you have the opportunity

to have any of these things in front of you mixed in with your ice cream.'
Then, as we fold them in, you have the opportunity to take your ice cream
and put it in a waffle cone – which comes with your purchase – or a bowl.
The customer has the opportunity to come in, get a completely indulgent
experience, and enjoy the process, because we have interacted with them
throughout the entire process'." He concludes: "It's fun, it's entertainment,
it's wholesome … It's premium quality."

It is also a great example of Branded Product Experience.

Self-analysis

Some questions to ask when creating a product experience:

1 Which values underpin our brand and do customers strongly
   associate these with our products?

2 Which features of our products could be enhanced to emphasize
   our brand promise?

3 What services could we bundle with our product that would be
   consistent with these values and which would heighten the
   experience and pleasure of usage?

4 How can we bring the five senses into play to heighten the
   uniqueness of our product by building on those characteristics
   that typify it in the minds of consumers? E.g. the sound of a
   Harley-Davidson engine, the smell of a Krispy Kreme, the look of
   a Porsche.

5 How can we bring target customers together so that the use of
   the product becomes an integral part of their lifestyle?

6 How can we provide stimuli or clues that trigger a memory of our
   product and the experience of using it? E.g. The Hot Donut sign
   at Krispy Kreme.

7 How can we recruit people who are passionate about the
   product and who can speak knowledgeably about it?

So far we have examined the impact of people, processes, and
products on delivering a Branded Customer Experience® and seen
that this is a powerful way to win in the marketplace. The next
question is how do you sustain this over time?

10

■■■■■■■■■■■■■■■■■■■

Keeping the edge

The levels of service that employees are expected to provide have to be measured constantly against changing customer demands and the competitive marketplace. We constantly survey our customers and make sure that we understand what services are required, and adapt accordingly. You have to do a tremendous amount of research in understanding what your customer profile is

Bill Fatt CEO, Fairmont Hotels

> **Strong brands survive the product life cycle through constant updating and reinvention.**

Life, including business life, seems to be made up of a series of cycles. Brands achieve preeminence by not just surviving the ups and downs, twists and turns, but by thriving in that process – indelibly embedding themselves in the minds of market constituents over time.

Strong brands survive the product life cycle through constant updating and reinvention. Fast moving consumer brands such as Heinz, Kodak, Colgate, Kellogg, and Gillette are in a constant state of reintroduction to the market. The slogan "New improved X" is known to generations of television viewers. Products like BMW, Sony, and Palm are altered, embellished, improved long before customers tire of the existing model. Lifestyle brands such as Chanel or Nike are re-launched every season. The same applies to those strong service brands that have survived the cultural life cycle – brands like Tesco, IBM, British Airways, Sears, Continental, and American Express have all reinvented themselves at one point or other. The fact is that as customers' needs and values change so must the customer experience change to satisfy them. Those leading organizations that fail to stay in touch simply die – think of Pan-Am, Wang, or C&A.

Whether the constituency is internal (employees, management, contractors) or external (customers, clients, shareholders, members of the public, governments), the challenge is to create a clear and powerful presence in the marketplace, signified in language – a name, a brand, a reputation that is evergreen.

Audit data shows that strong brands are more profitable. Being the #3 brand in a category can often mean unprofitability. The difference between first in market and third is often to do with customer acquisition and retention; and these are a function of customer advocacy, as we saw in Chapter 3.

In other words, consistency of delivery is paramount – and consistency of delivery is one hallmark of the Branded Customer Experience®. To sustain that consistency, your business must significantly expand its measurement systems – from providing a mere accounting of past business performance to anticipating and measuring customer needs. You must produce accurate, ongoing assessments of your capacity to fulfill the evolving brand promise. Sophisticated customer research allows you to uncover what customers really value, determine your performance gaps, and then track your progress in closing them. This ensures that you stay ahead of changing customer needs and can shape your offering to appeal to emerging customer groups. More basically, it involves really listening to the customer on a regular basis.

Krispy Kreme uses mystery shoppers who use pinhole cameras to record details of the customer experience and then feed this back to managers on a frequent basis.

Brand revitalization

*To improve is to change; to be perfect is
to change often.*

Winston Churchill

Old brands can be re-energized or they can be left to fade away. Brand
revitalization is all about physics. You can either let the energy dissipate
or you can make the conscious, intentional decision to put new energy
into an old brand. Engineers use the term entropy: the natural tendency
for things to decay and become less effective over time. In the broader
sense, a firm can decide to enrich and enhance the total brand experience or it can allow a brand that does not fit into its future to die or be
sold off.

The time when you really need to focus on revitalizing your brand is
when you are on top. The UK retail chain Sainsbury's lost its leadership
position to Tesco some years ago. But, thanks to a renewed focus on its
target customers and what these customers value, it has developed a brand
promise and begun to implement this throughout its stores. As a result,
Sainsbury's has regained much of its edge. As we write, a survey has
appeared showing Sainsbury's beating Tesco on key service dimensions.[1]

While the rebirth of Sainsbury's is underway, look at how the airline
Continental was revitalized – in contrast to many other airlines.

In 1994, when Gordon Bethune became chairman and CEO of Continental, the company lost $204 million. Continental's market capitaliza-
tion of $230 million was actually less than the trade-in value of its
planes. Things were bad. "We even had pilots turning down the air con-
ditioning and slowing down planes to save the cost of fuel," Bethune
later recounted. "They made passengers hot, mad, and late."

On arrival, Bethune took the double locks off the executive offices on
the 20th floor. He ordered the planes repainted so they were all the same
color. He instructed staff to ensure that the planes were cleaned three
times more often. He announced that every month that Continental was
in the top five airlines for on-time performance everyone would get $65
– the company had lost $6 million per month by being late. In the first
month Continental was seventh; in the second it was fourth; and in the
third, first.

Fortune selected Continental as the Most Improved Company of the 1990s. "We don't spend a lot of time on strategy; we spend more time on implementation, making sure we get it done," says Bethune.

Continental's success is built on meeting the demanding needs of business travelers. It needs to get the customer experience right for everyone who boards one of its planes. It does so by giving responsibility to its people and having rewards systems linked to the customer experience. In an age of product parity, the differentiating factor is people.

Continental executives continually emphasize the importance of their people and are in constant communication with them. Leaders connect with the customer experience and the work of staff on the front line. Continental executives now spend time with baggage handlers and gate agents to see things from their side. They can no longer take their vacations during peak travel times. This is symbolic, but important nevertheless. The message is that executives and cabin crew are working to the same ends. The result is that staff turnover is down 45 percent and customer satisfaction is up dramatically.

As the Continental story suggests, revitalizing or re-energizing a brand is much more than repainting the airplanes or changing the letterhead. Revitalization is about exploring the deepest, darkest, and most powerful corners of your brand and what it means, both rationally and emotionally, to one's clientele. This is not a small deal. Nor is it simple. It is about the entire "branded experience" that your firm creates.

Keeping the edge through a visionary goal

Throughout the 1980s Cadillac sorted out its quality problems and went on to win a Baldrige Award in 1990. The trouble was that it no longer had any buyers for its quality cars. A new generation of car buyers had emerged and Cadillac had been too busy getting its house in order to notice.

It takes real vision to recognize when the brand has become obsolete or a limitation to growth. You have to put your head above the parapet to survey the competitive battlefield.

Few CEOs take the bold step of totally changing the brand as did Bill Fatt of Fairmont Hotels. "Building the brand is absolutely critical and was a central part of why we acquired the Fairmont Management Company in

1999. We had been using the Canadian Pacific brand and we wanted to grow outside of Canada. Our belief was that the Canadian Pacific brand would not travel well outside of the country. So, having a brand name that represented an image in consumers' minds that was comparable or compatible with our properties and that had a reasonable degree of recognition in the very large US marketplace was critical to our strategy."

Having the vision is one thing, making it a reality is another. There is tremendous pressure on companies to produce short-term results and the tendency is to fall back on cost cutting or price promotion to achieve forecasts. Fatt's answer is that "It's really a question of prioritizing. We can come up with hundreds of ideas on things that would be nice to have but we recognize that these things are expensive and take time, training, and effort to put in place and execute. So we've tried to focus on the things that we believe are a priority. Guest service is priority number one and so there is nothing that takes us away from trying to provide guests with the absolute best service possible."

> **"We don't spend a lot of time on strategy; we spend more time on implementation, making sure we get it done."**

That, in turn, requires organizations to maintain their focus on changing guest expectations as indeed Fairmont Hotels does. "In order to build and sustain the brand you have to make sure that the product meets today's needs," says Bill Fatt. He goes on: "One of the things that has happened over the last few years is the increasing need for technology both to be able to serve guests, and to be available for guests to use when they're visiting our properties. So, a very important function for us is keeping up with the changing needs of consumers, particularly in the technology area – whether it's restaurants or food services that we provide, or the types of property experiences that guests want, or any one of a number of things. The levels of service that employees are expected to provide constantly have to be measured against changing customer demands and the competitive marketplace. We constantly have to survey our customers and make sure that we understand what services are required and we adapt accordingly."

Sir Stuart Hampson of the John Lewis Partnership offers similar advice: "Have a clear understanding of what you're setting out to do and follow it relentlessly. It's not a recipe for complacency, it's not a recipe for no change because by focussing on what you're trying to achieve enables you to look at the constantly changing environment around you and adapt. We are facing change in retailing, not just because the competitors change but because the customers change and if you are looking at that, monitoring it, thinking about it, and aiming to satisfy those customer expectations and to do it within your set of values, then you can adapt and constantly lead."

The emotional dimension

How do companies manage the issue of the emotional attachment to a brand? Some years ago Coca-Cola launched New Coke and were quickly forced to withdraw the product because of the pressure from legions of loyal Coke drinkers who had strong affiliations to the traditional product.

Building long-lasting customer relationships requires appreciation of two insights. First, we can learn from living relationships between individuals. Human relationships are the best model for building durable commercial relationships. There are human characteristics that we seek in our personal dealings, like being reliable, trustworthy, and being there when needed. They can be applied to customers to provide a rich and mutually beneficial exchange. We all enjoy the companionship of like-minded individuals. Customers will naturally appreciate involvement with like-minded suppliers.

The second insight is the need to focus on the most valuable customers (as discussed in Chapter 2). In a portfolio of customers, some will be substantially more profitable than others. In the European mobile telephone market, there are many more customers using pre-pay programs than contract customers, but the latter group use their phones far more.

Combining these two insights, think about how you feel when a company that you have done business with or worked with for many years is acquired or merges with another firm.

In situations such as these the mechanics of the merger opportunity – the growth potential, reorganization, harmonization of the pension schemes, re-sizing the workforce, etc. – tend to dominate the management agenda. In fact, what should be most important is what will the merger or acquisition do to our customers' perception of our brand? Will it increase brand loyalty or decrease it? The reality is that most mergers erode brand value because management becomes internally focussed during the transition and the brand promise and customer experience can become confused or diluted by the new combination. Similarly, the employees' attachment to their brand can be a stumbling block to the successful integration of the two organizations.

When Philip Satre, chairman and CEO of Harrah's makes acquisitions he thinks very carefully about the impact on the customer and employee experience. "One of the major hurdles we had to cross as a company when we decided that we were going to become a consolidator was, 'How will these companies fit into our culture, our brand, what we stand for?' In some cases we said we are going to leave them with second brands. We did that with Rio and we did that with Showboat. In most of the cases we've made the conscious decision we are going to convert these to Harrah's. Convert the experience to the brand."

Note   1 *Retail Week,* January 25, 2002.

11

■■■■■■■■■■■■■■■■■■■

Putting it all together

A brand used to be a promise, but as we move forward, a brand is a relationship, a living thing.

Kyle Shannon chief creative officer, Agency.com

The real issue for many companies is sustaining growth over the long term while meeting the expectations of the shareholders in the short term. How does customer loyalty help this corporate goal? Quite simply, loyal customers are profitable customers, so building brand loyalty is the most effective strategy for growing shareholder value. This principle was clearly illustrated during the stock market crash of 1987 when the market value of companies with the strongest brands rose by $7.1 billion, while that of the weakest brands plunged $19.8 billion.

The reality is that there has been a remarkable shift in the marketplace. We have charted the move toward the experience economy. But there is more to it than that. The experience economy is built around brands that create real value and meaning for customers and employees. It is not a superficial trend or experience. The brands that will succeed create genuine, powerful experiences which touch and affect people. Sincerity cannot be faked. In the wake of September 11, 2001, this move to powerful experiences as the commercial cornerstone has gathered even greater momentum. People are now actively seeking out deeper values in their lives and commercial transactions. Daniel Pink, author of *Free Agent Nation*, talks about "the flight to meaning." He uses the example of car advertisements and suggests that in the future we are less likely to see soft focus ads with thumping sound tracks featuring coupes taking corners at speed and more likely to see scenes of families in SUVs having meaningful discussions.

The economics of creating a Branded Customer Experience® are increasingly recognized and increasingly persuasive. The value of differentiation has long been recognized. Now, however, we are not talking about differentiating products – though that is still important – but differentiating experiences. Products are in the process of being redefined, bundled with experiences to create loyalty. Truly differentiated experiences create true brand advocates.

> **The economics of creating a Branded Customer Experience® are increasingly recognized and increasingly persuasive.**

None of this is possible without people who are wholly committed to the creation and delivery of the experiences. An organization's people are its key source of profit. Instead of being divided and ruled through functional demarcations, people power requires that functions dynamically interact and support each other.

The first and final part of this process is the role of the leader, which we explored in Chapter 4. The leader is now potentially a brand in his or her own right who can have a huge impact on shareholder value and the experiences created and delivered by the organization. What leaders do and stand for has rarely been more critical to organizational success or failure. We are witnessing the advent of the values-based leader – witness Rudy Giuliani's remarkable leadership after September 11. Values make the leader and leaders make the values that epitomize truly successful organizations and brands.

None of this happens by chance. The organizations featured here spend time, energy, and resources to create Branded Customer Experiences that set them apart. It is part vision from their leaders, part passion from their people, part art in finding just the right proposition, and part science in aligning the organization with it. Our observation in helping organizations create Branded Customer Experiences is that the journey is one well worth making.

The secrets of uncommon practice

Managing brands is going to be more and more about trying to manage everything that your company does.

Lee Clow chairman and chief creative officer,
TBWA Worldwide

In the book *Uncommon Practice*, which Shaun Smith co-authored with Andy Milligan of Interbrand, we discovered what it was that leading brands do to create unique customer experiences. We wanted to find out what made these brands unique, how they have managed to create enthusiastic customers and levels of employee loyalty that competitors dream of. Our premise that these companies have cultures uniquely developed to meet the needs of their customers in a distinctive way was certainly validated; however, while each of these companies is very different there are also some striking similarities in the way they operate. These characteristics, while shared with each other, are still uncommon practice as far as the majority of organizations are concerned and explain why these brands are so powerful. *Uncommon Practice* described *who* these brands are and *what* they do that makes them unique. The story was told in the words of their executives and very much in their individual "tones of voice." *Managing the Customer Experience* has set out to delve deeper into the *why* and the *how*.

The examples we have discussed in this book echo the stories related in *Uncommon Practice* and touch on many of the same themes. Subsequent to writing *Uncommon Practice*, Forum conducted an extensive survey with people in several of the organizations we interviewed. This was of a quantitative nature and featured surveys with executives and employees. This data was then statistically analyzed to validate the themes and create a diagnostic instrument that we could use with our clients to help them deliver their own Branded Customer Experiences. Our findings supported the themes emerging from the interviews but also created a way of organizing the information that was statistically valid and capable of being used as a diagnostic survey. For this reason, for those of you who have already read *Uncommon Practice* much of what follows will be familiar but from an internal perspective. This chapter will report on our major findings and give some examples to illustrate them. Further information, including the research methodology as well as the best practices analytical structure, can be found in the Appendix to this book.

Forum's research themes

Leadership

- **Leaders deliver a Branded Customer Experience®**

The leaders of these organizations take personal responsibility for driving the customer experience and creating cultures that support the delivery of it. Amazon.com's Jeff Bezos was very clear: "Our mission is to be the earth's most customer-centered company." Now many organizations have mission statements that say similar things but few have leaders who take personal responsibility for holding the organization true to them. According to Jeff Bezos: "It's the job of every person in this company to reinforce the culture, including me, so I'm a broken record on the customer experience. I've spent a lot of time over the last 18 months making sure people understand that as we focus more and more on operating efficiency there is no trade-off on the customer experience."

In talking with Jeff Bezos it quickly becomes clear that he is a wonderful example of the next practice.

- **Leaders are profoundly customer-focussed**

There is probably not a large organization today that does not feature customer service as a core value. Read their annual report and customer service will often be mentioned as a key performance indicator. However, the difference between the way most executives talk about customers and how the leaders featured in this book do is very marked. It is not *one* of the things that they pay attention to, it is the *main* thing they pay attention to. It is the way that they lead their business lives every day. Concepts like the Balanced Scorecard have been helpful in introducing the notion that the bottom line is just one of the metrics that a company must focus on. However, it does not go far enough; it implies that there is a trade-off to be struck between doing what is right for customers and the costs of doing so and, in the pure business sense, this is correct. But it implies a logical approach to customer experience whereas many of these leaders take a passionate approach to it.

These leaders believe that creating a consistently superior experience will lead to profitable growth. For example, Carphone Warehouse offers a free repair service to people who have not purchased their phone from the company. These decisions are not taken on the basis that they are the best way to optimize profits; they are taken because they are the right thing to do for customers. In the words of CEO Charles Dunstone: "We basically have a very child-like dream really, we absolutely fervently believe that if you have to buy a mobile phone there is nowhere better; no organization that will care more about you than we do."[1]

People

- **The customer experience and the employee experience are inextricably linked**

This theme seems so self-evident that to state it seems almost unnecessary, yet how many companies intentionally set out to create a culture that is designed to complement the customer experience? Midland Bank was so aware of this that it realized it needed to create not only a new brand called First Direct to communicate the proposition but also a totally separate company and culture to deliver it. This alignment of the employee experience with the customer experience was a conscious decision at First Direct. As First Direct's Peter Simpson puts it "We ensure that our internal brand values are the same as our external ones. It seems to me that there must be a mirror between the two. You can't pretend to be one style of brand to your consumers if you're a different style of brand to your people." This linkage is so strong that we found two different schools of thought in the companies we interviewed. One group are passionate about focussing on customers and aligning the internal culture with that imperative. Amazon.com, Fairmont Hotels and Resorts, and easyGroup are examples of this approach. Equally common, however, are those companies that are of the view "take care of the people and trust them to take care of the customers." Pret a Manger, John Lewis, and Harrah's are examples here. In reality, the two are so intertwined that you end up by satisfying both stakeholder groups.

Julian Richer of Richer Sounds makes this link between the customer experience and the employee experience even more explicit and takes a very uncommon approach to creating a distinctive employment experience for his best performing "colleagues" by providing Bentleys for the weekend, trips on the company jet, and vacation homes.

Common sense would say that this is a very expensive way of rewarding people and most organizations would opt for the more conventional Employee of the Month award. Julian Richer has a very different view: "My definition of culture is your perception of the organization as an employee," he says. "So for the culture to be a good, positive, happy one, employees have to believe in it, and that will only come through lots of effort. At the end of the day the Bentleys cost very little, the jet is flying anyway, the

> It is possible to be employee focused as well as have very tight financial controls.

holiday homes we provide cost a few thousand a year but the downside cost of having disgruntled or demotivated employees is phenomenal. It's absenteeism, labor turnover, theft, bad customer service. So I would argue that what I spend on these things is worth every penny."

If you think that Julian Richer is a soft touch when it comes to employee welfare, Richer Sounds is one of the tightest run retail operations that you will find anywhere. Rather, what it shows is that it is possible to be employee focussed as well as have very tight financial controls. Uncommon practice is about managing dilemmas so that business moves from a mindset of either/or to one of and/both. This mirroring of the employee and customer experiences requires HR departments to become much more strategic in their development of HR practices to support the business.

We find it amazing how many organizations talk about offering the most friendly call center employees, or having the best trained financial advisors, but have HR policies that are essentially the same as everyone else's. Uncommon practice requires that different strategies have different capabilities, different capabilities require different attitudes and skills, and these, in turn, come from different hiring, training, and reward practices.

David Mead at First Direct makes this link between HR practices and the customer experience: "We passionately believe that every customer is an individual and requires unique and personalized service. To make sure that our people genuinely believe that, and believe that principle on each and every occasion, we also focus very strongly on the individual within First Direct."

As a result, First Direct offers employees a package of benefits that enables the individual to tailor their particular remuneration to their stage in life. "In order to reinforce the primary importance of individuality with the customer we seek to do the same with our people, so we talk about individual people here in the same way as we talk about individual customers externally," says David Mead.

- **Managers engage employees around the customer**

Engaging employees around the customer is about creating regular means to exchange information about customers and company performance, and reaffirm the direction. Some organizations do this via video, some by newsletter, and some by the CEO taking personal responsibility for meeting with employees – as in the case of two of our airline examples.

"I have quarterly Talks with Tim. I go over to the hangar every quarter, and I have three different meetings, one during the morning, one late in the evening, and one midday, so we cover all of our technical service systems. It's just an hour and a half open session of Q and A, and I just get some terrific questions, and enhance people's understanding," says Midwest Airlines CEO Tim Hoeksema.

Virgin's Richard Branson also believes in the personal touch. "Once a year we have a staff party where everybody gets together. There are so many people working for Virgin that the parties last for six days, they have it in my home in the country and the last one we had was for about 70,000 people. I try to make sure that I shake hands with everyone as they arrive and then try to get out and about and party and mix as much as possible, by the end of the week I need a new body." Branson also ensures he spends as much time as possible with employees to listen to them and exchange views: "Anytime I'm on a plane I try to make sure that I'm not sleeping the whole way; that I get out and about and talk to everybody. I always have a notebook on me, I don't just talk to my staff about ideas for service but also ideas for improvements for them personally."

Business practices

- **The business is managed around the customer**

The companies we researched organize around the customer rather than functions or geography. That is not to say that they do not have similar functions to other companies but that these are aligned around a common agenda on "triad power" principles. This strong alignment is very much evident at easyGroup. Stelios Haji-Ioannou founded easyJet by identifying an unmet market need for a low-cost airline in Europe. He realized that in order to create assurance for customers, the airline had to have the latest aircraft and high standards of operational efficiency so the only way to achieve the lower costs that the strategy demanded was by cutting out the sales intermediaries and travel agents and having a direct channel to market. That in turn created the need for a low-cost, fast moving, highly communicative culture. If you visit easyGroup's London headquarters in Camden you will find a large open plan room with Stelios seated at the very center of the room sharing a central desk with his fellow directors. Radiating out are the various functions of marketing, finance, operations, etc. Everyone shares a common computer directory with total access to company information so that all customer data is shared.

It is easy to talk about paying attention to the non-financial measures rather than the bottom line but harder to do in practice. Carphone Warehouse refunding $15 million to customers because the price of their mobile phone had fallen *after* they had purchased it is a rare example of putting the principles of the company ahead of the bottom line, although interestingly, Charles Dunstone went on to say that the company had been even more profitable since implementing that policy.

Placing the customer at the center of the company is also about making decisions which sustain the customer culture. One of the most common growth strategies for companies is to acquire others or merge. It is also one of the quickest ways to erode shareholder value if the intended synergies fail to materialize. In the rush toward consolidation it takes a clear head to remember the core values of the brand and stay true to them even though the opportunity is a profitable one. Phil Satre of Harrah's recalled one such opportunity: "I remember considering a decision – 12 years ago – to acquire a company in the lottery industry. It was a very attractive opportunity. But we said, 'Where does that fit with our values? There's no relationship with the customer. We don't know who those customers are. They're buying a lottery ticket. Yes, it's the gambling industry, but it isn't what we stand for ...'" As a result, Harrah's declined that opportunity even though it was very attractive financially and would have made money for the organization.

- **Customer feedback is zealously acquired**

Sustaining the customer experience over time depends on really understanding what your customers expect and value and measuring this constantly. This knowledge comes from listening to customers and measuring the customer experience in a variety of ways as opposed to the more common customer questionnaire approach that so many organizations take. Krispy Kreme uses digital cameras to record the customer experience so that managers can see the actual problem not just read about it.

Measuring customer satisfaction is the norm, measuring the customer experience is not. Krispy Kreme captures data from a number of sources. 'Instead of looking just at quantitative sales measures, we established measures through mystery shoppers and our own internal inspections as well as solicitation of off-premises customers through surveys that are performed internally. We are receiving information all the time. We try to bring it to a level where we have a great deal of confidence in the information,' says CEO Scott Livengood.

Understanding its customers has become a key differentiator for Royal Bank of Canada. The organization initially introduced a CRM system in order to be more targeted in its promotional activity but is increasingly using the system to acquire knowledge of customers to enhance the service the bank provides. This is moving the bank from Customer Relationship Management to Customer Managed Relationships, placing the control in the hands of customers to determine how and when they wish to be served.

These companies don't just acquire information – they use it to run the business. Pizza Express uses the feedback from members of the Pizza Express Club to ensure a constant flow of information to inform operational decisions.

In summary, these six factors represent those practices that set exemplary companies apart from others. The strongest factor of the six, **Leaders deliver a Branded Customer Experience®**, confirms how important it is for leadership to manage the business around the customer. Not surprisingly, employees in these exemplary companies feel extremely committed to their company and feel an equally high level of personal responsibility for the customer experience. In fact, employees rate the "quality of the customer experience" as the number one reason why they believe customers do business with their company. In stark contrast, "low prices" received the *lowest* rating as a reason for doing business.

So why do your customers do business with your company? Is it because your product or service is so unique or differentiated? If so, how quickly do you think a competitor could catch up? Are you the price leader in your category? How likely is it that another company could undercut your price leadership over time? Or is the overall experience you provide to your customers so extraordinary that they couldn't imagine taking their business elsewhere? If this idea is the path your company is on, then our final chapter should be of great interest as it paints a detailed picture of one company's journey to achieve just that: the creation of a customer experience for a targeted set of customers that would drive loyalty and advocacy beyond what had ever been achieved before.

> **Employees in these exemplary companies feel extremely committed to their company and feel an equally high level of personal responsibility for the customer experience.**

Note

1 Smith, Shaun and Milligan, Andy, *Uncommon Practice: People who deliver a great brand experience*, FT/Prentice Hall, 2002.

12

■■■■■■■■■■■■■■■■■■■

Loyalty by design
in practice

*This case study is based on Forum's work with
Harrah's Entertainment Inc. However, we have
taken the liberty of changing some of the detail
to protect the confidentiality of Harrah's as
well as to align the case study with the steps
outlined in Chapter 3: Loyalty by design.
Inevitably, in our work with clients we find
that we are rarely starting with a blank sheet
of paper and so we seek to build on the good
work that already exists. In the case of
Harrah's we were able to build on a strong
foundation. So, we have created a semi-
fictitious company in order to illustrate the key
steps of Loyalty by design in a comprehensive
way. Our thanks to Harrah's for allowing us to
work with them and relate something of our
experience.*

Throughout the mid-1990s, significant shifts in the gaming entertainment industry fueled an over-supply of providers and intense competition
for customers. For example, as new "riverboat" market locations became
available to entertainment companies, they would quickly become satu-
rated as competitors rushed to build properties and seize market share.
They would aggressively compete for their share of customers through
marketing and advertising, greater amenities, promotions, and more
sophisticated properties. Soon, however, it was becoming clear that the

services and experiences offered by nearly all the companies were becoming commodities. The experiences customers had at various properties didn't seem that different. By targeting a mass market of potential customers, these entertainment companies weren't serving any specific segment particularly well. As a result, their business results were suffering. Out of all the players in the industry, one particular entertainment company decided to take dramatic steps to do something about it.

Define customer values

As with most gaming entertainment companies, this particular company was swimming in existing data about its customers. It had introduced a rewards card program that allowed it to track the behavior of a significant portion of its customers. The key question it now had to consider was which segments of its customers were most profitable?

A team began a dedicated effort to analyze the playing behavior of its customer base, and soon discovered a critical segment. Referred to as "middle customers," this group sits between the large segment of customers who come to properties and spend smaller amounts of money to play, and the relatively small segment of "high rollers." This target segment is made up of customers who enjoy playing, and set aside a budget and dedicated time to play. The team found that this group represented 24 percent of customers in the US, and accounted for 53 percent of total US entertainment revenues. For this company in particular, these customers were even more important. They accounted for 36 percent of all guest visits and generated 81 percent of the company's revenues. In addition, the team determined that this segment was growing.

Once the team had identified this pool of customers, they were now in a position to begin carefully understanding what these customers wanted most in a visit to this company's properties. The researchers used a variety of methods to gather, refine, and retest data that would determine these player's unique preferences. After they had mined the data in the company's customer tracking system for clues, they used specially designed focus groups to begin to build an in-depth understanding of these players – what they prize most in a visit, as well as what they most dislike. This data was then built into surveys sent to groups of target customers that began to help quantify and, most importantly, prioritize their expectations. Statistical analyses helped show how distinct expectations could be clustered and combined to form a core set of value drivers. Some of these key drivers included fast, efficient service and feeling like employees really know them, and what they like. After extensive work, the team had created a clear, comprehensive profile of what this segment of target customers values most in a visit to a property – what turns an occasional visit into a continuous stream of repeat business.

> **Statistical analyses helped show how distinct expectations could be clustered and combined to form a core set of value drivers.**

The company was now poised to crystallize its findings into a clear, memorable customer promise. The analysis ultimately resulted in a set of five value drivers. Forum helped to craft these drivers into a carefully worded acronym that both captured the essence of the findings, and enabled employees throughout the company to easily remember the drivers and eventually build them into their daily work. A round of meetings with senior managers throughout the company ensured that everyone was fully committed to making these series of promises to their target customers, and more importantly, doing whatever it would take to deliver on them.

Design the Branded Customer Experience®

The company had to choose a place to start. It decided to select one of their poorest performing properties and deploy a comprehensive strategy to retool the entire hotel and casino experience to consistently deliver their new promise to target customers. The plan was, once the experience had been designed, tested, and delivered at the pilot site, for the company to carry the strategy to groups of properties simultaneously, until their Branded Customer Experience® was installed at every location. Because market dynamics and customer bases tended to vary across locations, it was expected to shape the experience and their approach as needed to match local requirements.

With the pilot site, the company had to start by gaining a comprehensive understanding of how it was doing, in relation to delivering on the five value drivers. To develop a profound understanding of the customer experience, Forum conducted 80 job observations across the 15 key job categories in the hotel and casino that have customer contact. In addition, Forum deployed "mystery shoppers" to act as target customers and document employee behavior across 42 separate visits covering the same 15 job functions. The data was analyzed to look carefully at how target customers were currently treated at each key touchpoint throughout their experience.

Results showed that in relation to delivering on the five value drivers, performance varied greatly within and across all jobs, and job families (i.e. table games, or hotel check-in). Employees demonstrated an inconsistent grasp of even baseline skills, and few examples of service excellence were observed. Forum also compared service levels to external benchmarks and best practices research, to further clarify and evaluate existing service levels. Rather than revealing focussed trends in how expected service differed from how target customers actually experienced service, the research showed a comprehensive need for all employees to learn how to deliver the new promise. The gaps were everywhere.

The standard had to be set. For each touchpoint that a target customer had with the company/the property, the question was asked: What would make this interaction outstanding, in the eyes of a target customer? What would these interactions be like for the target customer: in the casino – playing table games, ordering a drink, or getting change – waiting for a table in one of the restaurants, or checking into their room? How could these five value drivers be infused into each touchpoint, delivered consistently by each employee?

To answer these questions, Forum reviewed the customer research, job observation, and mystery shopping data to begin to identify specific behavioral standards for each touchpoint. Working closely with key people from the company, Forum then began to access a network of high performers representing all 15 job functions from across the company. In-depth interviews and, where possible, additional job observations were conducted to collect a full range of phrases, actions, creative service ideas, and subtle tricks of the trade that were used to enrich the behavior standards being developed for each job and touchpoint. Through an intricate process of testing behaviors against the customer research/value drivers, and the real experience of high performers, Forum and the company emerged with a refined set of behavioral standards for all key touchpoints across the target customers' experience.

These behaviors were soon published in a "Phrases and Actions Guide" that became a core component of the front-line and manager learning systems.

The company was now ready to make the new experience a reality. It needed to transform not only how employees behaved with customers, but also how managers behaved with employees. People at all levels needed tools, support, training, and systems to channel their daily behaviors toward ensuring the company delivered on the customer promise. Forum worked closely with an extensive team from both corporate functions and the pilot property to think through and build a comprehensive change strategy. The strategy began with ensuring managers at all levels were fully equipped to lead the new organization.

Equip people and deliver consistently

As with the assessment of target customers' current experiences with front-line employees, Forum also had to get a clear sense of executives' and managers' current capabilities. A number of data sources helped to create a clear profile to work with, including executive and management interviews, a benchmarked survey assessing executives' ability to lead customer-intimate companies, and focus groups with supervisors. Among the findings were:

- Gaps in executives' stated vs actual understanding of the Branded Customer Experience® strategy the company was following.

- A lack of involvement and consultation of employees around decisions and customer needs/issues – infrequent two-way communication.

- Executives and managers scored low against benchmarks of customer contact.

- Management viewed the organization as under-committed to quality and poorly prepared to deliver – 50 percent of managers cited service quality problems as a key barrier to execution.

- Seventy-two percent of managers reported a lack of "ability to execute" as a key barrier to success.

One-on-one coaching for executives

In order to prepare and support executives in leading the rapid execution of the customer experience, the general manager and all of his direct reports were each paired with an executive coach from Forum. The coaches worked as a team to: saturate themselves in the business and new strategy, study the customer/property research findings, uncover individual executives' needs, and select critical tools and skills that would have the greatest impact on the executives' ability to lead the transformation. Each executive was given access to the same tools and skills, quickly building a common language and method of operating that broke down barriers, drove efficiency, clarified communication, and increased their presence and impact across the property. Respecting confidentiality, the coaches shared lessons, observations, and strategies with each other to further sharpen their approaches and accelerate development. The coaching lasted throughout the implementation of the customer experience at the pilot property.

Building leadership opportunities and capabilities on-the-job

Forum's findings showed that managers and supervisors had little experience or opportunity to engage the people they managed in meaningful ways. Many were even apprehensive about leading a meeting with their employees where they would be asked questions about the customer experience initiative. To build their capabilities, Forum designed a series of structured opportunities for managers and supervisors to engage their employees around:

- key communication messages for the customer experience initiative;
- input and ideas to improve the initiative and its execution;
- questions to be answered either by them or senior managers;
- feedback on approaches the manager/supervisor would like to take with the team to execute the initiative.

To equip managers and supervisors to be successful in these opportunities, Forum conducted just-in-time training sessions, provided agendas, frequently asked questions/answers, talking points, tips, and preparation steps for managers to use, and also created a "buddy system" giving managers permission to help each other.

The structured leadership opportunities throughout the implementation of the customer experience initiative included:

- *All-manager meetings* – weekly meetings to keep the full management team informed about implementation activities and reinforce the role of managers as leaders.

- *30-minute musters* – weekly managers' meetings with their direct reports (floor supervisors) to keep them informed about the initiative and reinforce their role as leaders.

- *Management by wandering around (MBWA) assignments* – scheduled half-day periods, once a week where managers spend time on the floor following agreed-to behavior standards that increase management support, presence, and involvement with customers and employees. Managers were also assigned to one shift working in a customer contact job once a month.

- *Senior manager skip-level meetings* – monthly, special small-group meetings where more senior managers share information and answer questions from supervisors and employees.

- *Buzz sessions* – bi-weekly one-on-one or small-group meetings held by front-line supervisors with employees to collect/answer questions and share information.

The communications strategy

While building the capacity to lead at all levels would make a significant difference, assessment data showed that more would be needed to rebuild the kind of culture where employees would enthusiastically

A comprehensive communications strategy was needed.

deliver the Branded Customer Experience® at every touchpoint with a target customer.

After Forum conducted a communication audit, assessing the effectiveness of current communication channels on the property, they determined that a comprehensive communications strategy was needed that was driven by clear objectives and made up of simple, compelling messages. The objectives of the strategy were to:

- build enthusiasm and commitment to the strategy;
- provide information to build assurance;
- give all employees information critical to their understanding of the upcoming changes at a level of detail that was appropriate to their positions and roles;
- ensure employees were clear about how changes would impact them and what would be expected of them in the coming months and beyond;
- foster a climate of openness and honesty to build morale and employee effectiveness;
- provide two-way communications channels that would help employees feel their feedback and ideas were valued;
- support management's credibility throughout the change process;
- prevent surprises.

Driven by these objectives, Forum designed a strategy that drew on a wide range of communication media that all brought to life, and reinforced, three core messages: focus on employees, focus on customers, and focus on their property is leading the way (for the company). The communication strategy was also cast in a theme, "Future So Bright," that capitalized on a popular song, generated added excitement around the changes, and further illuminated the messages.

Examples of the media used around the property included:

- *Viewpoints* – an existing employee suggestion system on the property that Forum helped to revitalize and support with reliable systems ensuring that suggestions were promptly responded to.
- *Q&A feedback postings* – boards placed in prominent back-of-house locations that posted responses to employee questions raised in any of the management/supervisor meetings or Viewpoints.
- *Reinforcement memos* – consistent memos from the general manager of the property to all managers, reinforcing key

information, guiding implementation activities, recognizing contributions, and emphasizing their role as leaders and models.

- *InfoZone* – a periodic video news magazine played on the televisions in employee dining and lounge areas. Regular features included Rumor of the Week and employee recognition.

- *Straw poll – "Take 5: Say What You Think"* – a six-question survey designed to periodically test the general feel around the property on specific issues. Results were posted and e-mailed to managers and supervisors.

- *"Spirit" employee newsletter* – the existing employee newsletter featuring property activities that covered key elements of the customer experience implementation.

- *Posters and table tents* – placed in back-of-house areas like the employee dining room and used to reinforce key messages, offer reminders, and announce upcoming events.

- *Payroll stuffers* – a colored card carrying similar information to the posters and table tents.

- *Future so bright: roadmap to the future* – a brightly colored illustration mapping out a winding road to the property's new customer-intimate future, designed to engage employees and build understanding of the overall initiative. The graphic was used in a variety of communications media, such as large posters, the newsletter, and InfoZone.

- *Mass rallies* – large all-employee meetings to build understanding, ownership, and excitement. Elements included custom videos featuring employees across the property set to music, and presentations from the general manager and other senior managers.

The learning strategy

To help create a learning strategy that would teach all employees and managers to deliver the Branded Customer Experience®, two additional assessments were conducted: Forum reviewed and analyzed all existing training that employees and managers had experienced, and focus groups were conducted with front-line employees to bring additional insight to the data from job observations, mystery shopping, and high performer interviews/observations.

Once these elements were complete, the Forum learning design team was ready to architect a systematic learning strategy that would integrate all of the elements of the Branded Customer Experience® initiative. These elements could then be channeled into practical tools, behaviors, and new ways of thinking that would make the Branded Customer Experience® come alive every day.

Front-line classroom learning

The classroom training experience essentially focussed on building capacity in four areas:

- ideas, phrases, and actions that would deliver on the five value drivers for each of the 15 job categories;
- a unique "interaction cycle" designed to give a consistent, intentional, yet natural structure to each interaction with a target customer;
- skills, approaches, and the development of judgment to handle challenging situations that could undermine the branded experience; and
- new ways of thinking and skills that forge partnerships across the property to seamlessly manage the branded experience across the entire target customer touchline – covering hand-offs, teamwork, knowledge sharing, and other elements.

Manager classroom learning

All supervisors, managers, and executives participated in their own versions of the front-line training, allowing them to fully understand, guide, and model the Branded Customer Experience® actions and ideas. A significant component was added to the manager training that concentrated on helping them coach employees and other managers to consistently deliver the experience. This coaching focussed on the four areas of the front-line training, teaching such things as acute observation skills and creative ideas for both allowing employees to be themselves, and yet aligning them with the standards of the branded experience.

Certification sessions

To ensure that all employees and managers were capable of demonstrating the new behaviors, Forum worked with the company to design a comprehensive certification process. This involved a half-hour to 45-minute session with each individual employee or manager where a qualified examiner from the company has the person demonstrate skills and apply tools based on scenarios that replicate relevant interactions with target customers. The individuals were evaluated and offered additional, customized coaching and development actions to further enhance their capacity to deliver the experience. The company estimated that close to 90 percent of the staff successfully passed the certification sessions. Special strategies were put in place for those who weren't certified the first time.

Property-wide, on-the-job reinforcement sessions

To further ensure that everyone consistently delivered the experience, Forum designed a series of 14, 20–30 minute reinforcement sessions for employees led by their supervisors. The topics of the 14 sessions spanned the four key areas of the front-line classroom training, targeting specific value drivers, steps in an interaction, challenging situations, or aspects of teamwork across the touchline. After the classroom training was complete, the entire property devoted one week to each of the 14 topics/sessions. To ensure supervisors were successful in leading the sessions on the floor with their employees, Forum created specialized guides for each of the 14 sessions including scripts to follow, process steps, tools, and tips. Throughout that particular week, across all three shifts of the 24-hour operation, supervisors conducted the sessions multiple times, ensuring they touched every employee. The centerpiece of each session was a creative, focussed assignment that each employee committed to completing on-the-job before the next session that further improved his or her ability to deliver the experience. At the next session, employees discussed success stories, lessons learned, issues, new ideas for enhancing the experience.

In addition to leaders reinforcing performance by following through on all leadership/employee meetings and communication methods that were designed, a number of measures were used to track the effectiveness of the Branded Customer Experience® initiative at the pilot site. In addition to these measures, the company planned to watch overall company revenue growth as the initiative was implemented at other properties.

Site-specific measures included:

- Results from employee/manager behavior certification sessions, measuring the extent to which each individual throughout the property was able to demonstrate the Branded Customer Experience® behaviors.

- A second administration of the executive benchmark survey, used in the initial assessment to measure senior leaders' ability to lead a customer-intimate company. The survey was given several months after the initiative was complete.

- Target customer interviews to determine any shifts in the share-of-wallet they were providing to the property – preferences to spend proportionately more money at the company's property than they used to.

- A customer satisfaction survey, comparing findings to original data from initial customer research.

- Figures tracking total average spend per customer, per visit, compared to data before the initiative.

- Overall property revenues compared to prior revenues.

- Conducting an employee focus group survey several months after implementation and comparing satisfaction scores to data gathered in employee focus groups conducted before the initiative.

Sustain and enhance performance

The implementation at the pilot property generated countless new ideas for improving execution of the initiative at the other properties. Once all adjustments had been incorporated into their implementation plans, the company executed the Branded Customer Experience® initiative at four properties at a time, until all properties had been transformed.

The primary mechanism for enhancing the experience consists of listening to employees. The leadership, communication, and learning initiatives implemented at each property open up vast channels for employees to package and share specific ideas and approaches that can upgrade the target customer experience. Executives and managers collect these ideas and, with employee involvement, create ways to consistently embed them into relevant touchpoints with the customer – from feedback on products used in the hotel, to advice to eliminate a company policy, to ways to make hand-offs of customers more seamless.

> **Both monetary and non-monetary rewards were used to reinforce behaviors.**

The company focussed on aligning reward systems and customer satisfaction metrics to the delivery of the customer experience. Both monetary and non-monetary rewards were used to reinforce behaviors. Throughout the implementation of the initiative, a number of the communication media and manager/employee meetings described earlier were used to directly recognize examples of employee behavior that noticeably impacted the Branded Customer Experience®.

Concerning monetary rewards, the company eventually created a formal Target Player Satisfaction Survey and established a Performance Payout Incentive Plan that rewards employees for meeting customer satisfaction goals, based on results from the survey. Eligible employees receive bonuses, and those who are not eligible for bonuses get cash awards. In the first year, the company paid out $7 million to employees for achieving improvements in service.

Many of the elements of the original communication strategy used at the pilot site are now being used at each of the company's properties. From weekly employee newsletters to themed meetings, each property continues to communicate progress and results to embed the Branded Customer Experience® as the "way they do business."

Results

While the property-specific results detailed below demonstrate the short-term impact of the Branded Customer Experience® on the pilot site, longer-term measures of business results have been directly attributed to the customer experience work by company representatives. For example, the company's 2000 revenues were $3.5 billion, a record for the company and up 15 percent over the year. While some of the revenue increases are due to newly acquired properties, the notable fact that same-store gaming revenue growth was up 13 percent over the prior year is considered by the company to be a direct result of the customer experience initiative. Also, in *Casino Player* magazine's annual reader's poll the company won 80 awards, more than any other entertainment company. Among the honors were first-place awards for best service in the Rio market, best service in the Atlantic City market, and a second-place award for best service in the Las Vegas market.

Measures conducted at the pilot site during the months after the customer experience initiative was fully executed showed the following:

- the property was capturing significantly greater share of the target customers' wallets;
- revenues increased by 15 percent;
- customer satisfaction scores jumped from the 22 percent baseline to 86 percent;
- average spend per customer increased by 17 percent;
- overall gaps in employee satisfaction closed significantly.

Employee satisfaction results

A comparison of employee satisfaction scores on four key indices – rewards/recognition, communication, teamwork, and the role of managers – between the initial site assessment and the results of an employee focus group survey several months later demonstrated marked improvements.

Leadership results

Several months after the Branded Customer Experience® implementation, Forum's executive customer focus survey was distributed to the entire management team, with the intent of measuring changes in leadership confidence, competence, commitment, and ability to execute since the site assessment. Overall results illustrated that the gaps had narrowed between the pilot site and "best in class" organizations recorded in Forum's database. Also, these results appeared to reflect an increase in the confidence and enthusiasm of the pilot site management team in executing and sustaining the Branded Customer Experience®.

Most dramatic were the improvements in the People area related to Competence, Capability, and Empowerment. The pilot site's scores went from the 36th percentile to the 98th percentile before and after the rollout. When it came to action, scores climbed from the 12th to the 88th percentile: "Rather than having to undo mistakes, we aim to do things right the first time." In addition, the follow-up survey results showed a much stronger aptitude for implementation. The pilot site management team appeared to have increased confidence in their ability to deliver against customer expectations. Overall, follow-up survey results indicated that the level of customer intimacy at the property had improved since the site assessment. This appeared to suggest that the right ingredients were present to successfully sustain the Branded Customer Experience®.

Communications strategy results

Overall, management demonstrated an increased competence and capability to communicate customer requirements throughout the organization. Comparing survey results prior to implementing the initiative and a follow-up survey several months after execution was complete shows a rise in percentile scores across several communication indices.

Learning strategy results

The notion of continuously upgrading the customer experience appeared to have become embedded in the pilot site culture.

A comparison of survey results before the implementation and several months after shows overall improvements in employee understanding of customer requirements and ability to deliver on the customer experience across customer, process, and people dimensions.

In addition, the notion of continuously upgrading the customer experience appeared to have become embedded in the pilot site culture, as demonstrated by dramatic increases in continuous improvement-related scores.

The end or the beginning?

We hope that this example has provided a clear road map of one company's journey toward delivering a Branded Customer Experience®. Clearly the results have been worth the investment and the journey itself has led not so much to an "ending" as to a new "beginning" for how they manage their business around the customer.

And so we reach the end of our journey with you. We hope that we have provided enough insight to have potentially created a view to a new beginning for your company, centered around delivering a Branded Customer Experience®. We have provided some tools in the Appendix to help you chart your own course which may be valuable, but in so much as we have come full circle, we are guided back to the Introduction and what Steve Anderson of Krispy Kreme advises: "The most important thing to do is to decide what you're about, decide who you are, what you hold as important, and what you value." It would be hard to find better advice since what is required for the journey ahead really does begin with what senior leadership decides is important, and what it creates direction around.

Abraham Lincoln once said: "Determine that the thing can and shall be done, and then find a way." At the time of writing this book, the world economy has experienced a recession that has challenged many industries and organizations. Perhaps your company is one of them. And perhaps, this idea, of committing to delivering a Branded Customer Experience®, could provide a platform toward finding your company's "way" forward. If so, we wish you the best of luck in the journey ahead!

Appendix

■■■■■■■■■■■■■■■■■■■

I Forum's Uncommon Practice Research

Background

The Forum Corporation, in association with Performance Measurement Associates (PMA), undertook a Customer Experience research project that explored the actions leading brands take and their overall organizational philosophy in delivering great customer experiences. The project involved the identification of twenty companies (six with headquarters in the United States, two in Canada, and twelve in the UK) that are unique in their creation and delivery of a customer experience. The project centered on leading and emerging service brands to identify the practices they engage in to deliver a differentiated customer experience. The underlying research assumption was that companies with a strong record of providing exceptionally superior customer experiences would broadly share a set of business and organizational practices that explain their success and that differentiates them from other companies.

Research approach

The identification of approximately 130 candidate companies began by conducting an initial literature search and expert survey to identify and nominate exemplary companies. These nominees were validated as offering strong brand experiences through a consumer e-survey process. The consumer e-survey was conducted in the US, Canada, and the UK. A total of 730 consumers rated companies in target industry segments and nominated additional companies. Candidate companies spanned a variety of industries including retail, hospitality, financial services, transportation, and e-commerce. The primary selection criteria for the targeted companies included: strong customer experience, image and reputation, and consistent (or promising) financial performance:

1 Strong customer experience
   - customer satisfaction scores (from the consumer e-survey)
   - positive anecdotes (from the consumer e-survey)
   - industry/consumer awards.

2 Image and reputation
- strong or emerging service brand
- high customer awareness.

3 Consistent financial performance
- third-party/trade sources
- Wall Street analysts
- 10-K's, public documents.

Intensive due diligence was conducted on each of the 130 companies around these criteria, with the end result being a final list of 40 top-rated companies that were shortlisted to participate in the research.

Based on our research and this shortlist, we approached those organizations in each of the sectors that we felt were the best examples of strong branded experiences. Twenty companies agreed to be interviewed. Interviews were conducted with senior executives within each of these companies. The purpose of the interviews was to gather the views of leaders of successful brands whose people play a major role in delivering the customer experience, and to identify their organization's practices. A total of 73 executives were interviewed. The senior executives interviewed within each company typically included representatives from the following functions: Chief Executive Office, Operations, Sales, Marketing, Human Resources, and Customer Experience/ Management.

Once the interview process was complete, the executive interviews were reviewed and content coded. Through the executive interview process, 60 discrete practices were identified and selected for testing in an employee survey. Additional items were added to measure outcomes such as customer loyalty, employee loyalty, and personal commitment. Employee opinion was used as a surrogate for customer responses regarding customer satisfaction. A body of research, including a major cross-industry study conducted by The Forum Corporation, established that employee opinion is, in fact, a reasonable surrogate.

The organizational practices were then tested and validated through the employee survey process. The employee survey was administered within a sample of the participating companies to validate the interview findings and the practices, and was provided through the internet and in hard copy form to employees and executives. The employee survey period took place from October through December 2001, with 664 employees (executive and front-line) responding. Overall, 87 percent of the survey sample was front-line, supervisory, and middle managers. The remainder was senior managers and professional/independent contributors.

Additionally, for general information purposes, respondents were asked to select the main reason why customers might do business with their company, and the main reason why employees might choose to remain with their company. The latter set of questions was largely based on Frederick Herzberg's Motivation Theory. Finally, respondents were given a set of demographic questions, including organizational level, work unit, tenure with the company, age, and gender.

To minimize response bias, the 60 practice items were presented to online respondents in random order. For the same reason, two versions of the paper questionnaire were used with the remaining respondents.

Identification of the practices

A factor analysis reduced the 60 practice-based independent variables in the survey questionnaire to 25 items combined in six factors. The six factors (coming under the headings of Leadership, People, and Business Practices) are:

I Leadership

(a) Leaders deliver a Branded Customer Experience®
(b) Leaders are profoundly customer-focussed

II People

(c) The customer experience and the employee experience are inextricably linked
(d) Managers engage employees around the customer

III Business practices

(e) The business is managed around the customer
(f) Customer knowledge is zealously acquired

On average, the participating companies responded in a similar manner to the study. This result is consistent with the assumption that the participating companies were appropriately selected and that they, as a group, are distinctly different from other companies.

The following items are the final practices that explain the participating companies' ability to deliver great customer experiences.

I Leadership

(a) Leaders deliver a Branded Customer Experience®

1 The company believes that giving customers a consistently superior experience will lead to profitable growth.

2 We have customer-focussed leaders at the top of our company.

3 Leaders have the courage of their convictions when it comes to the customer experience.

4 The quality of the company's interactions with customers is monitored.

5 We have a brand identity that promises customers a unique and satisfying experience.

6 Our leaders believe in our customer experience strategy.

(b) Leaders are profoundly customer-focused

7 Our company's leaders follow through on our customer experience strategy.

8 Our leaders are passionate about customers.

9 Customer-focussed employee behaviors are rewarded.

II People

(c) The customer experience and the employee experience are inextricably linked

10 The interests of employees are put ahead of the interests of other stakeholder groups.

11 The interests of customers are put ahead of the interests of other stakeholder groups.

12 In the interest of customers, we avoid creating bureaucratic processes or policies.

13 Front-line employees are involved in decisions about which potential co-workers to hire.

(d) Managers engage employees around the customer

14 Managers know what to do to improve customer loyalty.

15 Employees are kept informed about business results.

16 Our leaders provide an engaging customer-focussed vision for employees.

17 Managers make sure that employees behave in ways that benefit our customers.

III Business practices

(e) The business is managed around the customer

18 Our business is organized as much or more around the customer than it is around functions or geography.

19 Customer data is used to manage the business.

20 We work to develop products or services that are more appealing to our target customers than those of competitors.

21 As much attention is paid to non-financial measures, such as customer satisfaction or loyalty, as to financial measures.

22 Rather than rely on customers to suggest new product or service ideas, the company sees innovation as its responsibility.

23 Our products and services are designed to provide value to targeted customers.

(f) Customer knowledge is zealously acquired

24 Feedback is gathered from customers on a continuous basis.

25 Feedback from customers is gathered using a variety of methods.

Diagnostic instrument

The research described above supported The Forum Corporation's design and development of a diagnostic instrument that allows organizations to assess their use of best practices in delivering great customer experiences from an organizational practices perspective. This provides companies with a practical tool that can be used in a cost-effective way to identify opportunities to enhance their customer experience. The diagnostic instrument also provides a normative database against which client comparisons can be made. For more information about this instrument or to receive a copy of the "Branded Customer Experience® Uncommon Practice Research Report," please visit us at www.forum.com

II Tool Kit

Branded Customer Experience® Assessment

What it is

The **Branded Customer Experience® Assessment** is a self-assessment tool based on Forum's proven four-step methodology used to help organizations develop and implement a Branded Customer Experience®. The assessment is made up of four sections.

Why do it

This assessment will help you understand where your organization is in the process of creating a valuable and differentiated customer experience.

When to do it

This tool should be used to stimulate a dialog with colleagues as you create a common understanding of where your organization is along the journey to delivering a Branded Customer Experience®. Your team will derive the most value from using the tool in the early stages of your customer experience work. As you embark on defining and executing your customer loyalty strategy, it will also be useful to revisit the assessment at critical milestones in the initiative. At these points, it will provide a good reality check on your progress, and will also provide indicators for the path forward.

Who is involved

The maximum value will be derived from the tool when it is completed by the leadership team involved in driving the change implementation which aims to make customer loyalty an integral part of your business model.

How to do it

As a first step, the assessment is best completed individually by members of your leadership team. This should be followed by a team discussion, reviewing areas of agreement and disagreement in your individual scores.

Completing the assessment:

- There are four sections to the assessment. Each section has five questions, and each question has a 1–7 rating scale.

- Complete each section in full before progressing to the next. You will end up with a total score for each section (by adding your ratings for the five questions in each section).

- This score should be entered in the box at the end of each section titled "Our Score." The total score for the section will be somewhere between 5 and 35.

- On the right-hand side of the questions is the scoring menu. This provides you with a clear interpretation of your score for that section.

- As a final step, you should total your scores for the entire assessment. Your total score will be between 25 and 140. At the end of the tool you will find a final summary scoring menu. This provides an overall interpretation of where your company stands in its quest to create, implement, and sustain a Branded Customer Experience®.

Branded Customer Experience® Assessment

Section 1: Defining Your Customer Values

Please rate the following questions on a 1–7 scale,
where 1 = Not yet, 7 = Completely

A We have identified our targeted customer segments and the profit they represent
to our company

   1   2   3   4   5   6   7

B We have a factual understanding of what our most profitable customers expect
and value from our company

   1   2   3   4   5   6   7

C We know which customer expectations impact our target customers intention to
re-purchase and recommend us

   1   2   3   4   5   6   7

D We have a factual understanding of how customers rate our performance vs our
competitors against these loyalty drivers

   1   2   3   4   5   6   7

E We have a compelling brand promise that clearly communicates what target
customers can expect in their relationship with us

   1   2   3   4   5   6   7

Our Score = ☐

Scoring:

Complete your assessment for each item, total your score, and record it in the box at the bottom.

Scoring menu

5–10 Understanding who your most profitable target customers are should be your key priority.

11–20 You have an understanding of your target customers. The challenge now is to really gain an intimate understanding of what they expect and value.

21–30 Your focus should be on those few expectations that drive attraction, retention, and referral, and then building them into a compelling brand promise and customer experience.

31–35 You are making great progress in defining a brand promise that provides real value. The challenge is to constantly upgrade your knowledge of your most profitable customers, what they expect, and ensure your promise is aligned with it.

Section 2: Designing Your Branded Customer Experience®

Please rate the following questions on a 1–7 scale,
where 1 = Not yet, 7 = Completely

A We thoroughly understand the experience our customers currently have with us
    1   2   3   4   5   6   7

B We have clearly identified the critical "touchpoints" which make up the customer experience touchline
    1   2   3   4   5   6   7

C We have designed new service experiences which will deliver our customer promise in a way which is consistent, differentiated, and valuable to target customers
    1   2   3   4   5   6   7

D We have defined the specific employee behavior required to deliver the customer promise at each touchpoint
    1   2   3   4   5   6   7

E We have developed a comprehensive and fully integrated change strategy to implement the new brand promise and experience
    1   2   3   4   5   6   7

Our Score = [＿＿＿＿＿]

Scoring:
Complete your assessment for each item, total your score, and record it in the box at the bottom.

Scoring menu
5–10 Understanding the nature of the experience that your customers have of you should be your first priority.
11–20 You have a good understanding of what your customers experience. The challenge now is to clearly define the critical touchpoints from the customer perspective.

21–30 Your focus now should be on designing a customer experience which delivers your promise and defining how employees must deliver it.
31–35 It is all about execution now! Creating a fully integrated change strategy to align the organization will ensure your success.

Section 3: Equipping People and Delivering Consistency

Please rate the following questions on a 1–7 scale,
where 1 = Not yet, 7 = Completely

A   We have an internal communications plan to build commitment, understanding, and clarity around implementing the customer experience

   1   2   3   4   5   6   7

B   Leaders at all levels of our organization understand their role as champions of our customer experience and are prepared for their role in leading its implementation

   1   2   3   4   5   6   7

C   Leaders have clearly communicated to our employees what our brand promise is and their important role in delivering it

   1   2   3   4   5   6   7

D   We have prepared our people with the skills and knowledge required to deliver our customer experience

   1   2   3   4   5   6   7

E   We are taking specific action to improve people, processes, and products, to deliver our Branded Customer Experience®

   1   2   3   4   5   6   7

Our Score = [   ]

Scoring:

Complete your assessment for each item, total your score, and record it in the box at the bottom.

Scoring menu

5–10 The key to delivering the customer experience is communicating the promise throughout the organization and your people's role in keeping it.

11-20 You have begun to communicate the brand promise and new experience. The challenge is to equip leaders and employees with the skills to deliver it.

21-30 People are beginning to understand your brand promise and how it can be delivered. Your focus now should be on equipping people throughout the organization with the skills to deliver it consistently.

31-35 You are making great progress in delivering your customer experience. The challenge is to constantly upgrade your people, processes, and products to improve the delivery of your promise over time.

Section 4: Sustaining and Enhancing Performance

Please rate the following questions on a 1–7 scale,
where 1 = Not yet, 7 =Completely

A   We have a formal process for continually collecting customer and employee
feedback on our customer experience and how this can be improved
1   2   3   4   5   6   7

B   We have a balanced set of performance metrics that provide executives with
objective, timely feedback on how well we are delivering against our promise
1   2   3   4   5   6   7

C   We have a reliable, effective training system that continuously builds our capability
to deliver our customer experience
1   2   3   4   5   6   7

D   We have performance management and HR systems aligned with and supporting
the delivery of our customer experience
1   2   3   4   5   6   7

E   We have an effective process for continually communicating to our people
progress and results in delivering our customer experience
1   2   3   4   5   6   7

Our Score = [   ]

Scoring:
**Complete your assessment for each
item, total your score, and record it
in the box at the bottom.**

Scoring menu
5–10 Creating systems to gather
customer and employee data should
be an important focus for you.
11–20 You are collecting data but will
need to ensure that this is
communicated to executives in a way
that creates action and improvement.

21–30 You are seeing results. The
challenge is to sustain the effort and
focus by recognizing and rewarding
these results through your HR
systems.
31–35 You are making great progress
in delivering a customer experience
that provides real value. The challenge
now is to sustain and refresh this over
time through ongoing communication
and improvement activity.

Customer Experience Analysis Summary
Scoring menu

20–35: You are becoming increasingly aware of the need to understand your most profitable customers and how you can differentiate through offering them a Branded Customer Experience®. Awareness is the first step to your success.

36–70: You have begun to understand how you can differentiate your customer experience and create value for target customers. The challenge now is to design the customer experience that delivers your brand promise. A comprehensive and integrated plan is key to your success.

71–104: You have begun many of the activities necessary to implement a Branded Customer Experience® throughout your organization. The focus now should be on ensuring that your employee education, HR, and business systems support your people and their ability to deliver the promise. Consistent execution is now the key to success.

105–140: You are seeing results from your focus and improvement activity. You are delivering your customer experience and measuring performance against your promise. The challenge now is to refresh and upgrade the customer experience so as to build lasting loyalty and brand equity. Continual measurement, feedback, and improvement will ensure your long-term success.

Developing a comprehensive change strategy

What it is

A major step in designing and branding the customer experience involves developing **a comprehensive change strategy** to implement the new customer experience. This tool helps you identify your strengths for achieving customer-driven change, as well as areas that you might not have considered or need to improve. The organizing framework for the tool is based on Forum's three-phased approach for achieving customer-driven change – Alignment, Improvement (people and process), and Measurement (AIM). As part of the AIM approach, we use a three-phased implementation process to help you navigate through the change in becoming a customer-driven organization. The three implementation phases include:

- Building the foundation
- Developing organizational capacity
- Sustaining customer-driven performance.

This tool presents a series of questions that cover each stage of the AIM approach and the three implementation phases of building a customer-driven company.

Why do it

Customer-driven companies achieve superior results in today's marketplace. To stay ahead of the competition, growing companies must continually change to meet or exceed their target customer expectations and maximize value. To be effective at this, you need to see customer-driven change as an ongoing *process* rather than as a series of one-time events. You must also ensure that the elements to support the change are in place in your organization. This worksheet will help you identify the strengths of your current process for achieving customer-driven change as well as areas you might not have considered or need to improve. The more robust your change process, the better your results are likely to be.

When to do it

This tool should be used at the outset of any organizational change effort aimed at driving customer loyalty. It can also be used to assess how your company is doing throughout the change process, and can help you identify necessary actions to ensure that you are able to achieve your goals.

Who is involved

The maximum value will be derived from the tool when it is completed by the leadership team involved in driving the change implementation which aims to make customer loyalty an integral part of your business model. There are a number of options that the team can go through in completing the tool. You can complete it individually, then get together as a team and, through a facilitated workshop, discuss your respective assessments and identify appropriate actions for the team.

Alternatively, the team could go through the exercise of completing the questions together, and working together to build the course of actions for the change implementation.

How to do It

Step 1
Materials preparation

1   Create a large flipchart to mirror the customer loyalty change grid provided below.
2   Type each question provided below on a separate card. You should end up with 24 cards, one question on each card.

Step 2
Make sure that you and the team(s) going through this activity are clear on the direction that your company is taking. It may be a good idea to write up on a flipchart or on a whiteboard two or three key words that describe your current business situation on the left side of the flipchart/board, and on the right-hand side, write down your goal as a customer-driven company.

Step 3

Place the cards in a pack in sequence, and prepare to work through the cards one at a time, as each question is a building block in the *process* of driving customer focus and building customer loyalty through your organization.

Take about two hours to work through the cards in sequence. For each card, read the question aloud to your group. Discuss (briefly) the answer to this question, based on the current situation in your own organization. Identify examples that support your answer. Each card has three possible answers:

- **YES** (completely, or to a large extent) – in this case, mark the appropriate square on the Customer Loyalty Change Grid with a large green X in the corresponding numbered box on the red and white grid.

- **PARTIALLY** – in this case, mark the corresponding square with a large orange X.

- **NO** (or hardly at all) – place a large red X in the corresponding numbered block on the grid.

Step 4

When you have discussed all the cards, as a group examine the pattern of the colors of the Xs on the grid. The red Xs represent "gaps" in your process. Likewise the orange cards on the grid show where a particular building block is not yet fully in place, i.e. a partial "gap." The pattern of colors may also indicate particular strengths or gaps within certain phases of the AIM approach, and/or in the different implementation phases of the change.

Use the "Conclusions" spaces on the bottom and to the right of the grid to record insights or conclusions that you feel may be significant as a result of these gaps, and discuss what actions the group agrees are appropriate as a result. It is up to you and the group to determine the level of detail you want to get into when action planning for the change process.

Figure 1

Customer Loyalty Change Grid

	BUILD THE FOUNDATION		DEVELOP ORGANIZATIONAL CAPABILITY		SUSTAIN CUSTOMER-DRIVEN PERFORMANCE		CONCLUSIONS AND ACTIONS
ALIGNMENT	1	2	9	10	17	18	
IMPROVEMENT (PROCESS)	3	4	11	12	19	20	
IMPROVEMENT (PEOPLE)	5	6	13	14	21	22	
MEASUREMENT	7	8	15	16	23	24	
	CONCLUSIONS		CONCLUSIONS		CONCLUSIONS		

Questions (Note that each question corresponds to a block in the grid presented above.)

1 Have you clearly defined the need for change, a compelling vision of the future, and the implementations strategy to achieve this vision?

2 Is a critical mass of leaders committed and capable of actively leading this effort?

3 Are you intentional about creating early wins to build momentum and credibility for the change?

4 Do you have an effective improvement methodology that will enable you to improve key processes quickly and reliably?

5 Have you identified the skills and knowledge required at each level and function of the organization to implement the desired change?

6 Is the new direction adequately supported by existing training and performance management systems?

7 Have you established baseline measures for customers, employees, and financial performance?

8 Are customer, employee, and process data being communicated to the organization in order to support the case for change?

9 Are leaders at all levels translating the new direction into specific unit action plans?

10 Do employees have opportunities to shape the direction and give feedback on its implementation?

11 Are key processes identified, measured, and in control?

12 Are key processes being rigorously improved to meet customer expectations?

13 Are you building competency quickly enough to achieve the vision?

14 Is the voice of the customer being translated into clear standards and desired behaviors for employees at all levels?

15 Are you systematically capturing and integrating multiple sources of customer, employee, and process data?

16 Are customer, employee, and process data used to monitor progress, set priorities, and drive decisions at all levels in the organization?

17 Is leadership reinforcing the desired change by their daily behavior and by making critical decisions consistent with the new direction?

18 Are incentive and reward systems holding employees at all levels accountable to acting in a way that is consistent with the new direction?

19 Is a critical mass of employees engaged in continuous improvement of key processes?

20 Have structural issues been addressed to maximize process performance?

21 Do you continually assess and revise your approach to building required skills and knowledge to ensure competitive performance?

22 Is leadership continuously removing barriers that keep employees from delighting customers?

23 Are you benchmarking critical best practices to establish corporate performance standards?

24 Does the measurement system enable top management to predict performance and take corrective action?

Customer experience scorecard

What it is

The **customer experience scorecard** is a management framework for more effective and responsive performance measurement systems. It is a process wherein metrics are causally linked to one another, and together form a coherent system that can predict future results. It is a strategic tool that focuses the organization on customer value creation, and provides a succinct and powerful way to communicate the essence of customer focus strategy to all employees. It helps everyone understand what is critical to the company and its customers, and ultimately drives employee behavior.

Why do it

Many organizations have multiple measures within their companies that are overwhelming, focus on financial results, and are control oriented against the annual strategic plan or budget. These metrics give after the fact, non-predictive information, and as a result, critical business changes are not captured until it is too late. This kind of measurement process can become an end in itself – long on effort and resourcing, short on strategic return.

The customer experience scorecard, however, is a management framework for more effective and responsive performance measurement. It balances financial with non-financial measures and reflects the causal relationship between the two.

It is a powerful tool that:

- Helps you manage your business as a totality.
- Creates the strategic line of sight to customer value.
- Aligns the organization around strategic goals, and links performance measures to strategy and goals.
- Provides a vehicle for communicating the essence of the customer experience strategy to all employees, and cascades measures and targets throughout the organization.
- Acts as a mechanism for change.
- Provides a means to measure the Return on Investment (ROI) of Customer Experience improvement efforts.

Installing the customer experience scorecard forces disciplined, sharp thinking about what really drives value for the customer and what leads to customer loyalty.

When to do it

Your company should consider creating a scorecard when you find that the current measurement system is cumbersome and cannot be leveraged to drive the business and employee behaviors. The scorecard can also be used and highly leveraged when an organization (or parts of the organization) is embarking on strategic change.

Scorecards can be created at multiple levels within your organization. It makes sense for the company to develop an organization-wide scorecard as a starting point. This provides the context for scorecards that can be created at the regional, functional, business unit level and so on.

Who is involved

The senior executive team should sponsor and be involved in the development of the organization-wide scorecard. The team that builds the scorecard should be representative of critical functions within the organization, who are able to define the specific measures within each part of the scorecard.

How to do it

Step 1
Review the major elements in the customer experience scorecard that are presented in Figure 18.

Step 2
1   Identify the critical measures for each of the elements of the scorecard, namely People, Product/Service, Process, Customer Experience, Customer Behavior, and Business Results.
2   Start on the right-hand side of the model, i.e. with the key business measures for your company. You should then work progressively through the model from right to left.

Figure 2

Customer experience scorecard framework

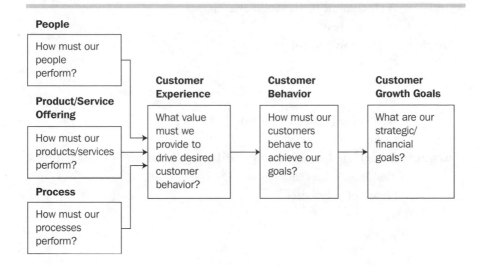

3 Each part of the scorecard has three elements that you need to define for your company. These include the goal, the metric, and the target. An example worksheet for one of the scorecard boxes is provided below.

Figure 3

Worksheet Example

Goal	Metric	Target	Drives...
Retain existing customers	Retention rate	89%	Revenue
Obtain new customers	New customer acquisition rate	10%	Orders
Increase customer profitability	Net profit per customer	$16,000	Net operating profit after taxes

4   As far as possible, ensure that each element within each scorecard
box meets the following criteria:

Goal   • A statement of strategic intent

        • A desired result

Metric • Measurable value of a goal

        • Obtainable

        • Reliable

        • Precise

        • Always expressed as a number

        • Controllable

Target • Based on baseline, capability, competition, process limits,
customer expectations

        • Near term hurdle

Reproduce the template provided below, and record all your scorecard data in the designated boxes.

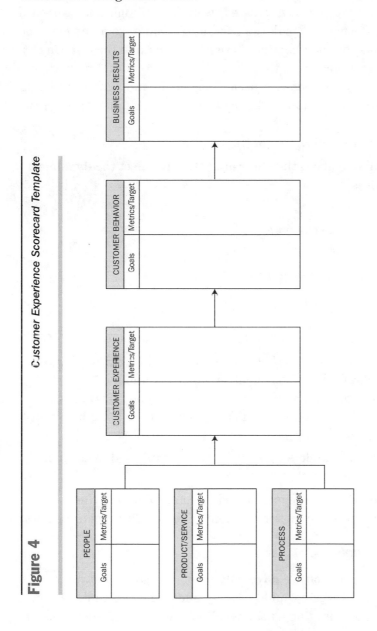

Figure 4   Customer Experience Scorecard Template

Step 3

In a team setting, or with a group of select individuals, review the straw-man scorecard that you have created, working through one scorecard box at a time. Review the goals, metrics, and if you have managed to do this, the targets that you have set for each box against the criteria outlined above. Also check to see that you can trace the causal link between, and explain how each measure drives, the goals, metrics, and targets in the box to its immediate right between all of the measures in the scorecard.

Ask the team the following questions:

– What do you like about the scorecard? Does it reflect the dynamics of the business?

– What is unclear?

– What do we need to change?

Step 4

Revise the strawman as appropriate.

Critical success factors

• Focus on the few key metrics that are critical to success.

• Choose the stakeholders that will be involved in creating the scorecard carefully. This is an opportunity to align key stakeholders regarding expectations and outcomes for the business, and provides an excellent opportunity to build buy-in, alignment, and commitment.

• Be sure that you understand how baseline data used in setting targets was calculated.

• Review the scorecard regularly and, in particular, test the relationship between metrics to identify the key leading indicators.

Scorecard examples

For ease of presentation we have only displayed goals and metrics on these scorecards. Targets could be easily added. For example, a target for retention rate in the Customer Behavior box of the chemical company scorecard might be 90 percent.

Figure 5

Retail Grocery Example

PEOPLE

Goals	Metrics/Target
Motivation to increase sales	Same condition sales per employee
Motivation to reduce costs/improve margin	Operating costs per employee
Increase competency levels	Appraisal aggregate score
Increase customer focus	Customer defection/retention data appraisals
Increase empowerment	Number of employee suggestions implemented
Improve morale	Sickness rate
	Turnover
	Survey scores

PRODUCT/SERVICE

Goals	Metrics/Target
Encourage switching to company by increasing relative perceived value	Relative value line positioning
Enhance margins	Performance by sector basket spend analysis
Target offering to most profitable customers	Performance by profitability segment

PROCESS

Goals	Metrics/Target
Reduce operating costs (buying price-supply chain costs)	Year-on-year comparison
100% availability	Number of off-sales
Optimize layouts to meet customer needs	Number of customer enquiries
Increase store productivity	Year-on-year (improvement)
Eliminate errors/rework	Errors rework in areas of biggest (financial) opportunity
More effective communication to target customers	Tracking studies

CUSTOMER EXPERIENCE

Goals	Metrics/Target
Competitively superior customer experience	Perceived performance: customer expectation gaps relative to regional competition

CUSTOMER BEHAVIOR

Goals	Metrics/Target
Retain existing customers	Customer loyalty index
Attract new customers	New customer accusision rate: Existing and new stores
Increase store visits	Average customer visits per week
Increase amount spent per visit	Average amount spent per visit
Increase profit per customer	Gross profit per customer

BUSINESS RESULTS

Goals	Metrics/Target:
Increase earnings per share	Earnings per share
Better same condition sales	Sales of store this year against last year's sales
Increase return on capital employed	Return on capital employed
Improve pre-tax operating profit	Pre-tax operating profit
Reduce risk	Borrowing; Net assets

Figure 6

Chemical Company Example

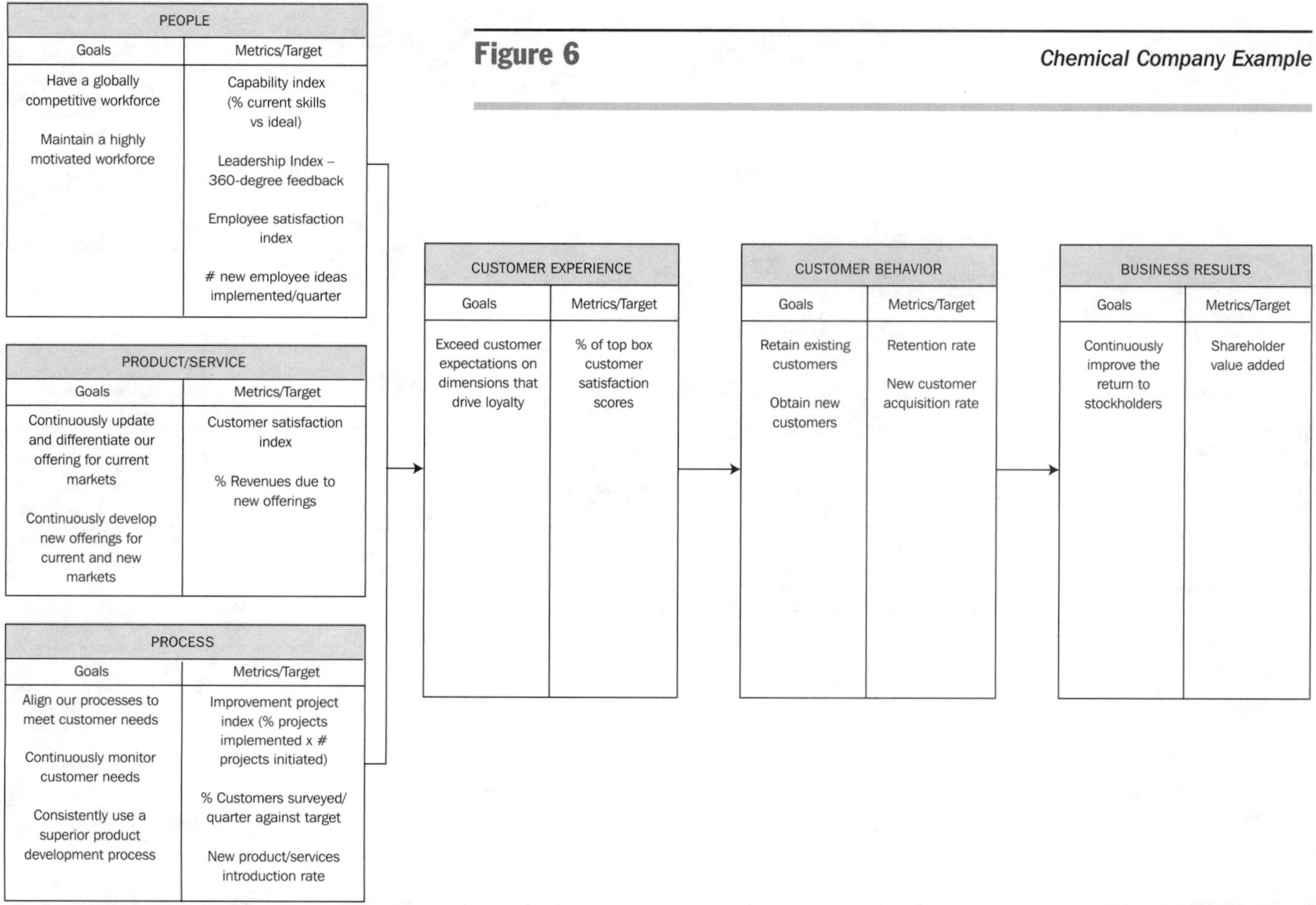

BUSINESS RESULTS

Goals	Metrics/Target
Continuously improve the return to stockholders	Shareholder value added

CUSTOMER BEHAVIOR

Goals	Metrics/Target
Retain existing customers	Retention rate
Obtain new customers	New customer acquisition rate

CUSTOMER EXPERIENCE

Goals	Metrics/Target
Exceed customer expectations on dimensions that drive loyalty	% of top box customer satisfaction scores

PEOPLE

Goals	Metrics/Target
Have a globally competitive workforce	Capability index (% current skills vs ideal)
Maintain a highly motivated workforce	Leadership Index – 360-degree feedback
	Employee satisfaction index
	# new employee ideas implemented/quarter

PRODUCT/SERVICE

Goals	Metrics/Target
Continuously update and differentiate our offering for current markets	Customer satisfaction index
Continuously develop new offerings for current and new markets	% Revenues due to new offerings

PROCESS

Goals	Metrics/Target
Align our processes to meet customer needs	Improvement project index (% projects implemented x # projects initiated)
Continuously monitor customer needs	% Customers surveyed/ quarter against target
Consistently use a superior product development process	New product/services introduction rate

Internal communications audit

What it is

An **internal communications audit** is an assessment of an organization's past and current internal communication activities. The communications audit captures data on formal and informal media, the different audiences within the organization, and the communication needs, networks, and challenges for each audience. The audit also gathers information on messages and activities that worked particularly well and not so well within the organization in the past.

There are three primary components of a communications audit:

- interviews
- focus groups
- sample media collection.

Why do it

The purpose of conducting an internal communications audit is to gather information that will help to inform any changes that need to be made to enhance or improve upon current and future communications efforts.

Within any organization undergoing change (e.g. a merger or acquisition, a strategic imperative to create and implement a Branded Customer Experience®), internal communication is a critical success factor to sustaining the desired change. The audit helps you understand the effectiveness of current communication practices and channels, what to leverage going forward, and what gaps need to be taken care of in developing your internal communication strategy. This data can then be used to narrow the gap between the desired outcome of the communication efforts and the current state.

When to do it

An audit should be done whenever there is a communication strategy put in place to support an organizational initiative. An audit may also be done when feedback is received that communications are not meeting the needs of the various constituencies.

Who is involved

Anyone who is accountable for internal communications or public relations efforts as well as the success of a major change initiative.

How to do it

Step 1

Position the audit as positively as possible, focussing on the opportunity to further improve current methods.

Step 2

Develop a protocol (which can be embedded into an interview, a focus group session, and/or a questionnaire) to assess the current state of communication in the organization. Sample questions can include:

- Which of the more formal communication processes in the organization seem to work best for you?

- When you think about all the ways you've received important company information, do one or two events or communications stand out as especially effective? If so, what were they?

- What do you think would be the most effective way for you to receive key organization information?

- When it comes to staying connected to other departments and higher levels of the organization, to which communications do you pay the most attention?

- How do most people like to receive information about important organization events or plans?

- Between (media) (event), and (media), which do you value most? Why?

- To which communications do you pay the least attention? What is it about (media/event), that makes it less interesting to you?

- Are there formal communications events or media that seem less effective for you? If so, why are they less effective?

- What opportunities do you have to respond to more formal communications methods?

- When you think about (media) (event), or (media), what opportunities do you have to engage in two-way communication or provide feedback?
- When you think about (media/event), how might it be improved?
- When you think about (message/strategy/plan), are there some better ways in which you think it could be communicated to (audience)? What might work best, given their needs and circumstances?

Step 3
Identify trends and patterns from the feedback to inform future internal communication decisions.

The "straw poll"

What it is

An employee communications survey – or **straw poll** – is a tool used to randomly collect opinions about the effectiveness of an organizational initiative. This initiative may be narrow or broad in scope, ranging from a procedural change to something as broad as an organization-wide customer-driven change initiative.

Why do it

As an initiative evolves, it is often helpful to obtain a "pulse check" or gauge of people's opinions about their feelings on the initiative. A straw poll provides immediate feedback about the issue at hand; this information can then be used to inform any future decisions. It can also be used to determine how your internal communication strategy should be leveraged to drive the desired change through your organization.

When to do it

A straw poll may be done whenever it is important to obtain a snapshot or "pulse" of the organization. The frequency with which it is done is driven by how often feedback is required. For an organization going through a rapid customer-driven change initiative (say of around three months in duration), you might consider doing a straw poll every two weeks. For a longer initiative, for example, closer to 12 months, you might consider conducting your straw poll once a month.

Who is involved

Employees, at all levels, can be polled for their feedback. A representative sample is important so as to obtain as broad a perspective as possible.

How to do it

Step 1

Select a representative sample of employees from all levels of the organization who are "vocal" and willing to express their opinions candidly. Ensure there is cross representation (i.e. organizational levels, departments, geographies).

Step 2

Develop a protocol (which can be embedded into an interview, a focus group session, and /or a questionnaire) to assess current opinions across the organization. Sample questions can include:

- How well do you understand the purpose and impact of the current changes that are underway?
- How clear are you on what these changes mean for you?
- How good has the internal communication around the changes been for people in positions or levels in the organization that are similar to yours?
- What do the changes (sample initiative, i.e. customer focussed) mean to you?
- How will this initiative affect your current role?
- How will this initiative affect the people with whom you most closely interact?
- What are the positive aspects of this initiative?
- What are the drawbacks to this initiative?

Step 3

Identify trends and patterns from the responses to inform future decisions.

Customer touchline map

What it is

A **customer touchline map** is a tool that visually displays how a customer interacts with your business. Unlike a process map, it is linear and illustrates only those points at which your customer 'touches' your product or service. A well-developed touchline map will show you how and when the customer experience is impacted.

Why do it

The purpose for mapping the touchlines from the customer's point of view is to ensure that your organization is delivering what your most important customers value most. It is vital to an organization's success to know if its employees are meeting and exceeding its customers' expectations and to know what is working and what is not working in delivering the desired experience. Knowing this information will help you delight customers and promote loyalty.

When to do it

A customer touchline map can be used when there is a need:

* to fully understand your customers' experience with your organization;
* to identify potential inefficiencies, redundancies, or inconsistencies in how customers experience your organization's products and/or services;
* to identify how the experience can be made more "seamless";
* to enhance the experience your customers have with your organization.

Who is involved

Anyone who is accountable for delivering a consistent, differentiated, and value-added experience to your customers by consistently meeting or exceeding their expectations.

How to do it

Step 1

Identify what your most important customers value most about the relationship they have with your organization.

Step 2

Put yourself in the customer's position and determine what steps he or she would go through if he or she were experiencing the current level of product or service from your organization. Be certain to consider the entire transaction or process; that is, from the time the customer first comes into contact with your organization to the very last point of contact, from the customer's perspective, not the organization's perspective.

Step 3

Map out all of the points (see example below) at which the customer has direct impact with your organization (face-to-face, telephone, e-mail, etc.). You could map one touchline that encompasses the entire customer experience from the point of initial contact to the last contact they have with your organization. For example, if you were mapping the touchline for a passenger intending to take a business trip, you could map the entire process from making the airline reservation through to baggage collection. On the other hand, it may either be too complex or illogical to map the customer experience as one touchline. If this is the case, go ahead and map a touchline for each key customer process. For example, say you worked for a cellular phone company. You could map the following separately:

- opening a new cellular account
- buying a phone
- reporting a lost or stolen phone
- querying an account.

Step 4

Use the touchline to identify inefficiencies, redundancies, or inconsistencies in how customers experience your organization's products and/or services. Consider the promise that you have made to these customers, and how well you are delivering on this promise at each point in the touchline. As you do this, make sure that you think about your most valuable customers and those aspects of your product or service on which they place the highest value.

Step 5

Identify ways to enhance, improve, or streamline the desired customer experience.

Example of a customer touchline

The example presented in Figure 7 (p. 232) covers one part of the overall travel experience with an airline. It maps out the in-flight experience for the customer.

The competitive win/loss debrief tool

What It Is

The **competitive win/loss debrief** is a process for speaking with customers right after they have made a major purchasing decision. It is protocol for interviewing your customer just after you have won or lost a major piece of business, and is a powerful and simple way for hardwiring the voice of the customer into your organization.

Why do it

The competitive win/loss interview will enable you to learn more than at almost any other time about your company from the customer. It is a tool that provides rich data on your customers' experience of your organization throughout the sales process. It provides clear indicators on how well you have delivered on your brand promise, as well as clear feedback on whether you have addressed and provided significant value to your customers. It is simple to complete, and provides rich information and learning to the organization.

Figure 7

Customer touchline example

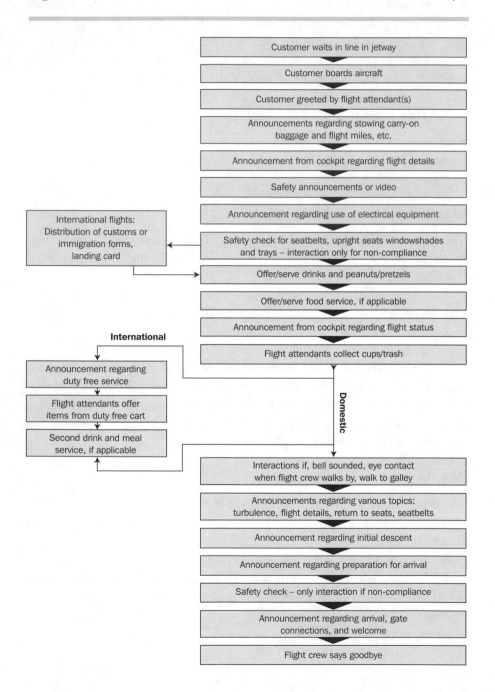

When to do it

As stated above, the competitive win/loss interview is best conducted with customers right after they have made a major purchasing decision on a piece of business that your company has pursued.

Who is involved

It is usually best for the win/loss interview to be conducted by a senior executive who was not the contact person during the selling process. Data gathered from the interview should then be fed back to the selling team, and should also be provided to the entire organization for learning. As part of the interview, the interviewer must discuss issues of confidentiality, and if the client feels that certain issues are too sensitive to be fed back to the individual or to the organization, this must be honored. At Forum, win/loss debriefs are posted on our intranet. Each time a new win/loss debrief is completed, it is showcased on the homepage of our intranet.

How to do it

Step 1
Prior to conducting the interview with the customer, the executive should be briefed on the situation background by key members of the sales team. He/she should review the protocol, and prepare additional questions relevant to the situation.

Step 2
The senior executive schedules the meeting, and at the outset, introduces himself or herself to the client and thanks the client for making the time.

At this point, the interviewer should discuss confidentiality, and explain that ideally, he/she would like to be able to share all feedback throughout the organization. However, if the client feels that certain items are too sensitive, the interviewer should ask the client to mention them during the conversation, and confidentiality will be observed.

Step 3

Conduct the interview. Here is a list of questions that form the body of our interview process at Forum. They are presented as if you are in the live interview:

1 Can you summarize the business issues that [our company] responded to? You may want to summarize what you have heard from your sales team, and check for clarity and then ask the customer to expand on this.

2 What factors led you to consider [our company name] for the business?

3 Which other firms were competing for the business? You may also want to elaborate here with the following if appropriate: How did you find out about us? Why did you make this competitive (especially if you are the incumbent)?

4 Overall, what were the main reasons [your company name] won or lost the business?

5 Can you tell me something about how your [the client's] decision-making process worked? What factors were important in the decision-making process? Can you tell me who made the decisions? What were the key criteria used for making the decision?

6 I would like to ask you some questions around the specifics of the selling process. (Probe for what, how, and why on the questions below. You may also want to adjust these questions to reflect your company's performance on specific elements of your value promise.)

   • How did you feel about the quality of our salesperson's management of the relationship?

   • Did you meet other people from our organization during the sales process? If yes, what was your impression of these people? Did you feel that we used our resources appropriately?

   • What about the sales process. Did you think we jumped to the solution too quickly before adequately understanding your situation? Did we meet or exceed your expectations on the

R.A.T.E.R. dimensions? (See p. 244 for explanations of R.A.T.E.R.)

- What about the quality of our proposal, the solution, and our presentation to your team?
- How did you feel about our pricing? Did the pricing match up with your perception of the value we would be providing?

7 Overall, how would you rate us against our competitors? What are the strengths and weaknesses relative to other firms that were involved in the proposal process?

8 Did we provide you with references? Did you call these references and were they helpful?

9 What advice would you give us for working with you in the future?

10 Is there anything else that you would like to add?

Step 4
After the interview, write up the details and distribute throughout the organization – if this is consistent with the customer's wishes. And lastly, send a thank-you note to the client.

Leading customer focus – tactics guide

What it is

The following **tactics guide** is for leaders and managers at all levels. It contains practical tips to support the four key leadership practices, which are as follows:

● Connect to customers and employees (Connecting).

● Create meaning and purpose for staff (Creating meaning).

● Mobilize people and help them see progress (Mobilizing).

● Inspire and develop others to be leaders (Inspiring).

The guide describes the actions managers and leaders should take to achieve a customer focus transformation among their teams. Each action is accompanied by specific ways in which a manager can accomplish the action. For example, as part of "Connecting," one of the actions is to spend time with employees who serve customers. Three specific tips on how to do this are provided, including the following: a manager devotes an hour each week to talking informally with employees about customer expectations and how your team can meet those expectations. Managers may modify these tips to suit their own leadership style and situation. The key is not to focus too much on the "how," but rather to accomplish the action – in this case, the action is to create a flow of ideas between the manager and those employees who interact with customers regularly.

Whether done using the tips listed here or through other approaches, leaders should be prepared to support the changes associated with a customer focus transformation. With no leadership support, employees may find it difficult to change behaviors and deliver the new customer experience. Leaders play a critical role by reinforcing good behavior, by coaching employees when the "old" behavior is exhibited, and by modeling the effective new behaviors themselves.

Why do it

As most leaders know, successful change campaigns require more than just a PR effort. Successful change requires leadership support – from the very top of the organization down to the front-line supervisors. Transforming a company into a customer-focussed organization is just like any other change effort in this regard. Leading your work team to deliver on its commitment to customers in all day-to-day operations is critical to the success of any transformation to customer focus. It reinforces customer focus, which is the practice of constantly striving to exceed customers' expectations on those things customers value.

When to do it

These tactics can and should be part of any manager or leader's repertoire in an organization that is committed to providing a unique, differentiated, and value-added experience to its key customers that drives their loyalty to the company. These are tactics that can be used at any point in a company's journey to become a customer-driven organization.

Who is involved

Anyone who has management and/or leadership responsibilities within your company.

Leadership tactics guide

These tactics are presented using four major leadership practices:

- connecting
- creating meaning
- mobilizing
- inspiring.

Figure 8   *Connect to customers and employees*

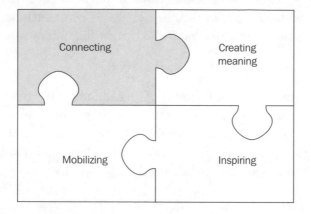

What to do	How to do it
Spend time with customers and employees who serve customers.	• Walk around (and/or call around) and talk to employees.
	• Tell customers and employees that you're interested in their point of view and offer them a way to give it to you (e.g. telephone, make an appointment, e-mail).
	• Devote one hour each week to talking informally with employees about customer expectations and how you can meet those expectations.
Listen carefully to what employees and colleagues are saying.	• Differentiate between facts and assumptions. Recognize personal constraints or biases that may affect your objectivity when you are listening.
	• Investigate employees' and colleagues' views sincerely and open-mindedly, as you might wish them to investigate yours.
	• Incorporate feelings and values, as well as the facts, when restating perspectives.

Model the behavior that builds your company's commitment to customers.

- Treat customers as you would like employees to treat them.
- Avoid talking negatively about customers, especially in front of employees or other customers.
- When you feel like acting in conflict with your customer-focus behaviors, pause, take a breath, and think of what you expect from others in a similar situation.

Figure 9   *Create meaning and purpose for staff*

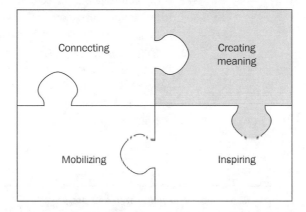

What to do	How to do it
Communicate a clear and compelling picture of your company's future.	• Make sure employees see how their work contributes to your company's strategy. • Communicate your company's strategy to your employees. Explain how it was developed and why it is crucial to your success. • Repeat the message ten times and use at least three different methods of communication. • Encourage discussions in which employees can ask questions about the strategic intent of the organization.

	• Regularly indicate to the people you talk with your interest in seeing the overall company benefit.
Use every opportunity to reinforce your customer focus strategy and supporting behaviors.	• At least monthly, provide specific information to employees about customers' expectations and experiences. • Initiate an internal publication or support an existing one that publishes customer quotes, experiences, horror stories, comments, compliments, and expectations as well as commends employees' efforts in serving customers well. • Share compliments and comments you have received from customers with all employees. Let them know how important their work is in serving customers. • Publicly reward and commend employees who are especially effective at delivering your commitment to customers.

Figure 10　　*Mobilize people and help them see progress...*
with a mix of both challenge and support

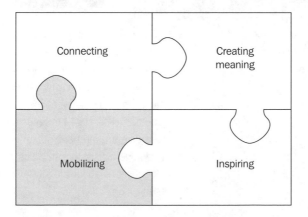

What to do	How to do it
Take decisive action on issues that impact customers.	• If a customer need and your company's policy are in conflict, fill the customer need whenever possible, even if it does bend the rules. If an exception cannot be made for an important reason, explain to the customer why the policy must be followed (government regulations, etc.). • Help employees to make judgment calls in regard to filling the customer need vs following the "rules." • Talk with a group of employees about how they have made successful judgment calls that have led to a delighted customer. Let them share stories with each other.
Engineer short-term wins and celebrate progress.	• Create ideas for how employees can improve customer relationships and implement those ideas. • Schedule a meeting of employees to discuss their views on customer needs and expectations. Gather improvement ideas and ways to implement them. • Inform employees of changes and decisions made in response to information you have received from them or why they could not be implemented.
Communicate clearly the results expected from your employees and help them to achieve the results.	• Explain clearly the purpose of tasks and conditions under which they are to be done (time pressures, low clarity, with or without resources). • Ask employees to state or restate their understanding of their roles and responsibilities in serving customers. • Ask employees questions that check their understanding of their role in delivering the commitment to customers. • Support the increased competence of employees by encouraging and supporting their training.

Figure 11   *Inspire and develop others to be leaders*

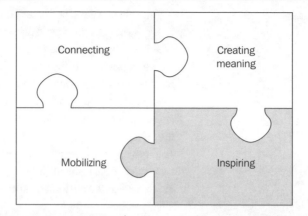

What to do	How to do it
Identify and celebrate your company's customer champions.	• Praise others publicly whenever they deserve it. • Let high-performing employees know you are proud of them. • Create tangible, short-term milestones for your employees that they can achieve and which contribute to the overall commitment to customers.
Encourage every employee to take responsibility for delivering on your company's commitment to customers.	• Identify typical problems you have seen or that can be expected in your environment. Ask employees to analyze the situation and develop approaches based on the data presented. • Form project teams or task forces, giving them the responsibility to produce results *without* your intervention.
Build enthusiasm about the future and your commitment to customers.	• Make a point of highlighting achievements. • Explain how success will benefit the individual and your organization. • Only speak positively about the company, its goals, and your job.

Customers' expectations framework and mapping

What it is

Forum has developed several unique and proprietary tools that we use with companies to identify, organize, and prioritize their key customers' expectations. We do not use these tools to identify all customers' expectations. In conjunction with our customer segmentation work (or the client's customer segmentation strategy), we use our customer expectation tools to ensure that our clients only focus on their most important segments (for example, most profitable, or most valuable customers).

Forum frequently uses two kinds of focus group techniques in its customer expectations work. The first is the Nominal Group Technique (NGT), which is based on bringing customers together for a focus group. The second type is the Virtual Group Technique (VGT), which can be conducted via fax or e-mail with individuals who are geographically dispersed. The NGT is an effective way to collect customer expectations, hearing customers describe what it is they value in their own words. NGT may be effective when more comprehensive data collection is not necessary. On the other hand, the VGT may take several days to complete, but it can reach a wider audience (even global). Alternatively, bringing a few customers together to gather expectations, then polling a larger group through fax/e-mail correspondence to score/rate expectations is a way to combine both methods to arrive at both qualitative and quantitative data.

These focus group methodologies provide:

- A clear understanding of customer expectations expressed in their own words.

- Insight into which customer expectations are most important.

- An assessment of your current performance against key customers' most important expectations.

- Data which shows how you are performing on key expectations vis-à-vis your competitors.

- Documentation of how customers describe their loyalty behaviors.

- The foundational work for building a unique Branded Customer Experience®.

Customer Expectations Identification, Organization, and Prioritization

The purpose of the customer expectations map is to present customer expectations in a format that provides insights about the relationship of expectations to each other and to attributes of customer service. The maps organize data into three levels: dimensions, clusters, and customer expectations.

Level 1: Dimensions

These are recorded in the first column of the expectations map. They describe the important service quality, product quality, and cost attributes that your customers may have.

SERVICE QUALITY

Following our customer expectation focus groups and analysis, we use the R.A.T.E.R. framework to organize customer service expectations. R.A.T.E.R. is the acronym for the five dimensions of customer satisfaction (as identified by Texas A&M University):

Reliability: Ability to perform the promised service dependably and accurately

Assurance: Knowledge and courtesy of employees and their ability to convey trust and confidence

Tangibles: Physical facilities, equipment, and appearance of personnel

Empathy: Caring, individualized attention the firm provides its customers

Responsiveness: Willingness to help customers and provide prompt service

PRODUCT QUALITY

Grade: Refers to the image, design, or quality of attributes or features, and the care with which the product or service is made or performed

Fitness for use: Refers to client needs or requirements for performance

Conformance to specifications: Refers to required standards and specifications

COST

Price: Has to do with the sticker or quoted price of the product or service; what the customer is expected to pay

Level 2: Expectation clusters

These are presented in the middle columns of the maps. Clusters help define the dimensions and they are summary statements for a group of thematically related customer expectations.

Level 3: Customer expectations

Customer expectations are found in the third columns. These expectations are gathered from focus groups, and identify what customers want from your organization.

Why do it

Many companies assess their performance with customers through customer satisfaction surveys. While these surveys provide some value, they do not identify your targeted customers' key expectations and drivers of value. They also fall short of providing insight into the extent to which your company is meeting or exceeding customer needs. What is missing is knowledge of what the target customers *expect* in their relationship with your company, and therefore what your most important customers *value* in their relationship with your company.

Once customer expectations have been collected, your company can then map its own customer experience and identify where expectations may be falling short, and therefore areas that may be targeted for improvement.

Using R.A.T.E.R. as the organizing framework for customer expectations will help your company focus on the behaviors that need to change to deliver an improved customer experience.

Armed with this information, your company can – through its products/services, processes, and most critically, its people – deliver a valuable and differentiated customer experience that will drive customer loyalty and retention.

When to do it

Identifying, organizing, and prioritizing customer expectations should take place at the start of any Branded Customer Experience® initiative, or for any major customer focus initiative. Customer expectations should be gathered periodically thereafter to ensure your company is still delivering a customer experience that drives loyalty.

Customer expectations map

A partial customer expectations map for a banking client is shown below for illustration:

SERVICE QUALITY		
Dimension	**Cluster**	**Expectations**
Reliability concerns dependability, meeting promises, personnel, and consistency in performance.	**Get things right the first time**	• Gets things right the first time • Accuracy during check encoding • Accuracy of processing (no errors that can affect continuity of customers or financial records) • Transactions done correctly
	Provide timely reporting	• Provides statements, reports, and tax information on a timely basis • Timeliness in receipt of monthly statements (three to seven days into next business cycle) • Delivery of reports on a timely basis, real time information connection made, information there
Assurance concerns the ability to inspire trust and confidence in customers.	**Communicate information clearly and completely**	• Clear explanations regarding issues raised • Complete and detailed service – provider should be as detailed as possible so I can relay information back to my staff • No hidden charges – make me aware of all charges when you quote pricing • Provide as much online information as possible (pull down information I need from system) and post real time

| *Empathy* concerns practices that suggest respect, caring, and the provision of individual attention. | **Build a personal relationship with me** | • Deal directly, personal touch
• Assign one person to my business and know my business, personal attention from a human being, give me my options, I don't want an 800#, I want to feel important
• Account officer who is dedicated to my needs, but may use other bank resources to respond to inquiries |

PRODUCT QUALITY

Dimension	Cluster	Expectations
Grade refers to the image, design, or quality of attributes or features, and the care with which the product or service is made or performed.	**Has a wide variety of products and services**	• Wide range of products and services • Ability to bring varied number of products (offer full complement of quality products – lending, investment, cash management, etc.) • Deliver a pretty broad product slate seamlessly across the bank's boundaries • Have total services, be all encompassing, provide the services I want, one branch that can provide total services

COST

Dimension	Cluster	Expectations
Price	**Limit service charges and fees**	• Don't charge me when a check is overdrawn the first time • Don't want to be charged for inquiries I make regarding problems that result from bank errors • Make money on interest rates, not nickel and diming on fees

Improving your customers' experience

What it is

This is a tool that gives service providers an opportunity to critically observe their experiences as customers and, in turn, gain personal insight into how they can enhance the experience they provide to their own customers. This tool uses the R.A.T.E.R framework, discussed earlier, to help the service provider evaluate his or her experience as a customer. This perspective is helpful in that it allows a service provider to better understand the level of product or service that his or her organization's customers desire. This understanding then provides a point of reference from which product or service enhancements can be made. (Note: This tool is best used when a customer expectations map has been developed.)

When using this tool to evaluate the service provided by another organization, the greatest value is derived when observing similar levels of product and/or service quality. That is, a premium-priced organization would be most interested in the products and/or services provided by another premium-priced organization.

The first column of the framework, Dimension, describes important service quality, product quality, and price attributes that have been derived from industry-wide research into customer expectations.

The second column of the framework, Expectations, translates the Dimension into specific customer needs and wants. They illustrate, for the service provider, what a customer expects.

Why do it

This tool provides a framework that guides and shapes the service provider's observation so that he or she is better able to evaluate the quality of his or her service experience. The data this framework yields can then be used to determine how to enhance the desired experience of the organization's most valued customers.

When to do it

Improving your customers' experience can be done:

* to highlight what enhances and detracts from a desired customer experience;

- when it is necessary to expand upon a service provider's current experience or perspective;
- to evaluate the products or services provided by another organization (i.e. a competitor);
- to determine if and how another organization's products and services, and the delivery of those products and services, can enhance your customers' experiences.

Who is involved

Anyone who is involved and responsible for creating predictably positive experiences for customers by consistently meeting or exceeding their expectations.

How to do it

Step 1

Review the Dimensions that impact a customer's experience (Column 1):

- service quality
- product quality
- cost.

Step 2

Develop specific, actionable Expectations that are critical in satisfying your most important customers (Column 2). These Expectations can be developed, in part, from information provided from the customer expectations map. Sample questions to help develop your customers' expectations may include:

- *Service quality* – What are the ways in which I can demonstrate reliability to my customers? In what ways can I provide assurance to my customers? On what tangibles do my customers place the greatest value? In what ways can I provide individual attention to my customers? In what situations can I demonstrate responsiveness to my customers?

- *Product quality* – What aspects of my products are most important to my customers? How user-friendly are my products?
- *Cost* – Do my customers perceive they are receiving value for the price they are paying for my products and/or services?

Step 3

Once the Dimensions and Expectations have been developed to support the desired customer experience, evaluate your experience in a similar organization against the expectations of your most valued customers. Take note of specific behaviors, actions, and phrases heard that enhance or detract from the Expectations. For example:

- At a place you go to frequently – the post office, your bank or building society, a restaurant – pay close attention to the "body language" and "tone of voice" of the service professional.
- When you are paying your bill – in a shop, restaurant, or any other situation – watch closely the behavior of the person at the register. Do they show appreciation for your business? Do they check for your satisfaction? Do they encourage you to return?
- Visit two or three different places (shops, cafes, bars, etc.) that offer a level of service you would like to offer to your customers. Describe and compare the greetings you receive in each of these places. Did you feel welcomed?
- When you find yourself waiting in line, watch to see if the service professional manages the situation positively. Does he or she acknowledge that you are waiting? When you reach the head of the line, does he or she thank you for waiting?

Step 4

Once you have completed your observation, evaluate the current products and/or levels of service your organization is providing to its most valued customers. Identify, from your observation experience, what enhancements can be made to your organization's current product offerings and/or service levels.

Index

██████████████████████████

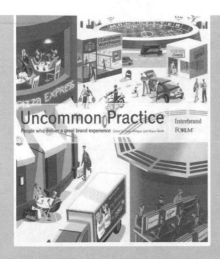

Uncommon Practice

People who deliver a great brand experience

"This is a terrific book. It paints a picture of what the 21st century company has to look like. In today's hypercompetitive markets the business has to be profoundly customer centric if it is to prosper. This is not about clever advertising but creating a genuine commitment among employees to provide customers with a unique, quality experience."
–Professor Peter Doyle, Warwick Business School

"This book takes an original approach to its subject and comes up with some uncommonly useful lessons."
–Rufus Olins, Editor-in-Chief and Publisher, Management Today

"... so if you want to hear direct from Richard Branson and his lieutenants, Carphone Warehouse's Charles Dunstone and other uncommon business leaders—many of whom are nortoriously reluctant to be interviewed *Uncommon Practice* is the book that lets you hear their story straight from the horse's mouth."
–Phil Dourado, Editorial Director, eCustomerServiceWorld.com

In an increasingly crowded market place, there are certain companies that really stand out from their competitors—companies like Tesco, PizzaExpress, Amazon.com, Virgin, easyGroup, First Direct, Harley-Davidson, Krispy Kreme and Pret a Manger.

This book by Interbrand and Forum shows how the companies above and other leading organizations provide remarkable experience for their customers and staff alike. The book demonstrates, through interviews with key executives, that success stems from their distinctive cultures uniquely developed to meet the needs of customers. The companies featured have defied conventional wisdom and broken the traditional rules of management to engender exceptional levels of commitment from their people, who, united behind a clear brand vision, translate their belief in the company into exceptional customer service.